The Sociopolitics of English Language Testing

Also available from Bloomsbury

Contemporary Second Language Assessment, edited by Jayanti Veronique Banerjee and Dina Tsagari
Learner Corpus Research, edited by Vaclav Brezina and Lynne Flowerdew
On Writtenness, by Joan Turner
Reflective Language Teaching, by Thomas S. C. Farrell
Second Language Acquisition in Action, by Andrea Nava and Luciana Pedrazzini

The Sociopolitics of English Language Testing

Edited by
Seyyed-Abdolhamid Mirhosseini
and Peter I. De Costa

BLOOMSBURY ACADEMIC
LONDON • NEW YORK • OXFORD • NEW DELHI • SYDNEY

BLOOMSBURY ACADEMIC
Bloomsbury Publishing Plc
50 Bedford Square, London, WC1B 3DP, UK
1385 Broadway, New York, NY 10018, USA
29 Earlsfort Terrace, Dublin 2, Ireland

BLOOMSBURY, BLOOMSBURY ACADEMIC and the Diana logo are trademarks of
Bloomsbury Publishing Plc

First published in Great Britain 2020
This paperback edition published in 2022

Copyright © Seyyed-Abdolhamid Mirhosseini, Peter I. De Costa and Contributors, 2020

Seyyed-Abdolhamid Mirhosseini and Peter I. De Costa have asserted their right
under the Copyright, Designs and Patents Act, 1988, to be identified as
Editors of this work.

All rights reserved. No part of this publication may be reproduced or transmitted
in any form or by any means, electronic or mechanical, including photocopying,
recording, or any information storage or retrieval system, without prior
permission in writing from the publishers.

Bloomsbury Publishing Plc does not have any control over, or responsibility for, any
third-party websites referred to or in this book. All internet addresses given in this
book were correct at the time of going to press. The author and publisher regret
any inconvenience caused if addresses have changed or sites have ceased to
exist, but can accept no responsibility for any such changes.

A catalogue record for this book is available from the British Library.

A catalog record for this book is available from the Library of Congress.

ISBN: HB: 978-1-3500-7134-6
PB: 978-1-3502-7794-6
ePDF: 978-1-3500-7135-3
eBook: 978-1-3500-7136-0

Typeset by Deanta Global Publishing Service, Chennai, India

To find out more about our authors and books visit www.bloomsbury.com
and sign up for our newsletters.

Contents

Preface *Seyyed-Abdolhamid Mirhosseini and Peter I. De Costa*	vii
Foreword *Paula Winke*	xvi

Part One The Ideologies of Testing in English-Speaking Countries

1. Who Me? Hailing Individuals as Subjects: Standardized Literacy Testing as an Instrument of Neoliberal Ideology *John Yandell, Brenton Doecke, and Zamzam Abdi* — 3
2. Standardized Testing and School Achievement: The Case of Indigenous-Language-Speaking Students in Remote Australia *Leonard A. Freeman and Gillian Wigglesworth* — 23
3. Where Language is Beside the Point: English Language Testing for Mexicano Students in the Southwestern United States *Luis E. Poza and Sheila M. Shannon* — 46
4. Language Testing in Service-Learning: A Critical Approach to Socially Situated Language in Use *Netta Avineri and James Perren* — 68
5. Moving beyond Deficit Positioning of Linguistically Diverse Test Takers: Bi/Multilingualism and the Essence of Validity *Jamie L. Schissel* — 91

Part Two The Politics of Testing in the Non-English-Speaking World

6. The Coloniality of English Language Testing *Ruanni Tupas* — 113
7. Reforming Foreign Language Teaching Policy in Japan: The Politics of "Standardization" *Masaki Oda* — 130
8. Sociopolitical Factors Surrounding the Rise and Demise of the National English Ability Test (NEAT) in South Korea *Gwan-Hyeok Im, Liying Cheng, and Dongil Shin* — 147
9. The Disconnect between English Tests and English Proficiency: Two South Korean Jobseekers' Perceptions and Performances *Miso Kim and Mari Haneda* — 165
10. Sanctioning the IELTS for Enrolling in ELT: A Critical Perspective from Oman *Ali S. M. Al-Issa* — 185

11 Neoliberal Placemaking and Ideological Constructions of
    Standardized Tests in Nepal's Linguistic Landscape *Prem Phyak*   208

Afterword *Constant Leung*   231
List of Contributors   243
Index   247

Preface

Seyyed-Abdolhamid Mirhosseini and Peter I. De Costa

Doctoral students in all Iranian universities are required to take an English language proficiency test and provide the official certificate as a compulsory requirement for a PhD degree, *regardless* of their field of study. This means that even for a doctorate in a field like Persian Literature, Islamic Theology, or Arabic Language and Literature, a certain threshold score of a high-stakes test of English is mandatory. The high point of the story is that no university, department, or individual presenting or pursing a PhD is exempted from this requirement and that no other foreign language is accepted. Thus, it is not unusual to see a doctoral student of History of Islam, Quranic Studies, or Ancient Iranian Languages struggling to obtain a certificate of an English proficiency test, after several rounds of failure to achieve the required score. If anything, cases of comprehensive exams and thesis approvals being delayed or halted are not uncommon because of a pending "language certificate," as it is usually called.

In a very different setting, literally far away in terms of geography and contextually different in terms of culture, society, economy, and politics, students and teachers in the United States also have to grapple with tests that sort and sieve K-12 students. Teachers in these settings thus have to negotiate the Common Core State Standards for English Language Arts and Literacy in History/Social Studies, Science, and Technical Subjects (the *standards*) as they prepare English language learners for success in college, career, and life by the time they graduate from high school. Students who do not pass tests administered by educational consortia, therefore, run the risk of being academically and socially left behind.

One way to understand the underlying layers of the two situations briefly sketched here is to scrutinize these instances in terms of the ideological and political essence of language tests and testing practices. Evidently, beyond the technicalities of test construction and administration based on mainstream views of formal linguistics and psychometrics, such bizarre entanglements of issues related to English language testing are to be understood as part of the politics of language and knowledge (Pennycook, 2001). Numerous questions can be raised about *why* policies that lead to such situations are adopted and *who* the policy makers and stakeholders behind them are. More profoundly, serious questions about the *fundamental beliefs* underlying such policies and practices of English language testing emerge, leaving us to unpack their ideological underpinnings (Mirhosseini, 2018; van Dijk, 1998, 2006). Elevating the English language to a point that creates such dilemmas is an ideological concern, one that casts its shadow on the cultural, social, economic, and political aspects of people's lives (Al-Issa and Mirhosseini, forthcoming).

* * *

Within applied linguistics and language education, language testing in the form of limited-scope assessment, as well as administering high-stakes international proficiency tests, continues to be a significant concern at the institutional, national, and international levels. Mainstream trends of language testing research and practice have been mainly viewed from *asocial* perspectives, often pivoting around cognitive considerations, linguistic constructs, and psychometric measurement technicalities that tend to overlook socially situated understandings of language assessment. However, related to earlier conceptual discussions of the ethical aspects and social consequences of language tests (e.g., Hawthorne, 1997; Messick, 1981; Sarig, 1989; Shepard, 1997; Spolsky, 1986, 1997), the notion of *critical language testing* has been proposed as a standpoint that "assumes that the act of testing is not neutral . . . [but] both a product and an agent of cultural, social, political, educational and ideological agendas" (Shohamy, 1998, p. 332). The scope of such discussions on testing acts was later extended to the realm of language policy and learner identities (Shohamy, 2007, 2013).

Among the later explorations of language testing as a critical and social practice (e.g., Fulcher, 2009; Khan, 2009; Lynch, 2001; McNamara, 1998, 2001; Schissel, 2010; Templer, 2004) are two landmark works. First, Shohamy's (2001) book *The Power of Tests: A Critical Perspective on the Uses of Language Tests* problematizes the ways language tests are used and the social and political consequences of relying on them. The applications of tests as means of exercising power and control as well as resisting the power and misuse of language proficiency tests are the focal discussions of this pathbreaking book. Second, *Language Testing: The Social Dimension* by McNamara and Roever (2006) also addresses the social dimensions of how language tests are used. It elaborates on—and attempts to move beyond—the notion of fairness in examining the social concerns surrounding language testing (for a more updated and in-depth discussion of fairness and justice in language assessment, see McNamara, Knoch, and Fan, 2019). Considerably, both of these books centrally deal with test *use* rather than the essence of English language proficiency tests and their integral ideological features that can also be scrutinized from a critical perspective.

Up to the present time, the literature of the field has steadily continued to accommodate a tiny stream of theoretical discussions and research reports of issues of the cultural, social, and political aspects of English language testing at global and national levels (Booth, 2018; Hamid, 2016; Karatas and Okan, 2019; Pearson, 2019; Schissel, 2019). However, the spread and dominance of internationally reigning high-stakes tests of English language proficiency—as briefly exemplified in the two instances raised at the beginning of this preface—demands extensive discussions and research that extend beyond the meager contributions that can be counted in the past two decades (Jenkins and Leung, 2019). This thin body of literature remains clearly marginalized in mainstream theoretical discussions of the field. Even Shohamy's (2019) own most recent contribution highlights the scarcity of critical accounts of English language testing by opening up new areas of inquiry. She argues that the perspectives of English as a lingua franca and translanguaging tend to be overlooked in language assessment, and that testing practices need to accommodate such views of language and language education (Shohamy, 2019). This can be counted as an invitation to expand the theoretical domain of sociopolitical debates surrounding English language teaching and testing.

In the actual practice of English testing in classroom life and local level, as well as national and international levels, there is arguably little trace of socioculturally sensitive testing practices. Even the limited considerations of such concerns in practice tend to fall within the conceptual confinements of measurementist views of language testing in the form of discussions of washback (Xu and Liu, 2018) and test fairness (Karami and Mok, 2013). "Fairness" has even been used as an index to accuse critical language testing of extremism in confronting psychometric perspectives (Karami, 2013). Therefore, the prospect of the actual embrace of sociopolitically sensitive understandings of language assessment is still far away, and an indispensable prerequisite for that prospect is considerable further development in the theoretical discussions and empirical investigations of the sociopolitics of language testing.

* * *

The contributions in this volume highlight marginalized but significant perspectives on the sociopolitical essence of English language tests and testing processes by exploring the implications of testing theories and practices from a critical perspective, that is, a view that foregrounds concerns surrounding power inequalities. In addition to further discussing the politics of test use, the book addresses issues of ideology, diversity, and dominance in English language testing. We hope this collection yields valuable insights for the language education community who have focused on positivistic and cognitively oriented conceptions of language testing and also sparks interest for a new generation of scholars and students who may wish to venture beyond the traditional boundaries of the field. The eleven chapters, which are organized in two parts, consider the contextual differences and the extant literature on English language testing concerns in English-speaking countries (e.g., Hawthorne, 1997; Schissel, 2010, 2019) and other contexts around the world (e.g., Crossey, 2009; Hogan-Brun, Mar-Molinero, and Stevenson, 2009).

"Part I" comprises five chapters that examine "The Ideologies of Testing in English Speaking Countries." In Chapter 1, John Yandell, Brenton Doecke, and Zamzam Abdi illustrate key moments of classroom life in a school in London that are overshadowed by the General Certificate of Secondary Education (GCSE) examination in English Literature as a high-stakes test. They explicate the ideological functioning of such tests through shaping everyday school activities. They argue that this very reconstructive role of testing mechanisms makes them a neoliberal apparatus but at the same time constitutes a possible means of resistance as enacted by both students and teachers. Also concerned with standardized national-level testing, Chapter 2 by Leonard Freeman and Gillian Wigglesworth turns to the context of Australia. They critique the National Assessment Program—Literacy and Numeracy (NAPLaN) in terms of how it measures the impact of school attendance on the literacy and numeracy achievement of children in remote indigenous communities. Through a reanalysis of school-level achievement data of schools in the Northern Territory of Australia, the chapter illustrates how the English language learning needs of students from indigenous-language-speaking communities often remain unnoticed within national standard literacy and numeracy assessment practices. Disturbingly, children who speak indigenous languages as their mother tongue are seen to be in need of specific procedures of teaching and assessment.

Luis Poza and Sheila Shannon, in Chapter 3, shift the focus to English language testing in the United States. They raise the concern that the burdens created by the use of English language testing as a measure of school achievement for bilingual learners is rooted in the hegemony of English. Referring specifically to certain settings in Southwest United States, Poza and Shannon view the uncritical embrace of tests by teachers as an element that perpetuates this condition, and they advocate a form of teacher education that encourages teachers' transformative roles. In Chapter 4, Netta Avineri and James Perren call for socially situated language testing within the practices of service-learning. Following extensive reviews of various issues related to language testing in service-learning, the chapter briefly examines two instances of service-learning in which the authors themselves were involved in order to illustrate aspects of their proposed critical language assessment framework.

In the final chapter of the first part of the book, Jamie Schissel's Chapter 5 provides a discussion of English language tests exploited as gatekeeping tools that rely on a deficit view of language-minoritized individuals. Broadly situating her arguments within the sociocultural context of the United States, she revisits some hitherto marginally considered aspects of language test validity such as cultural considerations and the role of values. The chapter culminates in a call for testing practices that are sensitive to sociopolitical dynamics as mediated through heteroglossic English language testing approaches that can be specifically developed for language-minoritized bilinguals. In depicting heteroglossic testing, in addition to referring to studies in the United States, Schissel presents a case of adopting such approaches in classroom-based English language assessment in Mexico and an example of the successful integration of students' multilingual background into large-scale language testing in South Africa. These examples from contexts where English is not the first language of the society transition us into the next part of the book that focuses on such contexts.

The six chapters in "Part II" explore "The Politics of Testing in the Non-English-Speaking World." Ruanni Tupas, in Chapter 6, investigates the politics of language testing within the context of a US development project—the Jobs Enhancement English Programme—that was committed to teaching the English language in the Philippines. Highlighting the role of colonialism on the lives and social relations of colonized nations that gained independence, the chapter concentrates on the coloniality of language testing. Tupas argues that testing practices can be shaped by sediments of colonialism and can, therefore, conflict with the values of test takers in these given communities. In Chapter 7, Masaki Oda explores the place of standardized tests in language teaching policies in Japan. He analyzes some Japanese newspaper articles that promote the application of commercial tests as part of university entrance exams. Based on his findings that reveal that these articles reflect Japanese educational policy makers' inclination toward the standardized language tests, he exhorts teachers to actively project more realistic images of such tests in the public sphere.

The next two chapters turn to the context of South Korea. Gwan-Hyeok Im, Liying Cheng, and Dongil Shin address issues of policies and public opinions with regard to the application and functioning of language tests in their discussion of the National English Ability Test (NEAT) in this country. They examine a number of official policy documents as well as media reports to understand the sociopolitical considerations related to the development and subsequent abandonment of the NEAT. The test is portrayed as a social practice intertwined with values and political purposes within the society. In the same national setting (South Korea), Miso Kim and Mari Haneda focus on the ideological climate surrounding the Test of English for International Communication (TOEIC) that forms a crucial part of the job market gatekeeping system. The authors examine jobseekers' perspectives of the problem of English proficiency and its assessment as well as the candidates' actual test performance. The chapter underlines the gap between the tests and real-life communication and, therefore, problematizes the exclusionary nature of these English proficiency tests.

In Chapter 10, Ali Al-Issa addresses the application of the International English Language Testing System (IELTS) as a measurement tool for selecting English language teachers at a university in Oman. Through a critical discourse analysis of semi-structured interviews with teacher candidates who took the IELTS, he probes the ideological underpinnings of the testing practices. The chapter demonstrates how some hegemonic aspects of such a high-stakes test can cause possible harm. Finally, Chapter 11 presents Prem Phyak's study of the construction of imagined communities through the promotion of international English language tests in Nepal. He analyzes a body of multimodal data comprising various promotional materials that were produced and displayed by educational consultancy institutions. The promotion of native-speakerism and the commodification of the English language are discussed as major ideological aspects of such discursive practices. Importantly, these issues are shown to be mechanisms for creating imaginaries of transnational migration and dream life opportunities in other countries.

* * *

Inevitably, the title of our volume invites comparison to Hall and Eggington's (2000) edited volume, *The Sociopolitics of English Language Teaching*. Nearly two decades ago, and underscoring macro-level cultural, social, and political concerns about English language teaching, they argued that such dimensions of language education are a crucial part of the decisions we make. Highlighting the *sensibilities* and *awareness* of language teachers with regard to sociopolitical issues, they maintained that their main purpose was "to introduce these issues to aspiring teachers of English from myriad educational contexts and geographical locations for the purposes of provoking their sensibilities, stimulating discussion, and ultimately raising students' awareness of these important issues" (p. 1). Building on Hall and Eggington's astute observations as well as the wider *critical turn* in language education that had started much earlier (e.g., Graman, 1988; Pennycook, 1990) and has continued to this day (e.g., López-Gopar, 2019), our volume was motivated by a need to usher in a much overdue discussion on the sociopolitical essence of English language testing. By initiating and extending this conversation on the ideological nature of standardized English language tests, we hope to inspire policy makers, academics, language educators, and English language learners around the world to be more aware of the inequalities embedded in language tests and testing practices and possibly to engage in concrete acts of transformation within English language testing.

April, 2019

References

Al-Issa, A. and Mirhosseini, S. A. (Eds.) (forthcoming). *English Language Education Worldwide Today: Ideologies, Policies, and Practices*. London: Routledge.

Booth, D. K. (2018). *The Sociocultural Activity of High Stakes Standardised Language Testing: TOEIC Washback in a South Korean Context*. Cham: Springer.

Crossey, M. (2009). The role of micropolitics in multinational, high-stakes language assessment systems. In C. Alderson (Ed.), *The Politics of Language Education: Individuals and Institutions* (pp. 147–65). Clevedon: Multilingual Matters.

Fulcher, G. (2009). Test use and political philosophy. *Annual Review of Applied Linguistics*, *29*(3), 3–20.

Graman, T. (1988). Education for humanization: Applying Paulo Freire's pedagogy to learning a second language. *Harvard Educational Review*, *58*(4), 433–48.

Hall, J. K. and Eggington, W. G. (Eds.) (2000). *The Sociopolitics of English Language Teaching*. Clevedon: Multilingual Matters.

Hamid, M. O. (2016). Policies of global English tests: test-takers' perspectives on the IELTS retake policy. *Discourse: Studies in the Cultural Politics of Education*, *37*(3), 472–87.

Hawthorne, L. (1997). The political dimension of English language testing in Australia. *Language Testing*, *14*(3), 248–60.

Hogan-Brun, G., Mar-Molinero, C., and Stevenson, P. (Eds.) (2009). *Discourses on Language and Integration: Critical Perspectives on Language Testing Regimes in Europe*. Amsterdam: John Benjamins.

Jenkins, J. and Leung, C. (2019). From mythical "standard" to standard reality: The need for alternatives to standardized English language tests. *Language Teaching*, 52(1), 86–110.

Karami, H. (2013). The quest for fairness in language testing. *Educational Research and Evaluation: An International Journal on Theory and Practice*, 19(2–3), 158–69.

Karami, H. and Mok, M. M. C. (2013). Editorial (Special Issue on Fairness Issues in Educational Assessment). *Educational Research and Evaluation: An International Journal on Theory and Practice*, 19(2–3), 101–3.

Karatas, T. O. and Okan, Z. (2019). The power of language tests in Turkish context: A critical study. *Journal of Language and Linguistic Studies*, 15(1), 210–30.

Khan, S. Z. (2009). Imperialism of international tests: An EIL perspective. In F. Sharifian (Ed.), *English as an International Language: Perspectives and Pedagogical Issues* (pp. 190–205). Clevedon: Multilingual Matters.

López-Gopar, M. E. (Ed.) (2019). *International Perspectives on Critical Pedagogies in ELT*. Cham: Palgrave Macmillan.

Lynch, B. K. (2001). Rethinking assessment from a critical perspective. *Language Testing*, 18(4), 351–72.

McNamara, T. (1998). Policy and social considerations in language assessment. *Annual Review of Applied Linguistics*, 18(3), 304–19.

McNamara, T. (2001). Language assessment as social practice: Challenges for research. *Language Testing*, 18(4), 333–49.

McNamara, T. and Roever, C. (2006). *Language Testing: The Social Dimension*. Malden, MA: Blackwell.

McNamara, T., Knoch, U., and Fan, J. (2019). *Fairness, Justice and Language Assessment: The Role of Measurement*. Oxford: Oxford University Press.

Messick, S. (1981). Evidence and ethics in the evaluation of tests. *Educational Researcher*, 10(9), 9–20.

Mirhosseini, S. A. (2018). Issues of ideology in English language education worldwide: An overview. *Pedagogy, Culture & Society*, 26(1), 19–33.

Pearson, W. S. (2019). Critical perspectives on the IELTS test. *ELT Journal*. http://doi.org/10.1093/elt/ccz006

Pennycook, A. (1990). Critical pedagogy and second language education. *System*, 18(3), 303–14.

Pennycook, A. (2001). *Critical Applied Linguistics: A Critical Introduction*. Mahwah, NJ: Erlbaum.

Sarig, G. (1989). Testing meaning construction: Can we do it fairly? *Language Testing*, 6(1), 77–94.

Schissel, J. L. (2010). Critical issues surrounding test accommodations: A language planning and policy perspective. *Working Papers in Educational Linguistics*, 25(1), 17–35.

Schissel, J. L. (2019). *Social Consequences of Testing for Language-Minoritized Bilinguals in the United States*. Clevedon: Multilingual Matters.

Shepard, L. A. (1997). The centrality of test use and consequences for test validity. *Educational Measurement: Issues and Practice, 16*(2), 5–24.

Shohamy, E. (1998). Critical language testing and beyond. *Studies in Educational Evaluation, 24*(4), 331–45.

Shohamy, E. (2001). Democratic assessment as an alternative. *Language Testing, 18*(4), 373–91.

Shohamy, E. (2001). *The Power of Tests: A Critical Perspective on the Uses of Language Tests*. London: Longman.

Shohamy, E. (2007). Language tests as language policy tools. *Assessment in Education, 14*(1), 117–30.

Shohamy, E. (2013). The discourse of language testing as a tool for shaping national, global, and transnational identities. *Language and Intercultural Communication, 13*(2), 225–36.

Shohamy, E. (2019). Critical language testing and English lingua franca: How can one help the other? In K. Murata (Ed.), *English-Medium Instruction from an English as a Lingua Franca Perspective: Exploring the Higher Education Context* (pp. 271–85). London: Routledge.

Spolsky, B. (1986). A multiple choice for language testers. *Language Testing, 3*(2), 147–58.

Spolsky, B. (1997). The ethics of gatekeeping tests: What have we learned in a hundred years? *Language Testing, 14*(3), 242–47.

Templer, B. (2004). High-stakes testing at high fees: Notes and queries on the international English proficiency assessment market. *Journal for Critical Education Policy Studies, 2*(1), 1–8.

van Dijk, T. A. (1998). *Ideology: A Multidisciplinary Approach*. London: Sage.

van Dijk, T. A. (2006). Ideology and discourse analysis. *Journal of Political Ideologies, 11*(2), 115–40.

Xu, Q. and Liu, J. (2018). *A Study on the Washback Effects of the Test for English Majors (TEM): Implications for Testing and Teaching Reforms*. Cham: Springer.

Foreword

Paula Winke

Language educators know that tests affect teaching and learning. But they do much more than that. They affect education policy, how textbooks and educational materials are written, and how society views individuals who perform below and above the critical test-score cut-points that serve as gateways to desirable (and often limited) goods. The higher the stakes of a given test, the more important it is to ask questions about the appropriateness of the test as well as the ethics and societal benefits of the uses of the test scores. Because more and more high-stakes tests are being developed and adopted around the world, language testers have moved more and more into modern test validation (Chapelle, forthcoming), an area of test research that includes understanding the benefits and scrutinizing consequences of the uses of test scores. Below, I explain this further and how this volume contributes uniquely to understanding high-stakes tests and the power they wield.

Testing Theory Is Predominately on the Periphery of the Social Consequences of Testing, but It Is Moving In

In 1995, Bernard Spolsky wrote that if a test has high stakes, that is, if it is used "to make some serious decisions affecting the future of the persons being tested" (p. 358), then the test developers and administrators have to be careful to fully acknowledge that the test will not be without flaws. This is because language testing is a "flawed technology," he wrote. Language testers have to calculate and document a test's reliability and validity, but more than that, they have to hold an "intelligent and sceptical interpretation of the multiple methods of measurement and assessment used" (p. 358). I often present these excerpts from Spolsky to the students in my graduate-level class on language testing. The individuals in the class are always an amazing mix of international graduate students from around the world. They are in my class as prospective English teachers, or they already are English teachers, and they are on the path toward a master's degree in teaching English to speakers of other languages. Or they are doctoral students who are going to be instructors of English or other languages at the high school or university level or who will go on to do applied linguistics research at universities, not-for-profit agencies, or international applied linguistics institutions. Over the years, I have also had a handful of students go on to take positions at testing agencies around the world. Their aim has always been to try to make large-scale and high-stakes tests of English and other languages as valid and reliable as possible. While I teach, and while the assessment work of my graduates goes on, larger forces are at play that are ingrained into societies and cultures that shape public opinions about tests and how tests take hold, change direction, and come to new purposes and uses. The larger forces are moving on their own but also being challenged, slowed down, and redirected by thoughtful and careful researchers and policy influencers and makers. I often explain to my students that language testers at any level (consumers, users, or creators), as Spolsky (1995) suggested, have to be skeptical of all test-score interpretations. Most importantly, those interpretations have to be overlain onto the sociopolitical landscape for them to be completely and systematically understood. As reviewed by Shohamy (2004, pp. 76–9), language testers must be skeptical and aim toward more inclusive and democratic language testing because of the following reasons:

- Language tests, especially high-stakes and powerful ones, often do not recognize test takers' home language(s) or bases of knowledge. Thus, minority groups often do not have their cultural capital or linguistic skills valued through testing (see Freeman and Wigglesworth, Chapter 2). Instead, what they bring with them as free human beings is ignored.
- Majority languages and cultures are prioritized and "enforced" (Shohamy, 2004, p. 78) through testing practices, which then become *de facto* language education policies (Menken, 2017), which perpetuate a disenfranchisement (and loss) of linguistic and cultural heritage, both locally and around the world.
- Through testing, groups from nondominate cultures and societies are compared to those of the dominate group. Test success (and thus overall success) is a one-size-fits-all policy, meaning that regardless of one's linguistic or cultural background, one just becomes a *test taker*, stripped of all rich identifying and discriminating information, and is passed through the test to come out as a number, as described by Yandell, Doecke, and Abdi

(Chapter 1). This can be seen as deficit positioning (Schissel, Chapter 5) and marginalizing (Poza and Shannon, Chapter 3; Al-Issa, Chapter 10).

The chapters in this volume stand as compelling evidence that high-stakes standardized English language tests around the world are part of a large moving fabric of centuries-long social norming as well as political and economic influence. This aspect of English language assessment, whether deliberate or not, is showcased, digested, and debated within this book's chapters in a frank and telling way. And the arguments the authors present are convincing. For example, Yandell, Doecke, and Abdi (Chapter 1) showcase how English tests are part of neoliberal reform. Poza and Shannon (Chapter 3) describe how English tests marginalize and discriminate against linguistic and ethnic groups. Im, Cheng, and Shin (Chapter 8) take a problematized look, through an exemplar, of how English language testing is difficult (psychologically, economically, and structurally) to wrestle away from the testing giants. And Phyak (Chapter 11) appraises how English tests help reproduce sociopolitical inequalities and a restrictive or reduced global political-economic ideology. The stories the chapter authors in this volume weave though literature reviews and quantitative and qualitative data are breathtaking. And, the chapters tend to point to one larger conclusion, and that is that high-stakes standardized English language tests present a type of *filtering bottleneck* through which only certain linguistic typologies, cultural and economic affordances, and ways of approaching English language study pass. This is not, I believe, uniquely the fault of the tests nor of the testing agencies themselves but rather is due to the historical, political, economic, and social nature of English language testing around the world, a complicated and often strife-ridden endeavor that exists as a historical and contemporary way of *access control*.

This *access control* or *filtering bottleneck* process of English language tests (see Figure 0.1) is in place due to a desire, requirement, or need by people to move from one side of the bottleneck to the other and a lack of resources for all to pass through or a lack of resources that would enable the bottleneck itself become wider and less taxing. It is a question of supply and demand, but not a simple one, for histories, cultures, socioeconomics, and current ideologies and politics shape and restrict the backdrop and flow through the bottleneck. The filtering bottleneck system is (or was) put in place contemporarily or historically (or both) by various stakeholders for a number of reasons. Nonetheless, in most cases, the system is (a) to promote individuals as potential test takers, (b) to sort them into categories in relation to established cut scores, and (c) to select from the actual

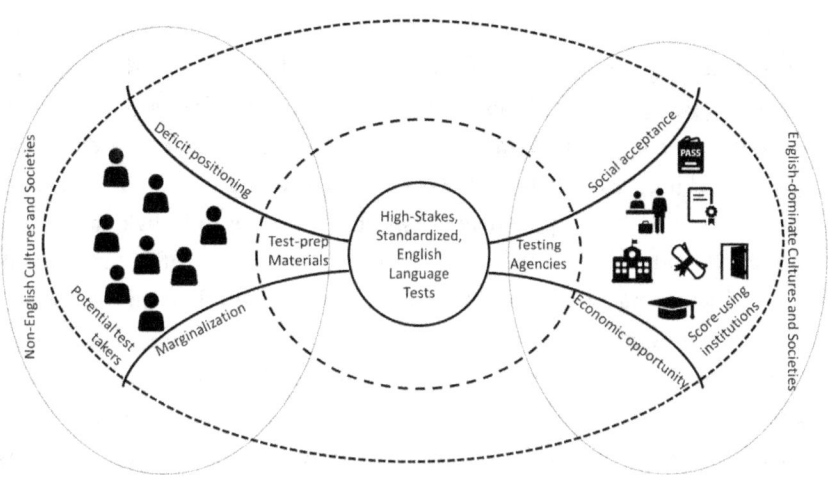

Figure 0.1 A negative (nondemocratic) view of English language tests as a *filtering bottleneck* through which only certain linguistic typologies, cultural and economic affordances, and ways of approaching English language study pass. Icons reproduced through subscription by the author to Freepik, www.flaticon.com.

pool of test takers, based on performances relative to the cut score, to enable individuals to pass through. Meanwhile, the desire to pass through the filtering bottleneck (from left to right) can be promoted by either side of the bottleneck itself, and therein the difficulties may lie. One's desire to pass through may be motivated by an intrinsic yearning to pass (ideally). In this case, the desire is on the part of the would-be test taker, who looks ahead and is determined to have something in the future, and the person's goal setting requires, consequentially, a substantial required plan to take a standardized test at the bottleneck (not ideal, especially for the individual who must take the test). Thus, the desire to test at the bottleneck is an ancillary goal, one tied to the person's larger personal goal, which may or may not have anything to do with language, really.

Or the desire to test at the bottleneck may be motivated and propelled by an external pressure immediately on the other (right-hand) side, perhaps (taking a skeptical view, as requested by Spolsky, 1995) in part to create a market for the assessment itself, that is, the testing agencies themselves may fuel a desire to take the test through the promotion of the test or test preparation materials that advertise or promote the soundness of the exam and/or the key-access opportunities that the exam will afford. Likewise, promotion of the filtering bottleneck may come from the institutions and opportunities on the far *other* right-hand side of the bottleneck. The test-score users, such as the universities or government agencies or certification bodies (the institutions), that require the tests may contribute to the demand for test preparation materials and may contribute to the growth and power of the test itself. Their enticing advertisements of unique opportunities (pictures of happy international students on a university campus in an English-speaking country, for example, or advertisements of English-speaking technology engineers engaged and invested in their work with sound and stable employment prospectives) may push individuals toward the filtering bottleneck, as the only way to pass through to the campuses or opportunities being offered by the institutions on the other side is through acceptable scores on the tests at the bottleneck itself. Such bottlenecks are useful for the institutions that receive and use the scores for filtering processes because, in general, the supply outweighs the demand. Test scores are an easy and rather objective (nonarbitrary-seeming) way of rendering (at least first-pass) decisions. In other words, the test saves the institutions money, while also promoting the institution as prestigious. The bottleneck process enforces the notion that what the institution has to offer is rare and can only be obtained through a rigorous selection process.

This situation of high-stakes standardized, English language testing as a filtering bottleneck is complicated and identity-stripping (Avineri and Perren, Chapter 4) at best and imperialistic (Tupas, Chapter 6) at worst. So what are language testing professionals to do? How can teachers and society at large promote English language tests that are democratic, inclusive, and that recognize the test takers' unique linguistic backgrounds and cultural capital? I turn to Shohamy (2004) and the chapters within this volume for guidance.

A Guide to Democratic and Linguistically and Culturally Affirming English Language Testing

While it is one thing to call out the sociopolitical problems and injustices that befall many, if not all, of the contexts of high-stakes standardized English testing today, it is another matter altogether to try to suggest ways to improve the current situation, which is complex, historically entrenched, and unfortunately catastrophically resistant to change. The task has been undertaken in this volume, even if it seems daunting and even Sisyphean. The task involves increasing the assessment literacy of language policy makers and the public at large, who are constantly changing generationally and who also ride the tide of sociopolitical climates that themselves drive educational and assessment policies, limiting or increasing access to goods and services. As outlined in the chapters that follow, several steps can be undertaken to make the sociopolitics of English language testing better and more inclusive of all stakeholder groups. A humble *first-step* list is presented below.

- First and foremost, channeling Shohamy (2004), the authors of the chapters call for *inclusion*, from all stakeholder groups, in English language testing. This means that for tests to be democratic and beneficial for all, the test designers must "consider the voices of diverse groups in multicultural societies" (Shohamy, 2004, p. 79). Language testing agencies and the institutions that use the test scores must recognize and include the voices of the test takers from linguistic and cultural minority groups (the groups not in power) and/or their advocates and take into consideration the test takers' sources of linguistic knowledge and cultural capital in innovative and convincing ways. This will necessitate test designers having claims about the test-score interpretations concerning the minority groups. The claims must be backed up and justified through robust and rigorous test-score validation research. If the validation arguments cannot extend to certain minority groups, then those minority groups should be exempted from testing.
- Second, Freeman and Wigglesworth (Chapter 2) and the authors of the other chapters in this book demonstrate how and why minority groups must not be ignored, discounted, and simply absorbed into the test averages. When an English-language-test bottleneck presents itself as the only pathway toward national or international affordances, accommodations or alternative testing pathways, or both, must be offered to culturally diverse groups who were not in mind when the test was originally created. In other words, when tests are designed, their technical test manuals must include a list of for whom (and for what purposes) the tests are intended. The one-size-fits-all policy cannot be supported. Results and technical-test-manual information should be separated by test-taker groups so that individual groups' performances can be ascertained and their scores judged externally as a fair or unfair application of the purported test purposes and test-score uses.
- A third guide was originally described by Shohamy (2004), who stressed that when a test has too much power to exclude and discriminate, especially against language and ethnic minority groups, the test itself must be disenfranchised of its strong power. Its power must be limited or taken away, she claimed. This can be done by allowing for alternative forms of testing (either additional tests, portfolios, or non-test evidence of performance or performance ability) to widen the bottleneck, so to speak, for the

minority groups (and, hopefully, as a positive consequence, for everyone). Shohamy noted, like Spolsky (1995) did, that test developers must "assume responsibility for their [tests'] consequences" (p. 79) and own up to them and make them right.

- As called out by Im, Cheng, and Shin (Chapter 8) and this volume in general, more research into sociopolitical factors in testing is needed. Qualitative studies, such as that by Kim and Haneda (Chapter 9), can strongly demonstrate and spell out well the disconnects between English-test-score interpretations and the values, experiences, and perceptions of English language learners from non-English-dominate societies. Qualitative research, such as that presented in this volume, is particularly powerful because it is inherently understandable and relatable. Numbers are, to be frank, *numbing*. No matter how much data one has, robust qualitative reporting is always more compelling, attention-holding, and influential. With a critical, skeptical stance and eye-witness reporting, we can change the world, one English-language-testing context at a time.

The takeaway at the end of the book will be for readers to widely share the chapters in this volume to promote and disseminate information on how and why high-stakes standardized tests of English are deeply embedded in history, economics, and the current sociopolitical climate. Knowing this and understanding this will help everyone, including the burgeoning language testers in my testing class, to understand the formidable and important work that lies ahead.

References

Chapelle, C. (forthcoming). Validity in language assessment. In P. Winke and T. Brunfaut (Eds.), *The Routledge Handbook of Second Language Acquisition and Language Testing*. New York: Routledge.

Menken, K. (2017). High-stakes tests as de facto language education policies. In E. Shohamy and I. Or (Eds.), *Encyclopedia of Language and Education* (Volume 7: Language testing and assessment) (3rd ed.) (pp. 385–96). New York, NY: Springer.

Spolsky, B. (1995), *Measured Words: The Development of Objective Language Testing*. Oxford: Oxford University Press.

Shohamy, E. (2004). Assessment in multicultural societies: Applying democratic principles and practices to language testing. In B. Norton and K. Toohey (Eds.), *Critical Pedagogies and Language Learning* (pp. 72–92). Cambridge: Cambridge University Press.

Part One

The Ideologies of Testing in English-Speaking Countries

1

Who Me? Hailing Individuals as Subjects: Standardized Literacy Testing as an Instrument of Neoliberal Ideology

John Yandell, Brenton Doecke, and Zamzam Abdi

Standardized Literacy Testing, Schooling, and the Reconstruction of Subjectivities

This chapter investigates the complexities and contradictions of standardized literacy testing when it is used as an instrument of neoliberal reform. Our focus is not primarily on the capacity of standardized tests to meaningfully represent the abilities of students but on the ideological work they are designed to achieve. In a policy environment where governments were committed to drawing on the best research available on language and literacy, the various critiques of the validity of standardized testing as a representation of students' literacy abilities might have had some impact. But standardized testing is primarily a mechanism for regulating what happens in schools, exerting a profound influence on curriculum (how knowledge is conceptualized and whose knowledge is valued) and pedagogy (how students are positioned in relation to that knowledge). Standardized testing *enacts* neoliberal ideology through restructuring the everyday life of the school, mandating certain practices in a bid to radically transform the school as a social organization and the roles that pupils are assigned within it.

James Britton suggested that education might best be construed as *an effect of community* (Britton, 1987, p. 25, original emphasis). Reflecting on the contribution made by Vygotsky to our understanding of pedagogy, Britton was envisaging the teacher as responsible for creating in each classroom a richly interactive learning community, thereby facilitating the kinds of intercultural dialogue that should ideally characterize the larger community. In the thirty years since Britton's essay first appeared, neoliberal governments around the world have sought to refashion schooling along totally different lines. In both England and Australia (the countries where we are located), bipartisan educational policies have seen the development of accountability systems that have radically transformed schooling, diminishing any sense of the need for schools to be responsive to the diverse populations for which they cater. Schools have been recast as businesses and parents constructed as consumers. The quality of the product that schools offer is measured by standardized literacy testing, supposedly enabling parents to make informed choices about the best school for their children (cf. Ball, 2012 [1990]; DES, 1987; DfE, 2014; Doecke et al., 2007; Jones, 1989; Jones et al., 2008; MCEETYA, 2008).

Regimes of standardized testing have been centrally implicated in this refashioning, constructing the individual learner as the unit of analysis without any recognition of his or her cultural identity. This is accomplished by the public spectacle of organizing students to take their seats in the examination hall and subsequently through the spreadsheet showing their results. Students' separate identities are announced in the disposition of the furniture in the examination room, that most undialogic of spaces. There is, likewise, a formal separation of one student from another when they are each placed in their own (aptly named) cell on the spreadsheet, their individual performance recorded as fact, permanently available to scrutiny and to statistical analysis, so that both they and their teachers may be held to account. And, in examination hall and spreadsheet, the ways in which individual learners are interpellated signal their equivalence, their interchangeability. For all relevant purposes of analysis and accountability, these are units that can properly be compared, one with another, placed in rank order, mapped against prior attainment, aggregated and averaged, set out on tables that show the overall performance of students at the school. Their individuality is thus of a somewhat rarefied kind: it is the uniqueness of the candidate number by which they are identified, not to be confused with the individuality of human beings, as that individuality is shaped by their cultures and histories.

Schooling, in this neoliberal model, becomes, in effect, a continual preparation for the test, since the test is the destination to which all stages in the process are directed and from which they derive their meaning. For learners, the test score represents a summative judgment made at various stages in their schooling. For teachers, the same scores become indices of professional efficacy or the lack thereof. Regimes of standardized testing thus become highly efficient mechanisms of the educational *Ideological State Apparatus*, operating to transform the very meaning of education (Althusser, 1971).

Standardized testing constructs ability as the property of an individual student that becomes visible when he or she performs certain arbitrary exercises under exam conditions. Such testing is blind to the learning that becomes manifest when students participate in collaborative activities, when—to draw on Douglas Barnes—they "come together in a meaningful communication—talk, write, read books, collaborate, become angry with one another, learn what to say and do, and how to interpret what others say and do" (Barnes, 1992 [1975], p. 14). The rituals of standardized testing, most starkly represented by the seating in an examination hall and the strict injunction not to talk to one another while the exam is in progress, seek to radically undermine the social conditions necessary for students to pursue genuinely intellectual and creative work at school that might have significance for them. Those rituals privilege a reified body of knowledge and skills that they must absorb and regurgitate, remote from their experiences and the languages and cultures of their communities.

Students nonetheless bring all their experiences to school, including their languages and stories. This is the stuff of their conversations with one another. You just have to stand in the middle of a school assembly area at the end of the summer break to sense how schooling provides an important social space for students, as they talk with one another, sharing their experiences. Yet standardized testing denies the legitimacy of those cultural resources for language and learning, focusing, instead, on what it constructs as an individual's cognitive level. This supposedly reflects the benevolent intention of equipping students to participate in a twenty-first-century economy, as in policy rhetoric that justifies standardized literacy testing as a key performance indicator of whether schools are producing a skilled and knowledgeable workforce. But what this rhetoric means, in effect, is that schools are being recast to mirror a neoliberal economy where everything is measurable and predictable, calculated to produce the required "value add."

Despite its pretense to test a level of "basic" literacy that is common to all (as in the notion of a "standard" English), standardized testing has differential effects on schools that cater for radically diverse school communities, ensuring that the system as a whole remains geared toward serving the interests of social elites. Standardized testing presupposes the very differences that it reveals. There is a fundamental difference between the way standardized testing is experienced by students in a comprehensive school located in a socially disadvantaged community and the impact that such testing has when it is implemented in a wealthy private school. Children from socially disadvantaged communities are being tested on their knowledge of a language that other people speak, whereas the children of the middle class are simply demonstrating their familiarity with the language they use at home.

This structural inequality is masked by mechanisms that are focused on differentiating between students according to their ability, constructed as a property of individuals without any regard to their place within the class structure or the type of cultural capital they bring to their education. Australia provides an especially crude example of this effacement of the social and cultural identities of students through the mechanism of standardized testing: each year all schools in Australia are required to administer the NAPLaN (National Assessment Program—Literacy and Numeracy) tests. The results of all schools, ranging from elite private schools in Melbourne to schools in remote Aboriginal communities, are then published on a website for people to make judgments about their effectiveness. This supposedly enables parents to choose the right school as well as allowing politicians and bureaucrats to determine whether schools are producing a literate workforce that will serve the interests of the economy (see Doecke, Kostogriz, and Illesca, 2010).

That, at least, is the ambition of neoliberal reforms. But our aim in writing this chapter is to argue that this is not and can never be the whole story. Althusser's understanding of ideology provides a theoretical framework for our analysis. By invoking Althusser's account of the way students are required to take on the identities that schools ascribe to them, we are also seeking to critically interrogate that account and to resist its bleak determinism. Standardized literacy testing shapes what happens in schools without fully comprehending everything that goes on within them. It seeks to construct students as competitive individuals, but such pressures continually misrepresent and conflict with the social relationships of the classroom and the way students and teachers experience those relationships from day to day.

Classrooms as Complex, Dialogic Sites

We want to look in some detail at one such moment of preparation for a high-stakes test, the General Certificate of Secondary Education (GCSE) examination in English Literature which is undertaken by almost all sixteen-year-old students in England. This moment, a single lesson taught by Zamzam (the third author of this chapter) as a student teacher during a practicum that was part of her preservice Postgraduate Certificate in Education, reveals not only the workings of the *Ideological State Apparatus* but also the tensions and contradictions within the system and the ways in which, within classrooms, such systems of control are questioned and resisted.

We remain interested in the complexity of what goes on in classrooms, a complexity of interaction and engagement, on the part of both teachers and students, that does not seem to us to be reducible to the neoliberal teleology of the test. And we retain a commitment to particularity, to the different meanings that are made and contested in different classrooms, and to ways of understanding these meanings that are attentive to the different histories, subjectivities, and interests of the participants in such acts of meaning making. This commitment is both political and methodological. Neoliberalism operates through mechanisms of abstraction and reification, reducing complex human processes of learning to the ciphers of test scores and thereby rendering invisible—insignificant, unworthy of notice—the processes themselves, most notably the deeply social character of learning when students engage in conversations and activities that are meaningful to them (Unwin and Yandell, 2016). But it remains possible to represent what happens in classrooms differently because what happens in classrooms is different from the sterile model of teaching and learning that neoliberalism imposes on schools.

Our focus on a single moment, and our attempt to represent that moment in narrative form, thus constitutes a way of resisting the systematic effacement of lived classroom experience that neoliberalism enacts. In this endeavor, we are working within a tradition of research and pedagogy (cf. Doecke, 2013; Yandell, 2013; Yandell and Brady, 2016), focusing on the rich particularities of a specific classroom setting, although we are confident in saying that the contradictory nature of Zamzam's situation is also being played out in other settings where neoliberal policy has been imposed. In a disadvantaged school in a southeastern suburb of Melbourne, Bella Illesca struggles as a remedial literacy teacher to bring her students up to the standards dictated by the literacy outcomes mandated for each year level by the state government (Illesca, 2014). In a school in the same region, Lisa Breen gives an account of her own struggle to move her students beyond the deficit constructions foisted on them by standardized literacy tests (Breen, 2014). In London, Anne Turvey, while visiting one of her student teachers, engages in conversation with the pupils, only to find one boy who is obsessed—and oppressed—by where he sits in relation to the levels imposed by government. "Do you think I'll always be on this level?" he asks her plaintively (Turvey, Yandell, and Ali, 2014). Such examples might be multiplied by drawing on other stories in England, Australia, and the United States, not to mention other policy environments that have all been radically reshaped by the implementation of standards-based reforms (see Abraham, 2016; Taylor, 2003).

We are stepping back, however, from constructing these reforms as part of a neoliberal policy juggernaut that no one can ultimately resist. Indeed, all the examples of classroom situations that we have just mentioned tell stories of teachers and students engaging in dialogue that challenges the hegemony of such reforms.

The Influence of Policy: Prescribing Texts and Identities

Before moving to Zamzam's story, we need to provide some contextual information on the current version of standardized testing in England. The GCSE English Literature exam, located within the framework of the English National Curriculum (DfE, 2014), manages to combine neoliberalism with an extreme form of cultural conservatism (cf. Jones, 2013). Its government-mandated specifications (DfE, 2013), which set out the prescribed content and assessment arrangements, adopt Arnoldian language to signal an attachment to a model of culture as a more or less fixed body of canonical texts:

> Through literature, students have a chance to develop culturally and acquire knowledge of the best that has been thought and written. (DfE, 2013, p. 3; cf. Arnold, 1993/1869)

The process that is envisaged involves more than the acquisition of a body of knowledge as it aims to enable students to "appreciate the depth and power of the English literary heritage" (ibid.). Students are positioned quite explicitly as passive recipients, not makers, of culture. They are required to genuflect before a literary culture that has been privileged by government, not one in which they might actively engage in issues of meaning and value as they arise through sharing their reading together. Questions of literary value are addressed with matter-of-fact confidence, indeed as matters of fact that brook no contradiction:

> Students should study a range of high quality, intellectually challenging, and substantial whole texts in detail. These must include:
>
> - at least one play by Shakespeare
> - at least one 19th century novel
> - a selection of poetry since 1789, including representative Romantic poetry
> - fiction or drama from the British Isles from 1914 onwards.
>
> All works should have been originally written in English (DfE, 2013, p. 4).

From the perspective of policy, there is, it would appear, a simple correlation between the quality of the text and the intellectual challenge it provides, and there is a complacent conviction that where quality is to be found is in the English literary heritage and the English language. The last of these bullet points is directly relevant to the lesson taught by Zamzam, since it is the injunction that the fiction students read must be "from the British Isles" that lies behind the choice of text: William Golding's (1954/1962) novel, *Lord of the Flies*.

The practice of literary interpretation as it is enacted in a GCSE English classroom might initially appear to be at a remove from how texts are used in standardized testing in the earlier years of schooling, when students are typically required to select the right answer from the multiple choices presented to them in order to demonstrate their understanding of a passage excerpted from a larger text. The word "literature" as it figures within the English curriculum (both in England and Australia) is usually taken to denote a level of sensitivity toward literary language that only the very best students can fully accomplish (Teese, 2011). This level is far above the standard measured by tick-the-box literacy testing. Yet both the curriculum and the pedagogy that Zamzam is required to implement are every bit as regulated as the standardized testing her students have experienced earlier in their schooling. The classroom situation that provides the focus of our analysis reveals the same standardizing pressures as standardized testing, as it is usually understood, and—crucially—the same capacity by students to register and judge what is happening to them, and thus to open up the possibility of alternative modes of thought and feeling, however they are being interpellated.

Zamzam's practicum took place in an inner London comprehensive school, with an ethnically diverse pupil population. Zamzam herself is of Somali heritage; she arrived in the UK with her family when she was a teenager and attended a London secondary school. For Zamzam, then, as for many of the students she was teaching, the curriculum with which they were confronted posed questions about identity and affiliation: where were they to position themselves in relation to a version of literary culture so exclusively tied to a particular notion of nationhood and belonging?

Zamzam's Story

Before I started my second and final practicum, I had not read *Lord of the Flies*. The only knowledge I had of it was a vague memory of a Peter Brook's 1963 film adaptation that I had seen as a child. I remember it fondly as my sister had read it at school and was quite excited to share it with us. As a child, I was unaware of the political and philosophical questions raised within the story; I had taken it as an innocent tale of adventure where young boys try to survive the wilderness without the help of adults. Reading the text as an adult, as a teacher, opened my eyes up to a lot of difficult questions. I found that the novel was an indictment of what was considered norms of our society—Western society. It brings to light the dichotomies of good and evil, civilization and savagery, and questions just how valid we are in our construction of them. It questions human nature and how, deep down, all of these opposing factors are within us. Throughout our reading of the text, we would often stop to consider what certain images may mean. Many students were able to identify the literal and figurative meanings of painting one's face (this is something I want to come back to). Students were also able to identify the allegorical aspects of the text, the representations of characters as aspects of our society: Ralph as order and democracy; Piggy as scientific and intellectual; Simon as religion; Jack as uncontrollable desire.

While reading the novel in class, something happened that left me considering the impact that texts can have on students' sense of self.

We had reached the penultimate chapter, where the boys have fallen out with each other, factions have been created, and there is a chance of all-out war. Jack and his tribe have painted faces, and Golding seldom refers to the boys by name: they have become "the painted face" or "the group of savages" (Golding, 1954/1962). I was reading the chapter aloud to the class; some students were reading along while others were just listening to me. In one of the moments of discussion a student, Andre,[1] said something rather interesting.

Andre: Miss, there is a bad word on the next page.

Zamzam: Oh really? It depends on how you react to it. Will you be sensible?

Andre was not as chatty and jokey as he usually was. There seemed to be something a little more serious in his tone. This left me a little confused but I strived to read on.

Piggy's character becomes infuriated; he can no longer handle the uncivilized behavior of Jack and his followers.

"'I got this to say. You're acting like a crowd of kids' . . . 'Which is better—to be a pack of painted niggers like you are, or to be sensible like Ralph is?'" (Golding, 1954/1962)[2]

The class was silent. One black student, who had not been reading along, shouted out, "What did he say? Miss, can you read that again?" There was a tone of anger in his voice. I was frozen by what I had read. I was experiencing the text along with the students. I had not rehearsed a dignified response to this situation.

This is when Andre commented, "I'm glad Miss Abdi is reading it instead of Mr Lewis."

I wonder whether he felt this way because of the solidarity we shared—the rejection we felt from the text. All along we had been discussing how the progression of the story was a sign of the "fall of civilisation," and we had agreed that the boys were falling into "savagery" and losing their "humanity." The students and I were comfortable with the themes and the dichotomies being presented. However, this changed when we realized that the "savagery" we had been discussing was being attributed to the color of our skin, our black skin. The class was in shock.

We were not allowed much time to consider what Andre had said as Mr. Lewis interjected:

> **Mr. Lewis**: No, why? Look Andre, we have to be objective here. This book was written in a different time. William Golding was not a very nice man. He went to a boys' school which is why there aren't any women in the story, he was a bit sexist. We need to be objective when we're reading.

Andre, however, kept his gaze on me and asked, "Are we allowed to talk about this in our essay? Can we talk about this in the exam?"

Whose Reading Counts?

What happens in Zamzam's lesson presents a series of challenges to the assumptions informing the specifications of the exam for which the students are being "prepared." The assessment-led curriculum positions students as empty vessels, beneficiaries of the knowledge that they are meant to acquire through becoming better acquainted with "the best that has been thought and written," that is to say, a reified vision of culture existing in a realm completely separate from their everyday cultures. The model of cultural development that is represented in policy is thus one of deficit (students start without culture and acquire it through literature) and of transmission (culture is imparted to the students from the literary text). In this model, students are defined wholly by their status as students: no other aspect of their identity, no dimension of their subjectivities, experiences, histories, affiliations, is pertinent when it comes to appreciating "the best that has been thought and written." But this simply does not reflect Zamzam's students' reading of *Lord of the Flies*: what they are reading is inflected by their sense of themselves, of who they are both within the classroom and in the world beyond.

Britton's suggestion that education is "an effect of community," which we quoted earlier, comes at the end of a sentence that begins, "The teacher can no longer act as the 'middle-man' in all learning" (Britton, 1987, p. 25). But this is precisely the role that the GCSE specifications assign to the teacher, as the purveyor of goods whose value has already been established elsewhere, by higher authorities ("high quality, intellectually challenging, and substantial whole texts"). And this is the role that Mr. Lewis attempts to maintain, with his claim to "objectivity."

For Zamzam, too, this is a moment that challenges her sense of herself as a teacher. Her first response to Andre—"Will you be sensible?"—is an appeal to shared (commonsensical) understandings of the mature behavior expected of a good student as well as of the detached scholarship that might be demanded by the process of individual cultural development that the specifications envisage. And such detachment, Zamzam suggests, is what might also be considered appropriate for her: with better planning, might she have been able to rehearse "a dignified response?" Her words at this point reflect received notions of teacher identity and behavior—in other words, the importance of maintaining control, distance, and professionalism (Britzman, 2003) that underlines the very notion of "objectivity" that Mr. Lewis is to assert.

But these authoritative discourses are robbed of their power by the force of Zamzam's own reaction to the text—and by her acknowledgment that, in the moment, she "was experiencing the text along with the students." This should not be construed as an admission that she has somehow failed in her role as a teacher but as a recognition of a shared reading position and—inseparable from this—of a common identity as people of color and of a common experience of racism. And, in the moment, this is what Andre, quite remarkably, also recognizes: the text's power to wound, to enact symbolic violence on its readers, their dignity, and sense of self-worth, is, at the very least, mitigated by the fact that it is mediated through Zamzam. Voiced by her, its strident reassertion of a vicious imperialist trope necessarily becomes problematized, open to scrutiny and contestation.

This recognition hardly sits easily with the class's white, male teacher. Intervening in the lesson, he attempts to reassert what might be regarded as normal pedagogic relations and simultaneously to shift the focus from the fraught question of the text's reception to the safer territory of the sociocultural circumstances at the time of its production conceived as a past that is both knowable and remote from the present. Creating distance is the vitally important property of Mr. Lewis's intervention—the distance between teacher and students and the historical distance that separates Golding from the students in this classroom—and it is the teacher's claim to knowledge in relation to the latter (biographical details as well as a sense of the social context) that bolsters his assertion of authority at once pedagogic and disciplinary.

What, then, of Mr. Lewis's injunction, "We need to be objective when we're reading?" His meaning is, in the immediate context of the classroom, clear enough. Subjectivity—any consideration of who the "we" are who are performing the act of reading—is to be avoided, particularly if that subjectivity involves difficult questions of power and oppression, of affiliations that might interfere with the serene contemplation of the textual object and the realm of values in which it is embedded. What is being recommended, then, is a particular, valorized reading practice, which construes the reader's extratextual experiences as irrelevant (and thus to be left at the classroom door). In this paradigm of reading, the text exists as an objective entity and the reader's task is to gain a proper sense of its value. Because the text is a piece of literature (and, *a priori*, an instance of "the best that has been thought and written"), to apprehend the text is to appreciate its worth. The concept of "literature" as it is framed by government specifications relating to texts written in English that are of "high quality" and "intellectually challenging" (DfE, 2013, p. 14) represents a standard against which students' responses are to be assessed. Their responses to a text are to be judged according to whether they properly acknowledge its canonical status and literally measure up to it.

The notion of the possibility of a "correct" reading of the text, free of any bias or ideology, is a key assumption behind standardized testing and the way it treats texts. There is only one correct answer, according to the psychometricians, one box that can be ticked. In most of its manifestations, where the test is constructed around single-word answers or multiple-choice questions, this takes a cruder form than it does here, where students will be judged on the basis of continuous prose responses to the "whole texts" (DfE, 2013, p. 4) that they have been studying. But the exam essay is likewise a culturally loaded form that privileges certain kinds of response and renders others unsayable, thereby advantaging those who have already attained fluency in particular kinds of discourse (Bourdieu and Passeron, 1977; Teese, 2011; Yandell, 2013).

Behind the teacher's words lies the history of the discipline, the repeated attempts to put the study of literature on an appropriately rigorous basis, from

I. A. Richards (1929) through to F. R. Leavis (1948) and beyond. Rigor, in this tradition, is to be found in the just appreciation of the value of the work, a value that is self-evident from its status within the canon. A literary education is meant to develop in students a capacity to exercise their powers of discrimination, which effectively means reaffirming the value of the work as they have been taught to see it. The teacher's intervention, in its utter disregard of the possibility of different readings, carries an echo of Leavis's famous phrase, "This is so, is it not?" which, as Perry Anderson observes, demands "one crucial precondition" that belies its apparently open and interrogative mood, namely,

> a shared, stable system of beliefs and values. Without this, no loyal exchange and report is possible. If the basic formation and outlook of readers diverges, their experience will be incommensurable. Leavis's whole method presupposes, in fact, a morally and culturally unified audience. (Anderson, 1969, p. 271)

The regime of standardized testing that is represented by the English Literature GCSE relies precisely on a nostalgic retreat into this premise of "a shared, stable system of beliefs and values," not only in its approach to text selection but also in its assumptions about how the canonical texts thus chosen should be read. This, too, might be construed as informing the counsel that the teacher gives: learning to read "objectively" offers instrumental rewards: this is how to pass the exam. The position that the teacher takes might be read as the enactment of the repression that Althusser described as part of the operation of the Ideological State Apparatus:

> For their part the Ideological State Apparatuses function massively and predominantly *by ideology*, but they also function secondarily by repression, even if ultimately, but only ultimately, this is very attenuated and concealed, even symbolic. (There is no such thing as a purely ideological apparatus.) (Althusser, 1971, p. 138)

The teacher is thus complicit in the construction of the neoliberal subject. But Andre will have none of it. The subaltern speaks (Spivak, 1988). He challenges the "we" imposed by the National Curriculum (and the figure of Mr. Lewis), invoking a community (an alternative "we") that judges *Lord of the Flies* differently. He refuses to be interpellated as either the docile acolyte of the teacher's reductive version of literary study or as the powerless victim of the text's symbolic violence. "Are we allowed to talk about this in our essay? Can we talk about this in the exam?" Andre's questions mount a challenge to the authoritative discourses of the teacher, of the high-stakes examination for which he is being prepared, and of literary study as it is constructed by the exam specifications.

What he envisages is a different—dialogic—form of reading, one that makes space for difference and for contestation, one in which the readers can speak back to the text and to the notions of authority inscribed in the canon. And the reading that he proposes is reading accomplished from a defined position, one that is indicated by the direction of his gaze toward Zamzam and thus by the fact that his questions are addressed to Zamzam and not to the (regular) teacher. In this context, there is a particular force to his use of the first-person plural: he is speaking representatively, on behalf of the students of color in the room, and he is looking to Zamzam for support and authorization precisely because of his recognition of their shared identity.

The Continuing Possibility of Resistant Readings

As Tony Bennett argues, literary interpretation has historically been differentiated from the functional literacy that people require in their everyday transactions. And this has not simply served to distinguish between the various ways that people use texts in their everyday lives, as with the distinction between transactional and poetic uses of language. The language that predominated in the elementary schools established for working-class pupils in the nineteenth century was an "administered" language (Bennett, 1979, p. 160) that took the form of textbooks comprising excerpts from literary texts that were used as vehicles to teach students new vocabulary and the rules of grammar, such as the functions of nouns, verbs, adjectives, and adverbs or agreement between subject and predicate. Language in such textbooks was constructed as something purely external to pupils, as a set of rules they were expected to learn and apply.

This contrasts, according to Bennett, with the reading enjoyed by children from middle-class families, who experienced the language of "literary" texts as their "own" (Bennett, 1980, p. 160). Bennett draws his examples of such practices from Renee Balibar's account of the French education system in the nineteenth century, using her example of a passage from George Sand to illustrate how a literary text was recast for the purposes of vocabulary and grammatical exercises that were targeted at students from working-class backgrounds. It would not be hard, however, to provide illustrations from both England and Australia over the nineteenth and twentieth centuries that show language being similarly deployed. Such practices effectively discriminate (albeit in a complexly mediated way) between the linguistic requirements of working-class students and those students from more socially privileged backgrounds. The famous Newbolt

Report (Board of Education, 1921) is instructive in this respect, for it can be read as a plea to provide working-class children with a richer, literary education, as distinct from treating books merely for the sake of "spelling and grammatical tests" (p. 50, p. 302)—a plea that arguably did little to affect the dominance of such practices in schools in England and elsewhere (Doecke, 2017).

Yet, as the foregoing analysis has shown, the assessment of literature at a more senior level is subject to similar determinants to those that obtain with standardized literacy teaching in earlier years. It is not as though, having shown that they have mastered the "basics" of literacy through standardized testing, students find themselves free of the constraints that they have experienced so far in their schooling and that they are then granted a license to use language in more creative ways. The concept of the "literary" in the GCSE curriculum that Zamzam was teaching is an equally powerful form of interpellation as the mechanisms of standardized testing at earlier levels of schooling. Like "functional literacy," the concept of "literature" in the GCSE is used to deny students an opportunity to make language their own and to become more fully aware of how language mediates their experience of the world around them.

There is, thus, a poignancy about Andre's question, "Can we talk about this in the exam?" since the examination does not allow for the kinds of dialogue and contestation that Andre has so emphatically inserted into the classroom. In the exam hall, Andre's prescribed role is to answer the question posed by the disembodied ("objective") voice of the exam paper. This is the form that such questions take:

> How does Golding present Ralph as a leader in *Lord of the Flies*?
> Write about:
>
> - what Ralph says and does as a leader
> - how Golding uses Ralph to explore ideas about leadership.
>
> OR
> "Ralph wept for the end of innocence, the darkness of man's heart . . ."
> What does Golding have to say about human nature in *Lord of the Flies*?
> Write about:
>
> - how the boys behave on the island
> - how Golding uses the boys' behaviour to explore ideas about human nature. (AQA, 2017, p. 10)

How, in responding to these questions, could Andre find an opportunity to debate the use of the word "nigger" in Golding's text? How might he register the impact that this word has had on him in the process of reading this novel and thus challenge its representation of universal human experience as quintessentially "British" and something that can only be rendered in the English language? He is invited to explore "ideas about leadership," to weep with Ralph for "the end of innocence, the darkness of man's heart," and to reflect on Golding's understanding of "human nature," without any opportunity to engage with the dialogical character of these words. What he is required to do is not to "talk" about how these words may have impacted on his sense of self and the history that constitutes it but to dutifully rehearse a taught response—to demonstrate an appreciation of a literary work of "high quality" as it has been classified by the National Curriculum. The response that is required here is not to question Golding's representation of "race" (this dimension of the novel is simply repressed by the questions set for the examination) but rather to parade a taught appreciation of how Golding has revealed some timeless truth about "human nature."

The assessment regime under which Zamzam is obliged to work is, in fact, every bit as standardized as those tests that require students to choose the correct answer from a range of alternatives that always presupposes one correct response. The very fact that literature is set as a subject for examination, and that this involves inducting students into the protocols of writing essays, typically involving formulae relating to the way an essay should be organized and even the structure of the paragraphs that comprise it (as in the injunction to "use the Point, Evidence, Explanation [PEE] structure to explain points" [Gill, 1989, p. 171]), is enough to show how students' responses to literature are being regulated. There is simply no opportunity for "talk" of the kind that Andre desires. Corresponding to these structures is the privileging of a certain type of response to literature, reflected in Mr. Lewis's comment to Andre that he needs to be "objective," which effectively excludes dissident interpretations, other views about the meaning of the words on the page that do not accord with the view that "we" hold.

Terry Eagleton (1985–1986) has critiqued the practice of "close reading" as privileging a kind of unanchored response on the part of readers to a text, a response that floats above any sense of the ethical and political issues that might be involved in reading a literary work. He argues that "literature" names more than a body of texts that are worthy of study but a particular way of responding to those texts that radically disables an individual's capacity to engage with the social and political issues that literary texts raise. Such an interpretive practice, according to Eagleton, interpellates readers as "subjects" who make a virtue of displaying their refined sensibilities (their openness to human experience as revealed to them through their response to the words on the page) while effectively remaining blind to the social and historical contexts that have shaped their own consciousness and being.

But are teachers and their pupils really locked into interpretive practices of this kind? What is ultimately so remarkable about the way Andre and his peers respond to *Lord of the Flies* is that they are showing a keen sense of the words on the page while simultaneously usurping the protocols that have traditionally underpinned close reading as an interpretive practice. For their response to the word "nigger" reveals that, far from being hostage to the words on the page in a way that occludes any consideration of larger social and historical contexts that are deemed to be extraneous to the text, they are supremely alive to the history that is refracted by a word and to the dimensions of social experience that are opened up when this word is spoken. This awareness of the dialogical character of language is also evident in Andre's reaction to Mr. Lewis's use of the word "objective." He senses that a text becomes a vehicle for the construction of other meanings than those that are officially validated, once it is read and appropriated by other reading communities whose values may be at odds with those being imposed on them. As Andre remarks, it is significant that Miss Abdi is reading the story and not Mr. Lewis.

Raymond Williams has observed that "a lived hegemony is always a process," involving continuing negotiation between people with respect to the roles assigned to them (Williams, 1977, p. 112). When pupils turn up at school each day and engage in the social transactions that occur in the school yard and the classroom, they are participating in this process. They might thus be said to be complicit in their own oppression. Yet there always remains the possibility that they—and their teachers—will experience their identities and relationships differently from the way they are defined for them. The machinery of the neoliberal state may declare that this is who "you" are and that this is where "you" belong in the social structure, but you do not need to accept the "self" defined for "you." The story at the center of this chapter shows that this refusal can be triggered by a word, that neoliberal efforts to contain language (to reduce it to a one-word answer, to treat language as though it can only mean one thing) always run the risk of foundering on the multiplicity of languages in which people are immersed from day to day, the shifts in dialect, the continuing negotiations that occur when people from different language communities interact with one another. Those interactions are mediated by a heteroglot environment (Bakhtin, 1987 [1981]) that cannot finally be contained by the regulatory mechanisms imposed by standardized testing.

That, at least, is an expression of hope with which we conclude this chapter. For what is at stake with the imposition of standardized testing is ultimately a capacity on the part of students and teachers to recognize in their social relationships an ineluctable condition for their growth as fully responsive and ethical beings and the possibility of organizing society as a whole along similarly humane and inclusive lines.

Notes

1   Names (of students and of the class teacher) have been changed to culturally appropriate pseudonyms.
2   This is the line as it appeared in the original 1954 edition of *Lord of the Flies* and in subsequent editions in the UK. Elsewhere, Piggy's words have been variously amended, as Robert Tally notes, recalling reading the novel in 1982, in his ninth-grade classroom in the United States:

> "Which is better—to be a pack of painted Indians like you are, or to be sensible like Ralph is?" ... At least, that is how the line reads in the copy we were given. In the terrific 1963 film adaptation, Piggy's line is slightly different: "Which is better—to be a pack of painted savages like you are, or to be sensible like Ralph is?" ... Somehow, my edition was expurgated, with the term "Indian" replacing the incendiary N-word. In other words, someone had Bowdlerized this passage, substituting "Indians" for a more offensive term, but one which was also apparently intended to refer to a similar though distinct sort of "savage." (Let us leave aside for the moment the proposition that the phrase "painted Indians" might be as offensive.) One other note about my *Lord of the Flies* experience in high school: nowhere in my volume does it say that anything in the novel has been altered. The copyright date is still listed as 1954, and there is no evidence that the author himself, an editor, or the publisher might have emended any part of the text. I am not sure just who, but someone had protected me and my fellow (American) pupils from an offensive word, without comment and apparently without any controversy at all. (Tally, 2013, 99–100)

References

Abraham, U. (2016). On their own but not alone: The difficulty in competence-oriented approaches to teaching reading and writing of thinking of "performance" in communal terms. *Changing English*, 23(3), 209–26. doi:10.1080/1358684X.2016.1203619

Althusser, L. (1971). *Lenin and Philosophy, and Other Essays* (B. R. Brewster, trans.). London: New Left Books.

Anderson, P. (1969). Components of the national culture. In A. Cockburn and Blackburn, R. (Eds.), *Student Power: Problems, Diagnosis, Action* (pp. 214–86). Harmondsworth: Penguin/New Left Review.

AQA (2017). *GCSE English Literature, Paper 2: Modern Texts and Poetry* (May 26, 2017). Online at: https://filestore.aqa.org.uk/sample-papers-and-mark-schemes/2017/june/AQA-87022-QP-JUN17.PDF

Arnold, M. (1993 [1869]). *Culture and Anarchy and Other Writings*. Cambridge: Cambridge University Press.

Bakhtin, M. M. (1987 [1981]). *The Dialogic Imagination* (C. E. M. Holquist, trans.). Austin, TX: University of Texas Press.

Ball, S. J. (2012 [1990]). *Politics and Policy Making in Education: Explorations in Policy Sociology*. Abingdon and New York: Routledge.

Barnes, D. (1992 [1975]). *From Communication to Curriculum*. Harmondsworth: Penguin.

Bennett, T. (1979). *Formalism and Marxism*. London: Methuen.

Board of Education (1938 [1921]). *The Teaching of English in England*. London: His Majesty's Stationery Office. [cited in text as Newbolt Report]

Bourdieu, P. and Passeron, J.-C. (1977). *Reproduction in Education, Society and Culture* (R. Nice, trans.). London: SAGE.

Breen, L. (2014). Creatively struggling with standard Australian English: Moving beyond deficit constructions of my students. In B. Doecke, G. Parr, and W. Sawyer (Eds.), *Language and Creativity in Contemporary English Classrooms* (pp. 173–86). Putney, NSW: Phoenix.

Britton, J. (1987). Vygotsky's contribution to pedagogical theory. *English in Education*, 21(3), 22–26.

Britzman, D. P. (2003). *Practice Makes Practice a Critical Study of Learning to Teach* (Rev. ed.). Albany: State University of New York Press.

DES [Department of Education and Science]. (1987). *The National Curriculum 5–16: A Consultation Document*. London: HMSO.

DfE [Department for Education]. (2013). *English Literature: GCSE Subject Content and Assessment Objectives*. London: DfE. Retrieved from https://www.gov.uk/government/uploads/system/uploads/attachment_data/file/254498/GCSE_English_literature.pdf

DfE [Department for Education]. (2014). *The National Curriculum in England: Framework Document*. London: DfE [Department for Education]. Retrieved from https://www.gov.uk/government/uploads/system/uploads/attachment_data/file/335116/Master_final_national_curriculum_220714.pdf

Doecke, B. (2013). Storytelling and professional learning. *English in Australia*, 48(2), 11–21.

Doecke, B. (2017). What kind of "knowledge" is English? (Re-reading the Newbolt Report). *Changing English*, 24(3), 230–45. doi: 10.1080/1358684X.2017.1351228

Doecke, B., Kostogriz, A., and Illesca, B. (2010). Seeing "things" differently: Recognition, ethics, praxis. *English Teaching: Practice and Critique*, 9(2), 81–98.

Doecke, B., Green, B., Kostogris, A., Reid, J.-A., and Sawyer, W. (2007). Knowing practice in English teaching? Research challenges in representing the professional practice of English teachers. *English Teaching: Practice and Critique*, 6(3), 4–12.

Eagleton, T. (1985–86). The subject of literature. *Cultural Critique*, 2, 95–104.

Gill, R. (2009 [1989]). Exploring *Othello* in the classroom. In W. Shakespeare, *Othello*. (Ed. R. Gill) (pp. 163–74). Oxford: Oxford University Press.

Golding, W. (1954/1962). *Lord of the Flies: A Novel*. London: Faber & Faber.

Illesca, B. (2014). (In-between) the complicities of the imagination: Teaching English in public and private schools. In B. Doecke, G. Parr, and W. Sawyer (Eds.), *Language and Creativity in Contemporary English Classrooms* (pp. 151–72). Putney, NSW: Phoenix Education.

Jones, K. (1989). *Right Turn: The Conservative Revolution in Education*. London: Hutchinson.

Jones, K. (2013). The right and the left. *Changing English*, 20(4), 328–40.

Jones, K., Cunchillos, C., Hatcher, R., Hirtt, N., Innes, R., Johsua, S., and Klausenitzer, J. (2008). *Schooling in Western Europe: The New Order and Its Adversaries*. Basingstoke and New York: Palgrave MacMillan.

Leavis, F. R. (1948). *The Great Tradition: George Eliot, Henry James, Joseph Conrad*. London: Chatto & Windus.

MCEETYA [Ministerial Council on Education, Employment, Training and Youth Affairs]. (2008). *Melbourne Declaration on Educational Goals for Young Australians*. Melbourne: MCEETYA. Available at: http://www.curriculum.edu.au/verve/_resources/National_Declaration_on_the_Educational_Goals_for_Young_Australians.pdf (accessed February 26, 2017).

Richards, I. A. (1929). *Practical Criticism: A Study of Literary Judgment*. London: Routledge & Kegan Paul.

Spivak, G. C. (1988). Can the subaltern speak? In Nelson Cary and Lawrence Grossberg (Eds.), *Marxism and the Interpretation of Culture* (pp. 271–313). Urbana, IL, and Chicago: University of Illinois Press.

Tally, R. T. (2013). Bleeping Mark Twain?: Censorship, Huckleberry Finn, and the functions of literature. *Teaching American Literature: A Journal of Theory and Practice*, 6(1), 97–108.

Taylor, D. (2003). Teaching reading and the new word order. In B. Doecke, D. Homer, and H. Nixon (Eds.), *English Teachers at Work: Narratives, Counter Narratives and Arguments* (pp. 29–49). Kent Town, South Australia: Wakefield Press.

Teese, R. (2011). The new curriculum for English in Australia and student achievement under the old curriculum: Understanding inequality and addressing it. In B. Doecke,

G. Parr, and W. Sawyer (Eds.), *Creating an Australian Curriculum for English* (pp. 5–20). Putney, NSW: Phoenix Education.

Turvey, A., Yandell, J., and Ali, L. (2014). English as a site of cultural negotiation and creative contestation. In B. Doecke, G. Parr, and W. Sawyer (Eds.), *Language and Creativity in Contemporary English Classrooms* (pp. 237–54). Putney, NSW: Phoenix.

Unwin, A. and Yandell, J. (2016). *Rethinking Education: Whose Knowledge Is It Anyway?* Oxford: New Internationalist.

Williams, R. (1977). *Marxism and Literature*. Oxford: Oxford University Press.

Yandell, J. (2013). *The Social Construction of Meaning: Reading Literature in Urban English Classrooms*. London and New York: Routledge.

Yandell, J. and Brady, M. (2016). English and the politics of knowledge. *English in Education*, 50(1), 44–59. doi:10.1111/eie.12094

2

Standardized Testing and School Achievement: The Case of Indigenous-Language-Speaking Students in Remote Australia

Leonard A. Freeman and Gillian Wigglesworth

Introduction

The Indigenous population of Australia comprises only around 3 percent of the total population, and their outcomes on various measures including life expectancy, health, and education are well below those of the general population. It is common practice for government reports in Australia to disaggregate their reporting of these important outcomes by Indigenous status thus making the deficit positioning of Indigenous peoples on these measures highly visible to governments and the wider population. In 2008, the Council of Australian Governments (COAG) reacted to the disparity between the outcomes of Indigenous and non-Indigenous Australians by setting up targets around these measures in a commitment to "Close the Gap." These targets included halving the gap in reading, writing, and numeracy for Indigenous children within a decade. The prime minister reports annually on the Closing the Gap initiative. At the same time, 2008 saw the first administration of the National Assessment Program—Literacy and Numeracy (NAPLaN)—a measure used by governments, education authorities, schools, and the community to determine the educational outcomes of young Australians (ACARA, 2011a), discussed further below. The first reported results in 2008 indicated large differences in the performance of Indigenous and non-Indigenous students, with the former performing increasingly less well depending on how remotely they lived from a major city (see Avineri et al., 2015, for a broader international discussion of these issues).

Ten years later, as Australia's national, state, and territory governments continue to try to "Close the Gap" between educational rates of achievement by Indigenous and non-Indigenous students, particularly on the NAPLaN, Indigenous education in Australia has been the subject of ongoing reviews, inquiries, and policy reforms (e.g., COAG, 2013; Education Council, 2015). The prime minister's 2018 report on Closing the Gap (Commonwealth of Australia, 2018) reveals two factors of relevance to educational improvement for Indigenous students. The first is that the gap in school attendance between Indigenous and non-Indigenous students has not been achieved, and the second is that the target to halve the gap between Indigenous and non-Indigenous students achieving minimum standards on the NAPLaN has not been achieved, although it has narrowed.

The children of the Indigenous population living in remote areas of Northern Australia attend state-funded schools in their communities, where the enrolled school population is mainly, if not entirely, Indigenous. For most of these students, English is not a first language—the local Indigenous language/s and the widely spoken Kriol is/are. Despite this, most schools adopt an English-only approach, with an English-speaking curriculum taught by English (only)-speaking teachers.

Concerns about the educational achievement rates of remote Indigenous students are often justified by citing the persistent gap between their literacy and numeracy outcomes and the national average. Scholars working in remote education contexts have argued that such "metro-centric" (Roberts, Piccoli, and Hattie, 2018) approaches are incapable of identifying the unique teaching and learning needs of students living in communities outside of the cities because their needs get hidden among the averages (e.g., see Bat and Guenther, 2013). There is also growing evidence that using NAPLaN tests to measure Indigenous students' rates of English literacy and numeracy skills often leads to deficit responses by policy makers, school leaders, and educators (Klenowski, 2016).

A key assumption that has underpinned Indigenous education reforms in Australia over the past decade is that improvements in Indigenous students' school attendance rates will directly improve Indigenous students' rates of literacy and numeracy achievement, as measured by national standardized literacy and numeracy assessments (Ladwig and Luke, 2014). The conventional wisdom is that students need to attend school at a minimum rate of 80 percent (i.e., on average, four days of the five-day school week) to meet year-level achievement standards (Ladwig and Luke, 2014; Wilson, 2014). This view that increased English input, use, and interaction as measured by time attending school in English positively predicts higher English second language (L2) abilities conforms with findings from virtually all studies in English second language acquisition (e.g., Paradis and Jia, 2017; Saville-Troike and Barto, 2016).

However, while research suggests that the relationship between school attendance and the English outcomes of multilingual learners is likely to be positive, a recent study by Paradis and Jia (2017) found more variance in the English outcomes of primary-school-aged multilingual children than their monolingual English-speaking peers. The finding was attributed to the complexity of the multilingual children's language environments and the resulting differences in the input, quality, and amount of English that the second language (L2) learners received (Paradis and Jia, 2017). The recognition that the language environments of multilingual children influence their English language and literacy development calls into question the appropriateness of Australia's approach of using common year-level achievement standards for all learners, particularly children learning in very remote Indigenous communities where English is not widely spoken and thus learned as a foreign language (Freeman and Staley, 2018; Wigglesworth, Simpson, and Loakes, 2011).

Guenther (2013) found that in Australia's very remote schools, where the proportion of Indigenous students enrolled was greater than 80 percent, the schools' attendance rates explained only 10 percent of the variance in their Year 3 National reading results, suggesting that where the majority of students are Indigenous, assumptions regarding the link between 80 percent attendance and educational success may not hold true.

To investigate the strength of the statistical associations between school-level attendance and achievement rates of schools in the Northern Territory (NT), we reanalyzed a dataset published in *A Share in the Future* (Wilson, 2014, pp. 273–80), a review of Indigenous education in Australia's NT. Here we question the rationale of current policies that problematize student attendance rates while overlooking a critical factor—that many of the Indigenous students in very remote communities are learning English as a foreign language—and argue that the current "one-size-fits-all" approach is not delivering equitable educational outcomes.

Background

The Northern Territory Department of Education (NTDoE) has developed a ten-year bipartisan Indigenous Education Strategy (NTDoE, 2015), which seeks to implement the recommendations of the Indigenous Education Review (henceforth IER), *A Share in the Future* (Wilson, 2014). In line with previous

Table 2.1 ARIA+ Service Center Categories

Service Center Category	Center Population
A	250,000 or more persons
B	48,000—249,999 persons
C	18,000—47,999 persons
D	5,000—17,999 persons
E	1,000—4,999 persons

reviews of Indigenous education, a central premise that framed the report's recommendations was that improvements in rates of student attendance will lead to improved performance on national literacy and numeracy tests, specifically the NAPLaN.

In Australia, communities with a population of more than one thousand are categorized into one of five categories based on population size and access to services in their community by the Australian Bureau of statistics (ABS, 2016) as illustrated in Table 2.1.

Relative accessibility/remoteness is represented using the Accessibility/Remoteness Index of Australia (ARIA+) published in the national census by the ABS (2016). The ARIA+ value for each populated locality is calculated by distance to services. The ARIA+ index score is a continuous scale with ranges from values of 0 (highly accessible) to 15 (limited accessibility/high remoteness).

When discussing the influence that the schools' level of remoteness had on educational outcomes, Wilson (2014) in the IER refers to schools by their "Geolocation," which are categories of remoteness based on the average ARIA+ index value for their locality (postcode area). As presented in Figure 2.1, the NT is divided into three categories of "Geolocation" or level of remoteness—remote, very remote, provincial. While Australia's major metropolitan cities, such as Sydney and Melbourne, have an ARIA+ index value of between 0 and 0.2, Darwin city and the suburbs of Palmerston, which lie outside Darwin, are categorized as "Outer Regional or Provincial" zones as they have an ARIA+ value between 2.40 and 5.92. Despite being the capital city of the NT, Darwin's population of approximately 120,000 people do not have access to the same level of services of a metropolitan city. All communities outside of Darwin and Palmerston are considered to be either "Remote" or "Very Remote" with Remote communities having an ARIA+ index that ranges from 5.92 and 10.53 because they are located within, or closer to, larger towns (e.g., Alice Springs, Katherine) than the localities classified as Very Remote that have an ARIA+ index higher than 10.53.

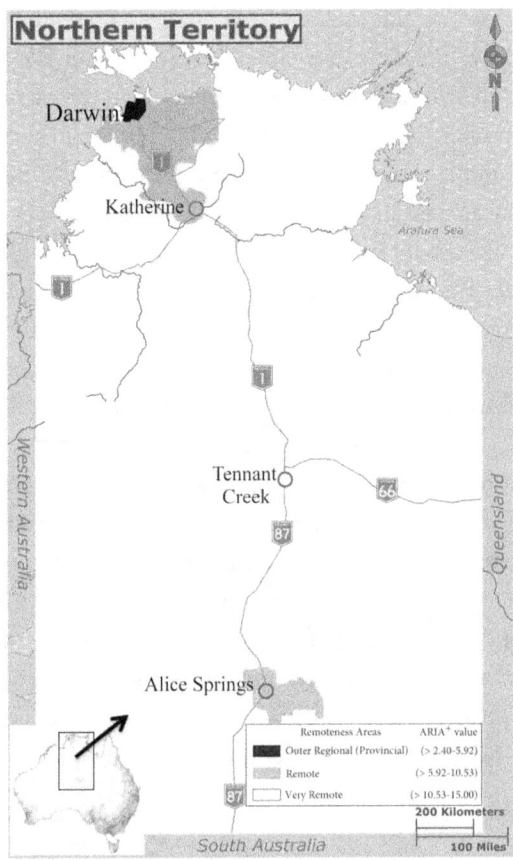

Figure 2.1 Map of the remoteness areas for the Northern Territory, adapted from (ABS, 2018).

Wilson (2014) claims that his analysis of achievement data indicated that "remoteness alone is not a key factor driving school performance" (p. 50). Rather, the IER identified school attendance as a major factor affecting student achievement. He states that "the dividing line between negative and positive attendance is 80%, the level at which the review's analysis suggests learning can be effective for the majority of students" (2014, p. 54). To provide a visual representation of the relationship between school-level attendance and school-level achievement, a color-coded data table is attached to the IER, as Appendix Six (Wilson 2014, pp. 273–80). However, Guenther (2013) argued that when it comes to the "red dirt" context of very remote Indigenous communities, assumptions regarding statistical associations between attendance rates and student achievement outcomes, as measured by literacy and numeracy tests, should be challenged.

This chapter rises to this call, and the analyses presented here investigate the degree to which linguistic diversity (see Simpson and Wigglesworth, 2018, for a discussion of Australia's linguistic diversity) and remoteness explain rates of literacy and numeracy achievement of NT schools situated in very remote Indigenous communities where English is not the majority language.

Without an awareness of the connections between literacy, education, and ideology, discussions about pedagogy are left weak and incapable of highlighting what is "wrong." This means the discussion has limited potential to drive real change by identifying an alternative that might be "right" (Cross, 2009). While presenting a reanalysis of the literacy and numeracy achievement data of very remote Indigenous community schools cannot solve the problems with respect to literacy education and remote Indigenous students, it is hoped that a reexamination of Wilson's (2014) school-level dataset may provide insights regarding the relationship between school-level attendance and achievement in the "red-dirt" remote Indigenous education context. The aim of this reanalysis is therefore to encourage policy makers, principals, and teachers to reevaluate the assumptions that currently frame the school improvement process by demonstrating that some principles (or ideas held as commonsense truths), which generally apply in mainstream urban contexts, may not hold when applied to the NT's very remote Indigenous community schools.

Evidence-Based Education

In Australia, the NAPLaN is the nationwide annual census of all Australian students' literacy and numeracy skills in years 3, 5, 7, and 9 (Lingard, Thompson, and Sellar, 2016). The four areas (or "domains") tested by NAPLaN are numeracy, reading, writing, and language conventions. For each year level and domain of literacy and numeracy assessed, the Australian Curriculum Assessment and Reporting Authority (ACARA) identifies a national minimum standard. Students' literacy and numeracy achievements in each of the domains of the test are reported as "above," "at," or "below" the national minimum standard (ACARA, 2015). Essentially, plotting all students on a standardized literacy development scale means that all students' literacy skills are judged against the milestones of students from a Standard Australian English-speaking background (Creagh, 2014). However, the provision of one developmental pathway does not account for Australia's rich linguistic diversity with approximately one in four students in Australian schools learning English as an additional language or dialect. It is also worth noting that while students from non-English-speaking migrant backgrounds are eligible for intensive English during their first year of schooling in Australia, this is not the case for Indigenous students who do not speak English as their first language (Lee et al., 2014) because the intensive English programs are only provided to students who migrated to Australia within the last twelve months.

Compared to migrant children living in communities where the language of school instruction is widely used in their community, Indigenous children growing up in very remote communities often face an additional challenge because English is not widely spoken in their language context (Wigglesworth and Simpson, 2018). Consequently, the majority of very remote Indigenous students in the NT commence school with knowledge of the sounds, patterns, and features of their first language but with little or no English language or literacy skills (Devlin, 2007). Wilson (2014) suggests that in some NT schools the proportion of students who start school with limited or no English approaches 100 percent. In addition, there are often limited resources in these schools to support the students' language development (Wigglesworth and Simpson, 2018), and resources and programs that are available to recent migrants in the NT are not available to these students (Lee et al., 2014).

Very remote Indigenous-language-speaking students are thus a geographical and linguistic subset of the English as an Additional Language or Dialect (EAL/D) category. Research suggests that because these students are attending school in a context where English is effectively a foreign language, their rates of literacy and numeracy development will neither conform to nor catch up to the English language and literacy developmental milestones of students from an English-speaking background during the primary or secondary school years (McKay and Scarino, 1991). This situation is exacerbated where there are few teachers who have specific training in the teaching of English to students from non-English-speaking backgrounds, as is the case in many of the remote schools across Australia.

Research Hypotheses

Our aim in this study was to empirically explore the relationships between patterns of student attendance and patterns of student achievement in very remote NT schools where the majority of students learn English as a foreign language. The hypotheses we investigated were the following:

1. School-level attendance rates significantly affect the literacy and numeracy achievement rates of NT schools, as measured by national literacy and numeracy tests.
2. The category of remoteness of NT schools significantly affects their rate of literacy and numeracy achievement, as measured by national literacy and numeracy tests.
3. When the proportion of Indigenous-language-speaking students enrolled in NT schools is greater than 80 percent, the influence that school-level attendance rates have on schools' achievement, as measured by national literacy and numeracy tests, is significantly reduced.

The Dataset

To address these hypotheses, we analyzed the school-level aggregated data presented in Appendix Six of the IER (Wilson, 2014, pp. 273–80). The dataset presents information aggregated at the school level for each NT government school. The variables relevant to this project were the following:

- Location—Provincial, Remote, or Very Remote
- Index of Community Socio-Economic Advantage (ICSEA) score
- Proportion of students who speak an Indigenous language as their first language
- Average school attendance rate during 2013
- The proportion of students who achieved the minimum standard (benchmark) measured across all NAPLaN tests domains during 2011, 2012, and 2013.

Strengths and Limitations of the Dataset

The NT has a population of 228,833 residents thinly spread over a large geographic area of 1.35 million square kilometers (ABS, 2016). Many of the NT's 154 government schools have relatively small student enrolment with 43 of the 154 schools listed in Wilson's data table having an average total enrolment of less than 50 students in 2013 (Wilson, 2014).

When less than five students in a year level sit for NAPLaN, the school's achievement data for that year level are not published on the Australian Government's *MySchool* website. ACARA (2015) explains this is to protect the privacy of students attending small schools. However, in Appendix Six of Wilson (2014) the variable "NAPLaN" in the IER dataset refers to the average proportion of students at or above national minimum standard across all NAPLaN domains and year levels over the three years to 2013 (p. 273). The variable "NAPLaN" thus represents the percentage of students from each NT school who met or exceeded the national minimum achievement standard across all the test domains during 2011, 2012, and 2013. The Wilson (2014) dataset is therefore the only complete publicly available source of NAPLaN achievement data for many of the NT's small schools.

The "problem of the levels" is a limitation of aggregated datasets such as Appendix Six of the IER and the *MySchool* website. The problem arises when statistical relationships are observed at one level, such as individuals, and then researchers (based on the findings at one level of data) assume that the phenomena will hold at another level. From aggregate-level datasets, we cannot determine whether or not the students who achieved the benchmark score were the students with higher or lower attendance. Therefore, the aggregated nature of the publicly available datasets means the problem of the levels restricts researchers from making claims about the influence that an individual student's attendance may have had on their NAPLaN achievement. For this reason, our investigation of factors that influence NAPLaN achievement was limited to drawing inferences about the statistical significance that school-level variables had on school-level achievement.

The final limitation arises because of a flaw in the construction of Wilson's (2014) cross-sectional dataset, which was that the variables included were calculated over different time periods. While each school's average enrolment and percentage attendance rates were calculated using collections from 2013, the rate of achievement data was averaged over three years. Wilson (2014) also fails to specify the timing of the collection for some of the demographic statistics, such as the proportion of students enrolled who speak an Indigenous language as their first language. While the physical location of the school building and thus its category of remoteness will be stable over time, much of the NT's remote Indigenous population regularly move between communities for cultural ceremonies and to access services (Simpson and Wigglesworth, 2008). The IER's school-level demographic data that were drawn from a single year (e.g., attendance in 2013) will therefore not account for the fluctuations in the schools' population and demographic profile during the three years from which the achievement data were collected. However, after acknowledging the limitations of the IER dataset, in the absence of an alternative comprehensive summary of the rates of achievement, attendance, and demographic variables for the NT's remote and very remote schools, the dataset represents a valuable source of publicly available information about school performance, particularly for researchers of very small remote Indigenous community schools.

Analyzing the Influence of Attendance on NAPLaN Achievement

Multiple regression analysis was used to investigate the combined influence of independent variables (attendance, remoteness) to explain the variance in a dependent variable (or outcome), in this case the schools' rate of NAPLaN achievement. The aim of regression analysis is to measure the responsiveness of the dependent variable to change in an independent variable, while holding the remaining independent variables constant (Berry and Sanders, 2000).

The analysis was also concerned with identifying whether a third variable, ESL versus EFL context, significantly moderates (interacts with) the degree to which an independent variable, such as school-level attendance rates, explains the outcome (i.e., schools' rates of NAPLaN achievement). Such an interaction effect would be said to exist when the degree that the explanatory variable affects the dependent variable differs depending on the value of a third variable (Jaccard and Turrisi, 2003). Interaction analysis therefore enables researchers to investigate whether or not specific school demographic variables reduce the statistical influence that school-level attendance rates had on rates of achievement for the schools in this sample.

Descriptive Statistics

A total of 10 of the 154 schools listed in the IER's Appendix Six dataset (Wilson 2014, pp. 273–80) were excluded from our analyses because no achievement data were included for these schools.

In Figure 2.2, the rates of NAPLaN achievement for all 144 schools are presented as a frequency distribution histogram with category interval bins with a range of 5 percent. Interpreting the graph reveals that there is a clear

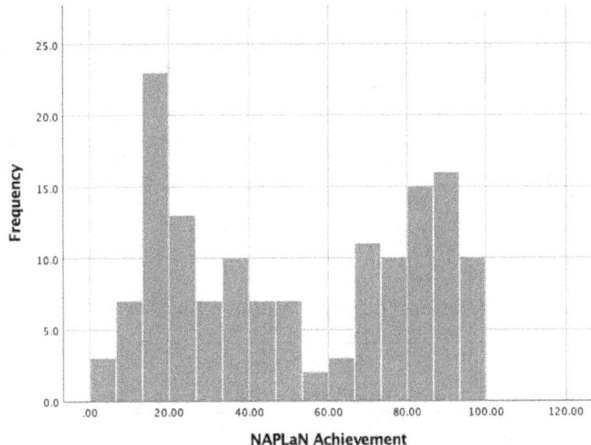

Figure 2.2 Distribution of Northern Territory government schools' rates of NAPLaN achievement.

global maximum score, which is the third bar from the left and caps out at a school-level achievement rate of 15–20 percent. There is also a local maximum score on the right-hand side of the frequency histogram at the thirteenth and fourteenth bars and peaks around 16 percent. This demonstrates that there is a second clustering of schools around a NAPLaN achievement rate of between 90 and 95 percent. The bimodal frequency distribution indicates that for NAPLaN achievement there may be two relatively distinct categories of NT schools.

Table 2.2 presents the distribution of the 144 schools by their category of remoteness with almost three-quarters (73.6 percent) of the schools operating in locations categorized as either Remote (18.8 percent) or Very Remote (54.9 percent).

Table 2.3 reports that the mean rate of school-level NAPLaN achievement for the 144 NT schools in this sample was 51.99 percent and provides a breakdown of the mean achievement rates of NT schools by category of remoteness. As identified by Wilson (2014), the mean school-level NAPLaN achievement rates of "Remote" and "Very Remote" schools are quite different from their Provincial counterparts. The differences in mean achievement rates between groups were both significant (ANOVA: $F_{(2,141)} = 136.684$, $p < 0.001$) and substantial. Provincial schools' average achievement on the NAPLaN was a little more than one standard deviation (1.08) above the mean for the 144 NT schools, while Very Remote schools' mean was almost three-quarters of a standard deviation (0.72) below. In practical terms, this means that the average provincial school was in the top 14 percent of NT schools while the average Very Remote school

Table 2.2 Northern Territory Schools Per Location

		Location				
		Metropolitan	Provincial	Remote	Very Remote	Total
Total	Count	0	38	27	79	144
	(%)	0	26.4	18.8	54.9	100

Table 2.3 Mean NAPLaN Achievement Rates by Location

Location	Mean NAPLaN Achievement Rate (%)	n	SD
Provincial	84.89	38	7.82
Remote	69.74	27	20.79
Very Remote	30.11	79	20.12
Total	51.99	144	30.44

was in the bottom 24 percent suggesting that remoteness, particularly very remoteness, could explain the bimodal distribution of NAPLaN scores observed in Figure 2.2. This hypothesis is investigated further below.

Analyzing the Relationship between Attendance and NAPLaN Achievement

As presented in Table 2.4, the mean rate of school-level attendance for this sample of 144 schools was 74 percent, while Figure 2.3 provides a visual depiction of the relationship between schools' NAPLaN achievement and school-level attendance (mean centered at 74 percent). The strong and positive correlation (Pearson's $r = 0.834$, $p < 0.001$) between school-level attendance and rates of NAPLaN achievement is highly significant with school-level attendance explaining nearly 70 percent ($R^2 = 0.695$) of the variance in their rates of NAPLaN achievement.

This shows that, on average, school-level attendance had a strong, significant, and positive affect on NT schools' NAPLaN achievement rates, supporting Hypothesis 1. In Figure 2.3, it is also clear that the majority of schools positioned to the right of the dotted vertical line representing 80 percent average school attendance have high rates of NAPLaN achievement—clustering between 80 percent and 100 percent NAPLaN achievement. Wilson's (2014) claim that in the "majority" of cases a school attendance rate of approximately 80 percent

Table 2.4 Mean School Attendance Rates by Location

Location	Mean School attendance rate (%)	n	SD
Provincial	89.05	38	3.03
Remote	81.63	27	9.94
Very Remote	64.15	79	13.98
Total	74.00	144	15.87

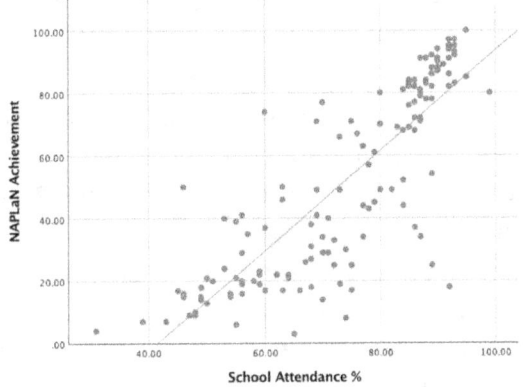

Figure 2.3 Scatterplot: NAPLaN achievement by school attendance (mean centered at 74 percent).

marks the line at which important educational outcomes are effectively achieved was therefore also supported by this initial analysis.

However, the scatterplot also reveals that there were about eight to ten schools that had more than the prerequisite 80 percent average school attendance and yet the rate at which their students achieved NAPLaN's minimum literacy and numeracy standards (benchmarks) ranged from about 20 to 50 percent. Therefore, while assumptions regarding the link between 80 percent school attendance and high NAPLaN achievement seems to work for most schools, it was not the case for all schools in the NT.

It is unclear the extent to which attendance explains NAPLaN achievement for schools in remote communities where the majority of students speak an Indigenous language as their first language because despite being a review of Indigenous education, the IER's dataset included Provisional schools, which typically have higher proportions of non-Indigenous students and speakers of English as a first language enrolled than is the case in Remote and Very Remote schools. To address these issues, the next section investigates how school-level rates of NAPLaN achievement are influenced by remoteness and the proportion of Indigenous-language-speaking students enrolled.

Isolating the Effect of Remoteness from Attendance on Achievement

Fox's (2016) methodology for incorporating categorical variables into multiple linear regression analysis was used to investigate the influence that remoteness had on schools' rates of NAPLaN achievement. The coefficient values reported in Table 2.5 for Remoteness and Very Remoteness represent the statistical influence that each level of remoteness had on school-level NAPLaN achievement rates while holding the effect of attendance constant.

Table 2.5 suggests that both Remoteness and Very Remoteness had a significant negative impact on the schools' NAPLaN achievement rates. On average, the statistical influence of Remoteness was a negative impact of almost 8 percent ($\hat{Y}_R = -7.73$, $p < 0.05$) and Very remoteness almost 30 percent ($\hat{Y}_{VR} = -29.94$, $p < 0.001$). The size of these negative impacts is depicted in Figure 2.4 by the vertical distance between the regression line for each Remoteness category and the Provincial category, which is the reference category (constant variable).

The effect of remoteness on schools' rates of NAPLaN achievement and the fact that the negative impact increased with the degree of the remoteness supports Hypothesis 2. However, Wilson (2014) and Guenther (2013) both suggested that remoteness alone did not explain the NAPLaN outcomes of Very Remote schools. Both studies concluded that a third variable that differed among Very Remote schools explained a key part of the variance in their NAPLaN outcomes.

A new category "Not-very remote" schools (Provincial and Remote schools) was created so that we could compare Very Remote schools with the rest of

Table 2.5 Influence of School Remoteness on School-Level Achievement

	b	(SE)	β	n
Constant	69.869***	2.74		38
Location (Ref: Provincial)				
School-Level Attendance CTR	0.996***	0.10	0.519	n/a
Remote	−7.731*	3.60	−0.099	27
Very Remote	−29.942***	3.76	−0.491	79

Notes: p* < .05; p** < .01; p*** < .001. n = 144. Ref = reference category. $R^2 = 0.791$***.

The continuous independent variable of school-level attendance has been mean centered at 74 percent.

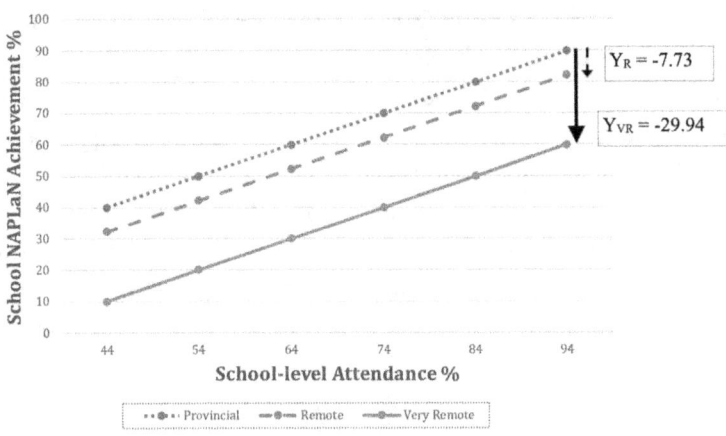

Figure 2.4 The impact of remoteness on school-level NAPLaN achievement while controlling for attendance.

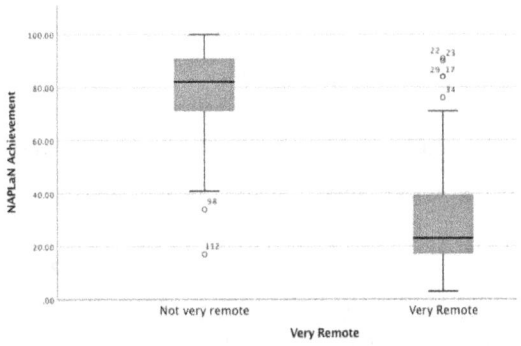

Figure 2.5 Rates of school-level NAPLaN achievement by Very Remoteness.

the sample. The boxplot in Figure 2.5 provides a visual representation of the distribution of school-level rates of NAPLaN achievement by very remoteness. "Not-very remote" schools (i.e., Provincial and Remote) are represented by the boxplot on the left and the boxplot for Very Remote schools is on the right. In line with the findings of previous studies, the clustering of the outlier Very Remote schools around 90 percent achievement indicates that another variable explains a key part of the variance in literacy and numeracy outcomes of Very Remote schools.

When the demographic profiles of the schools identified as outliers in the boxplots are investigated, some patterns emerge. First, each of the Very Remote outlier schools, Nhulunbuy High School (17), Nhulunbuy Primary School (22), Yulara School (23), Alyangula Area school (29), and Mataranka School (34), had relatively low proportions of Indigenous students enrolled (below 30 percent). Conversely, the two outlier schools in the "Not-very remote" group, Pine Creek School (98) and Barunga School (112), had relatively high proportions of Indigenous students enrolled with 83 percent and 97 percent, respectively.

Second, the ICSEA scores provided by Wilson (2014) in the IER dataset appear as another notable difference among the outlier schools. ACARA (2011b) explains that ICSEA scores are a measure that represents the average level of educational advantage for students attending a particular school. For Australian schools, the ICSEA scale ranges from about 500 to 1,300 with a mean score of 1,000 and a standard deviation of 100. A school's ICSEA score is determined by evaluating the types of work and level of education completed by the parents of the students enrolled at the school. ICSEA is a measure of educational advantage that is provided so that meaningful comparisons of the performance in literacy and numeracy of students in a given school can be made with the results of schools serving students with similar backgrounds (ACARA, 2011b). In this case, all of the Very Remote schools that were outliers with high rates of NAPLaN achievement also had ICSEA scores close to the Australian mean of 1,000, which was high compared to the other Very Remote schools. The difference in the parent occupations and qualifications is explained by the fact that the outlier Very Remote schools with high rates of NAPLaN achievement were located in regional centers with large mining or tourism industries. On the other hand, Pine Creek and Barunga schools had very low rates of NAPLaN achievement and low ICSEA scores (630 and 522, respectively) for schools classified as "Not-very remote." Unlike communities such as Nhulunbuy and Alyangula, no large mining industries were operating in either Pine Creek or Barunga that attract highly educated and skilled employees and their families (including their school-aged children) to move to these communities.

Examining the outlier Very Remote schools within this sample supports Guenther's (2013) claim that the negative influence that remoteness has on school-level achievement rates does not affect all schools equally, and that some Very Remote schools (those with high proportions of non-Indigenous students enrolled and high ICSEA scores) are indeed performing on par with their Provincial peers. This finding suggests that sociodemographic indicators, such as a high ICSEA and relatively lower proportions of Indigenous and Indigenous-language-speaking students at these schools, may interact with, or moderate, the influence that attendance rates, and living very remotely, have on achievement.

Investigating Achievement Rates in English Foreign Language Contexts

The analyses presented in this paper so far have demonstrated that both school-level attendance rates and remoteness have a significant statistical effect on NT schools' NAPLaN achievement. However, it may be the case that the impact school-level attendance had on NAPLaN achievement rates differ depending on whether English is a foreign language (EFL) as opposed to "mainstream" contexts where English is widely spoken in the community and students effectively learn English as a second language (ESL). Put another way, when the proportion of Indigenous language speakers enrolled is greater than 80 percent, the reduced amount of time students spend interacting in English with their classmates and in the wider community may affect (moderate) the influence that school attendance will have on NAPLaN achievement. We investigate this hypothesis in an effort to identify whether differences in language learning contexts (ESL vs. EFL) may explain some of the variance in the NAPLaN achievement rates of schools situated in "red dirt" contexts.

Three schools were excluded from the following analysis because the proportion of Indigenous-language-speaking students enrolled at these schools was not provided in the IER's Appendix Six dataset. The rates of school attendance and NAPLaN achievement for the remaining 141 schools by location are presented in Tables 2.6 and 2.7.

The analysis found that there was a significant interaction effect (ANOVA $F_{(3,137)} = 197.004$; $p < 0.001$), and the interaction equation explained more of the variance in NAPLaN outcomes for the schools in this dataset ($R^2 = 0.812$; $p < 0.001$). Table 2.8 summarizes the key statistics, and Figure 2.6 provides a graphical depiction of the moderating affect that a schooling context where more than 80 percent of the students speak an Indigenous language as their L1 (an EFL context) had on the relationship between school-level attendance and NAPLaN achievement. The reduced impact that school attendance had

Table 2.6 Mean NAPLaN Achievement by Location

Location	Mean NAPLaN Achievement Rate (%)	n	SD
Provincial	84.89	38	7.82
Remote	66.21	24	19.27
Very Remote	30.11	79	20.12
Total	51.01	141	30.00

Table 2.7 Mean School Attendance Rates by Location

Location	Mean School Attendance Rate (%)	n	SD
Provincial	89.05	38	3.03
Remote	80.17	24	9.55
Very Remote	64.15	79	13.98
Total	73.59	141	15.87

Table 2.8 Figures for the Interaction Effect Model

	b	(SE)
Constant	55.131***	2.21
Ref = Indigenous Language Speakers < 81%		
School-Level Attendance	1.801***	0.16
Indigenous Language > 80%	−19.835***	2.97

School attendance * Indigenous language > 80%

n = 141, R-squared = 0.812***, Ref = reference category.

Note: p*** < .001 and school attendance is mean centered at 73.59 percent.

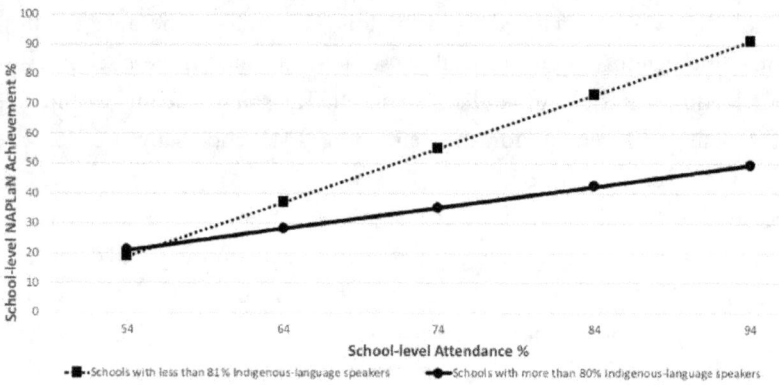

Figure 2.6 Interaction effect: The impact of school-level attendance and NAPLaN achievement rates among schools with more than 80 percent Indigenous language speakers and those with less than 81 percent Indigenous language speakers enrolled.

on NAPLaN achievement in EFL contexts (>80 percent Indigenous language speakers enrolled) is indicated by the difference in the slopes of the regression lines. The dashed line representing ESL contexts is significantly steeper ($b = 1.8$, $p < 0.001$) than the solid line ($b = 0.71$, $p < 0.001$), which represents EFL contexts. Interpreting the differences in these regression lines reveals that for every 10 percent increase in attendance in ESL contexts you would expect NAPLaN achievement to rise by 18 percent. However, for NT schools in an EFL context only a 7 percent increase in NAPLaN outcomes would be expected for a 10 percent improvement in attendance.

The results of the interaction regression analysis also indicate that for NT schools where more than 80 percent of the students speak an Indigenous language as their L1, even if the school's average attendance rates were 94 percent only approximately half (50 percent) of the NAPLaN tests attempted by the students at that school would be expected to achieve the minimum benchmark score. Therefore, while the relationship between attendance and NAPLaN outcomes is still positive in EFL contexts, the assumption that a school attendance rate of 80 percent will ensure that "learning will be effective for the majority of students" does not hold in "red dirt" school communities when most students are Indigenous language speakers. These findings support Hypothesis 3 and suggest that not only are rates of school-level achievement, as measured by NAPLaN tests, lower in contexts where Indigenous languages are the primary languages spoken in the community, but that the impact that teaching (attendance) has on learning (achievement) is also reduced.

Discussion

In recent times, the discourse regarding concerns of a general "literacy crisis" in Australia has morphed into a more nuanced "deficit discourse" that represents and frames Indigenous identity within a narrative of deficiency, negativity, dysfunctionality, and disempowerment (Fogarty, Lovell, and Dodson, 2015). The focus on "Closing the Gap" between the educational outcomes of Indigenous and non-Indigenous Australians has become the default approach to defining the Indigenous policy problems facing governments and their departments (Fogarty et al., 2015). Constructing the discourse in this way places the blame for failure on the Indigenous student, while simultaneously deflecting blame from the education system and policy makers.

The IER asserted that school attendance was a "major factor" affecting student achievement and stated "that student attendance is directly related to student achievement" (Wilson, 2014, p. 54). Wilson (2014) argued that "the dividing line between negative and positive attendance is 80%, the level at which the reviews analysis suggests learning can be effective for the majority of students" (p. 54). The key words here are *effective for the majority of students* where the "majority" are non-Indigenous students living in English-speaking communities. However, the findings of the analyses presented here challenge some of the assumptions that currently inform Indigenous education policies. The analyses indicate that the gap between Indigenous and non-Indigenous students' rates of NAPLaN achievement cannot simply be attributed to lower rates of attendance in very remote Indigenous schools. While the 80 percent attendance rule may hold on average for a dataset that includes all of the NT government's schools including those with high proportions of non-Indigenous students enrolled, our analysis demonstrates that this assumption does not hold for Indigenous community schools in remote areas when most of the students enrolled at the school speak an Indigenous language as their first language.

The findings presented in this chapter also suggest that current levels of resourcing, teaching programs, standardized national curriculums, and assessments are not delivering equitable outcomes for very remote schools where the majority of students learn English as a foreign language. This is concordant with the extensive literature that identifies problems with the use of norm referenced and standardized tests with minority children (e.g., Liddicoat et al., 2014; Scott et al., 2014; Valdes and Guadaloup, 1994). Our analysis also indicates that policy makers and educators working in remote Indigenous education should be cautious about simply assuming that applying principles or reforms drawn from the mainstream education contexts will be equally appropriate or effective in schools in remote Indigenous-language-speaking communities.

Conclusion

The evidence is clear that the myriad of "solutions" developed by education systems in concrete covered urban centers and implemented in the remote "red dirt" remote Indigenous communities of Australia and have failed to achieve the results the system itself has determined are required (Bat and Guenther, 2013). The analyses presented in this chapter demonstrate that assertions about education drawn from the mainstream, such as the direct statistical relationship between attendance and NAPLaN achievement rates, lack validity when applied to those schools in the NT where most students speak an Indigenous language as their first language, which is the case for the vast majority of the NT's very remote communities.

Currently there is only one educational pathway through Australia's national curriculum and assessment framework for the teaching and learning of English literacy and numeracy. The literacy and numeracy achievement rates of all students are interpreted against year-level milestones designed for students from an English-speaking background. The findings presented here suggest that this approach is not delivering equitable outcomes for very remote Indigenous community schools and their Indigenous-language-speaking students. Rather than problematizing the students and their rates of school attendance, the results suggest that policy makers need to truly recognize that in "red dirt" contexts, the majority of very remote Indigenous students speak an Indigenous language as their first language and thus require a differentiated approach to teaching, learning, and assessment.

References

Australian Bureau of Statistics (ABS). (2016). 2016 census quick stats Northern Territory. Retrieved from http://quickstats.censusdata.abs.gov.au/census_services/getproduct/census/2016/quickstat/7?opendocument

Australian Bureau of Statistics (ABS). (2018). Map of the 2016 remoteness areas for Australia, *Australian Statistical Geography Standard: Volume 5—Remoteness Structure*, map, cat. no. 1270.0.55.005, ABS, Canberra. Retrieved from http://www.abs.gov.au/ausstats/abs@.nsf/mf/1270.0.55.005

Australian Curriculum Assessment and Reporting Authority (ACARA). (2011a). *Why NAP?* Retrieved from http://www.nap.edu.au/about/why.nap.html

Australian Curriculum Assessment and Reporting Authority (ACARA). (2011b). *Guide to understanding ICSEA*. Retrieved from http://docs.acara.edu.au/resources/Guide_to_understanding_ICSEA.pdf

Australian Curriculum Assessment and Reporting Authority (ACARA). (2015). How to interpret standards. Retrieved 15 April 2015 from http://www.nap.edu.au/results-and-reports/how-to-interpret/standards.html

Avineri, N., Johnson, E., Brice-Heath, S., McCarty, T., Ochs, E., Kremer-Sadlik, T., …. and Alim, H. S. (2015). Invited forum: Bridging the "language gap." *Journal of Linguistic Anthropology*, 25(1), 66–86.

Bat, M. and Guenther, J. (2013). Red dirt thinking on education: A people-based system. *The Australian Journal of Indigenous Education*, 42(02), 123–35.

Berry, W. and Sanders, M. (2000). *Understanding Multivariate Research: A Primer for Beginning Social Scientists*. Boulder, CO: Westview.

Commonwealth of Australia. (2018). *Department of the Prime Minister and Cabinet, Closing the Gap Prime Minister's Report 2018*. Retrieved from https://closingthegap.pmc.gov.au/sites/default/files/ctg-report-2018.pdf

Council of Australian Governments. (2013). *The Stronger Futures Implementation Plans: Education*: Northern Territory Government. Retrieved from http://www.federalfinancialrelations.gov.au/content/npa/community_services/stronger_future_NT/Schooling_IP.pdf

Creagh, S. (2014). NAPLaN test data, ESL Bandscales and the validity of EAL/D teacher judgement of student performance. *TESOL in Context*, 24(2), 30–50.

Cross, R. (2009). Literacy for all: Quality language education for few. *Language and Education*, 23(6), 509–22.

Education Council. (2015). *National Aboriginal and Torres Strait Islander Education Strategy 2015*. Retrieved from http://www.scseec.edu.au/site/DefaultSite/filesystem/documents/ATSI%20documents/DECD__NATSI_EducationStrategy.pdf

Fogarty, W., Lovell, M., and Dodson, M. (2015). Indigenous education in Australia: Place, pedagogy and epistemic assumptions. *UNESCO Observatory Refereed e-Journal*, 4, 1–21.

Fox, J. (2016). *Applied Regression Analysis and Generalised Linear Models*. California, LA: SAGE Publications.

Freeman, L. A. and Staley, B. (2018). The positioning of Aboriginal students and their languages within Australia's education system: A human rights perspective. *International Journal of Speech-language Pathology*, 20(1), 174–81. doi:10.1080/17549507.2018.1406003

Guenther, J. (2013). Are we making education count in remote Australian communities or just counting education? *The Australian Journal of Indigenous Education*, 42(2), 157–70. doi:10.1017/jie.2013.23

Lingard, B., Thompson, G., and Sellar, S. (2016). National testing from an Australian perspective. In B. Lingard, G. Thompson, and S. Sellar (Eds.), *National Testing in Schools: An Australian Assessment* (pp. 1–17). New York, NY: Routledge.

Jaccard, J. and Turrisi, R. (2003). *Interaction Effects in Multiple Regression*. Thousand Oaks, CA: Sage Publications.

Klenowski, V. (2016). Questioning the validity of the multiple uses of NAPLAN data. In B. Lingard, G. Thompson, and S. Sellar, *National Testing in Schools: An Australian Assessment* (pp. 44–56). London: Routledge.

Ladwig, J. and Luke, G. (2014). Does improving school level attendance lead to improved school level achievement? An empirical study of indigenous educational policy in Australia. *The Australian Educational Researcher*, 41(2), 171–94.

Lee, P., Fasoli, L., Ford, L., Stephenson, P., and McInerney, P. (2014). *Indigenous Kids and Schooling in the Northern Territory: An in Introductory Overview and Brief History of Aboriginal Education in the Northern Territory*. Bachelor, NT: Batchelor Press.

Liddicoat, A., Heugh, K., Bigelow, M., and Ennser-Kananen, J. (2014). Educational equity for linguistically marginalised students. In M. Bigelow and J. Ennser-Kananen (Eds), *The Routledge Handbook of Educational Linguistics*. Routledge.

McKay, P. and Scarino, A. (1991). *ESL Framework of Stages: An Approach to ESL Learning in Schools, K-12*. Carlton: Curriculum Corporation.

Northern Territory Department of Education (NTDoE). (2015). Indigenous education review strategy. Retrieved from http://ed.ntschools.net/seto/team/ier/SitePages/Home.aspx

Paradis, J. and Jia, R. (2017). Bilingual children's long-term outcomes in English as a second language: Language environment factors shape individual differences in catching up with monolinguals. *Developmental Science, 20*(1). doi:10.1111/desc.12433

Roberts, P., Piccoli, A., and Hattie, J. (2018). How to solve Australia's "rural school challenge": Focus on research and communities. *The Conversation.* April 15, Australia. Retrieved from http://theconversation.com/how-to-solve-australias-rural-school-challenge-focus-on-research-and-communities-94979

Saville-Troike, M. and Barto, K. (2016). *Introducing Second Language Acquisition.* Cambridge: Cambridge University Press.

Scott, S., Webber, C. F., Lupart, J. L., Aitken, N., and Scott, D. E. (2014). Fair and equitable assessment practices for all students. *Assessment in Education: Principles, Policy & Practice, 21*(1), 52–70.

Simpson, J. and Wigglesworth, G. (2008). *Children's Language and Multilingualism: Indigenous Language Use at Home and School.* London: Continuum International.

Simpson, J. and Wigglesworth, G. (2018). Language diversity in Indigenous Australia in the 21st Century. *Current Issues in Language Planning, 20*(1), 67–80. doi:10.1080/14664208.2018.1503389

Valdés, G. and Figueroa, R. A. (1994). *Bilingualism and Testing: A Special Case of Bias.* Ablex Publishing.

Wigglesworth, G. and Simpson, J. (2018). Going to school in a different world. In G. Wigglesworth and J. Simpson (Eds.), *From Home to School: Language Practices of Indigenous and Minority Children and Youth* (pp. 1–20). Basingstoke: Palgrave Macmillan.

Wigglesworth, G., Simpson, J., and Loakes, D. E. (2011). NAPLAN language assessments for Indigenous children in remote communities: Issues and problems. *Australian Review of Applied Linguistics, 34*(3), 320–43.

Wilson, B. (2014). A share in the future: Review of Indigenous education in the Northern Territory. The Education Business. Retrieved from http://www.education.nt.gov.au/data/assets/pdf_file/0007/37294/A-Share-in-the-Future-The-Review-of-Indigenous-Education-in-the-Northern-Territory.pdf

3

Where Language is Beside the Point: English Language Testing for Mexicano Students in the Southwestern United States

Luis E. Poza and Sheila M. Shannon

Introduction

While the United States has always been a multilingual territory and nation (Wiley, 2014), its popular and official predilections for English are well documented, with Spanish being particularly marginalized (García, 2009; Macías, 2014). The vast majority of students labeled English learners (EL) (and thus subject to English language testing) in the United States use Spanish as a primary or heritage language (NCES, 2018), and a majority of these live in the Southwest. Thus, while noting the local particularities of different policy and sociolinguistic backdrops in other US regions and around the world, we focus our analysis on the contexts, history, and impacts of federal education policy and language testing on this subset, arguing that testing (like its preceding policies) consistently infantilizes and punishes bilingual students and disciplines their educators. We make our theoretical case through genealogy, a method of historiography and cultural critique that considers current circumstances not merely through chronology but rather thematically "to understand how various independently existing vectors of practice managed to contingently intersect in the past so as to give rise to the present" (Koopman, 2013, p. 107). Following Foucault (1975), our genealogy eyes mechanisms of power and considers how changes in policy and practice in the education of immigrant and bilingual youth correspond to enduring social relations between these students and dominant groups.

As such, this work begins with an overview of the linguistic ideological underpinnings of language testing in the United States, contending that it is an instrument of hegemonic English as a raciolinguistic project (Shannon, 1995). Bowing to it, educators adapt to the testing-related requirements rather than questioning and resisting them (Freire, 2005/1974) and in so doing cement language hierarchies rooted in ethnoculturalist (racist) constructions of an American identity that prizes whiteness, Christianity, and English proficiency (Schildkraut, 2003). We argue that testing regimes in this manner have made language a locus of discrimination and marginalization in lieu of previous characteristics such as race, ethnicity, and national origin. To demonstrate this evolution, we follow with a genealogical analysis of the relationship between Mexicans in the Southwest and the American government to show consistent political, economic, and linguistic hegemony and then connect these points to the testing regime of bilinguals in the United States today with further genealogical analysis of federal education policy. We close our theoretical argument including references to our empirical work in classrooms in California and Colorado offering pedagogical frameworks of resistance that disrupt US raciolinguistic hierarchies.

Language Ideologies and English Language Testing in the United States

We argue with a twofold theoretical framework that English language testing in the United States is an extension of the historical discrimination that we will describe in our subsequent genealogical analysis. First and foremost, we consider raciolinguistic perspectives (Alim, Rickford, and Ball, 2016; Flores and Rosa, 2015) and the broader field of language ideologies (Irvine, 1989; Kroskrity, 2004; Woolard and Schieffelin, 1994) to address how language is implicated in race-constructing projects (and vice versa), and how racial and linguistic—*raciolinguistic*—narratives underlie notions of national identity. Second, we consider language testing specifically as a mechanism of language planning (Shohamy, 2006, 2014) that sorts and punishes minoritized language users and coerces teachers into adaptation to unjust conditions (Freire, 2005). Regarding language testing in the United States, these two perspectives suggest that ideologies about *what*, *how*, and *by whom* language should be learned and often undergird current accountability regimes with assimilationist impulses toward a white, English-monolingual paradigm.

Language Ideologies and Raciolinguistic Perspectives

Language ideologies refer to the individual and societal beliefs and attitudes about language as a construct (what it is, how it is learned, how it should be used) and about the relative statuses among different languages and varieties (Irvine, 1989; Woolard and Schieffelin, 1994). Kroskrity (2004), meanwhile, cautions against monolithic understandings of language ideology by noting that language ideologies "are usually multiple, context-bound, and necessarily constructed from the sociocultural context of the speaker" (p. 496). That is, language ideologies are best understood as multitudinous, dynamic, situated, and at times contradictory.

This is plainly evident in US educational policy and jurisprudence underlying English language testing. On the one hand, it claims to protect the civil rights of minoritized linguistic communities by ensuring attention to their academic progress (or lack thereof) and, at times, advancing bilingualism as an asset. On the other hand, policy and court opinions often refer to these students as deficient and at risk because of their linguistic profiles. The contradiction is furthered by the reliance of these intended rights-protecting measures on high-stakes tests reflecting monolingual paradigms of language and language learning that, in fact, coercively incentivize English monolingualism (Menken and Solorza, 2014) while penalizing schools serving large populations of minoritized language users (Escamilla et al., 2003).

We argue that these impacts emerge from hegemonic English as a raciolinguistic American identity project. Scholars of *raciolinguistics* advance the term as a way to call attention to the intertwined constructions of race and language under colonial and postcolonial regimes. In the introduction of an edited volume by Alim, Rickford, and Ball (2016), Alim positions raciolinguistics as a commingling of linguistic and anthropological thought regarding "racialization as a process of socialization, in and through language, as a continuous process of becoming as opposed to being," that, in turn, necessitates "theorizing language and race together, paying particular attention to how both social processes mutually mediate and constitute each other" (pp. 2–3). Flores and Rosa (Flores and Rosa, 2015; Rosa and Flores, 2017), meanwhile, examine the role of whiteness in linguistic paradigms, beginning with the dehumanization of indigenous peoples and their languages through to current preoccupations with the inadequacy of minoritized vernaculars and languages other than English for academic achievement. The authors point to a continuous strand of Eurocentric surveillance and judgment of the communicative practices of people of color. Thus, they advance a "raciolinguistic perspective" to understand how the white gaze is attached both to a speaking subject who engages in the idealized linguistic practices of whiteness and to a listening subject who hears and interprets the linguistic practices of language-minoritized populations as deviant based on their racial positioning in society as opposed to any objective characteristics of their language use. (Flores and Rosa, 2015, p. 151)

Certainly this perspective is relevant anywhere that European colonialism imposed white supremacist racial hierarchy upon all facets of society, including language. In the US context, this linguistic coloniality (Mignolo, 1996; Quijano, 2000a) elevates English stylings of the white middle and upper classes and inscribes racialized deficiency upon other languages and varieties through overt repression and symbolic violence (García, 2009; Macías, 2014; Wiley, 2014). English language testing serves as one such coercive mechanism.

Testing as Language Planning

We argue that testing as currently constituted in the United States—atop a mountain of standards for academic content, teacher preparation, and teacher practice that minimally engage with the sociopolitical realities of immigrant and bilingual children—cements language hierarchies rooted in what Schildkraut (2003) calls *ethnoculturalist* constructions of US identity, which prize whiteness, Christianity, and English proficiency. It does so by instilling "a surveillance that makes it possible to quantify, classify, and punish" (Foucault, 1975, p. 18) those acquiring English in schools through panopticism, the ever-present gaze of the powerful (not as a group of people, per se, but as particular ways of being and knowing discursively inscribed as normal and desirable within a society) through observation, sorting, and discipline (Foucault, 1975). Drawing on this early framework, various scholars have argued that mechanisms such as high-stakes tests, teacher observations, and rigid curriculum pacing guides serve to mechanize and standardize teacher practice as means of such surveillance (Bushnell, 2003; Webb, Briscoe, and Mussman, 2009). With respect to the education of immigrant and bilingual learners in the United States, language testing and its subsequent regimentation of curriculum and teacher practice serves as a means by which to surveil and constrain teachers and students from questioning and resisting hegemonic English and its affiliated racist and linguistic ideologies.

The notion of testing as a language planning instrument is neither new nor unique to the United States, even though this is where we devote our focus. Shohamy (2006) notes that language testing links language ideologies and the societal linguistic realities they wish to foster, stating that testing "acts as a most powerful mechanism for manipulating language behaviors and the use of students, teachers, parents, and society as a whole" (p. 93). Shohamy adds that testing reinforces status hierarchies among languages and language varieties, perpetuates and legitimizes regimes of language standardization, and suppresses linguistic diversity and dynamism (p. 95). In separate work, Shohamy (2014) evokes Foucault's observations about testing as a sorting and punishing tool.

> The uses of test results have detrimental effects for test takers since such uses can create winners and losers, successes and failures, rejections and acceptances. Test scores are often the sole indicators for placing people in class levels, for granting certificates and prizes, for determining whether a person will be able to continue in future studies, for deciding on a profession, for entering special education classes, for participating in honour classes, for getting accepted to higher education and for obtaining jobs. (pp. 15–16)

Indeed, insofar as English language testing in the United States is instrumental in classifying students as EL and reifying this label, it is implicated in the tracking of EL-classified students into academic pathways with less engaging curriculum or college preparatory content (Callahan, Wilkinson, and Muller, 2010; Kanno and Kangas, 2014; Thompson, 2015; Umansky, 2016) and the inculcation of low self-efficacy among students who persist in this category (Dabach, 2014; Thompson, 2015). Moreover, high-stakes English testing has constricted access to bilingual education programs for EL-classified students as schools feel compelled to accelerate students to English proficiency at the expense of sustaining and developing their home languages (Menken, 2006, 2008; Menken and Solorza, 2014).

Beyond ethnocentric ideologies, testing also represents misguided ideologies about what language is and how it is learned. English language proficiency tests in the United States[1] examine language as segmented skills such as phonics, word knowledge, reading fluency, and grammatical conventions assessed against an orthographic norm, without account for the variations and communicative competencies of oral language. In addition, such skills are usually assessed in incremental and highly sequenced ways, presuming a uniform and linear trajectory of language development (see Leung and Scarino, 2016; Valdés and Figueroa, 1994; Valdés, Poza, and Brooks, 2014, for an in-depth critique of how language is conceptualized in assessment). Such a supposition runs counter to the burgeoning literature on sociocultural perspectives of second language acquisition, which highlights that language learning is nonlinear, never-ending, situated within the language user's interactional needs and experiences, and interwoven with the full linguistic repertoire rather than distinct monolingualisms (Atkinson, 2011; Cumming, 2008).

Thus, the underlying assumptions upon which assessments are written reflect ideologies rooted in Eurocentric and monolingual paradigms about how language is learned and how such learning can be demonstrated. To wit, reviews of the California English Language Development Test administered in the state to measure progress toward English proficiency found not only that most test items did not align with prescribed language standards (California Department of Education, 2013) but also that the test overidentified students as EL as even students who had grown up speaking only English would have been classified as EL based on their score on the exam (García Bedolla and Rodriguez, 2011). Conversely, the Arizona state Department of Education was compelled to a settlement with the federal Office of Civil Rights for using English language tests as a means to underidentify students as EL and to prematurely reclassify such students as proficient in English (leaving them to fend for themselves in mainstream classes taught in English without adequate linguistic supports) in order to avoid provision of language support services to thousands of children (OCR, 2016). While capturing opposite outcomes (overidentification and protracted EL classification on the one hand, underidentification and fugacious support provision on the other), both states demonstrate the injurious results of classifying and tracking students based on tests that reify faulty ideologies about language and language learning.

These fallacious beliefs about language learning and how to assess it are doubly true in the case of bilinguals. Prior work notes that it is erroneous to presume that bilinguals should conform to native-speaker paradigms of either language, and that to assess students' knowledge, even linguistic knowledge, in a single language misses important information that students hold bilingually in their communicative repertoires as well as cognitive processes and abilities that result from their bilingualism (Valdés and Figueroa, 1994). Building from these important foundations, numerous scholars have proposed methods of assessment that invite bilingual ways of knowing and demonstrating knowledge (García, 2009b; Shohamy, 2011; López, Turkan, and Guzmán-Orth, 2017). Such innovations in assessment, and the courage and leadership that teachers must exert to implement them in the face of high-stakes tests elsewhere in the curriculum, lead us to a third and final facet of our theoretical argument that we will examine at the close of this work: critical consciousness. However, we must first establish the savage and exploitative history informing the social order that we call upon educators to resist.

English Language Testing in the United States for Mexicans, Mexican Americans, and Chicanos: A Genealogy

Colonial Traces and the Coloniality of Power

English in the United States in the shape, form, and sound of a standard variety is perceived as a monolithic language. Its proliferation and ascent to hegemonic status was an important part of the colonial project extending into the present day within the coloniality of power. In writing about Latin America, Aníbal Quijano (2000b) shifts the notion of a postcolonial era to understanding that the colonial has become wherever power is continuously exerted over the colonized. This includes exploitation of labor, extraction and appropriation of natural resources, the dehumanization and exploitation of indigenous peoples, and the spread of capitalism that enriches the state. The coloniality of power includes Eurocentric capitalism and "the Eurocentric pretension to the exclusive producer and protagonist of modernity" (Quijano, 2000b, p. 544).

Walter Mignolo (2000) explores the role of national languages, particularly Spanish and English in the Americas, within the notion of the coloniality of power. He demonstrates that the insistence on monolithic national languages polices against the naturally occurring diversity of languaging practices that speakers use across and within imperialistically constructed borders.[2]

Recently, Fregoso Bailón and Shannon (2016, 2019) have extended the idea of the coloniality of power to transcoloniality—the particular case of Mexicans who immigrate to the United States. Applying this transcoloniality of power framework to US educational policy and practice, particularly language testing and accountability programs, sheds light on a regime of surveillance and discipline acting upon students and teachers alike.

We now turn to the historical construction of the speaker of languages other than English in the United States, in particular the Spanish speaker, as someone in need of detection, correction, and discipline (Foucault, 1975) through testing.

Mid-Nineteenth-Century United States

The coloniality of power of the United States in North America began in earnest with the westward expansion in the mid-nineteenth century dramatically ignited by the US war against Mexico from 1845 to 1848. Prior to this conflict, the United States had formed twenty-eight states from the east coast to mid-continent. In 1845, the large northern territory of Mexico was added as the State of Texas.³ The annexation of Texas and machinations of politicians, provocateurs, and entrepreneurs on both sides led to the war with Mexico (Conway, 2010). The Treaty of Guadalupe de Hidalgo ended the war, ceding Mexico's northern territory to the United States (comprising current states New Mexico, Arizona, California, Utah, Nevada, and Colorado) but also providing for the Mexicans who inhabited that territory to become US citizens and protect their land holdings (Griswold del Castillo, 1990). Del Castillo estimates that one hundred thousand Mexicans remained in the territory.⁴ Many of those in those communities spoke Spanish. And as San Miguel, Jr., and Valencia (1998) point out, the treaty insured that the Mexicans would have "the enjoyment of all the rights of citizens of the United States, including the right to maintain their language" (original text from the Treaty of Guadalupe Hidalgo, Art. 9, excerpted from Miller, 1937, p. 362).

As the educational system developed in the southwestern United States from Texas west to California and north to Colorado and into New Mexico, it increasingly shifted toward a public system that shunned and eliminated any use of Spanish in the schools (San Miguel, Jr. and Valencia, 1998). This move was a clear violation of the treaty and a solid example of the coloniality of power. No longer colonized by the Spanish crown, Mexicans in the US Southwest were recolonized by the United States and subjected to coloniality and the erasure of their language.

United States in the Nineteenth Century and Beyond

The border between the United States and Mexico, with a wall running through it or not, is an invention of the political economy that capitalism demands. The Mexicans were already in what was to be the United States in 1848 and continue to come north as the US economy relies on the cheap labor that unauthorized entry provides. This example of the transcoloniality of power involves welcoming labor across borders without guaranteeing citizenship and the rights and dignity it affords. Labor unions pressured legislators to curtail the flow of unauthorized workers, while businesses, on the other hand, desired a way to retain a "legal" workforce relying heavily on Mexican workers (Fregoso Bailón and Shannon, 2016).

In response to this conflict of interests and the increasing numbers of unauthorized persons, upward of 3 million at the time, the Immigration Reform and Control Act of 1986 (IRCA) was passed.⁵ Of most importance, however, the legislation would provide amnesty to certain qualified immigrants.

Nearly 3 million unauthorized persons applied for amnesty and over 2 million were granted temporary resident status. Once approved, recipients began the process of naturalization with the application for legal residency and taking steps toward citizenship. English language testing emerges as an issue. As White, Bean, and Espenshade (1990) point out, the applicants could "later adjust to permanent resident alien status provided they [could] demonstrate a minimal understanding of English and a basic knowledge of U.S. civics and history" (p. 94).

Up until IRCA of 1986, the requirements for citizenship did indeed include some testing of English and civics. However, as Kunnan (2009) concludes from his review about the testing requirements, the point of testing was not clear at all.

> The crux of the matter regarding the English language and the history and government requirements for naturalization is whether these tests have in any way been able to promote "civic integration," "political allegiance," "social cohesion," "social harmony" among immigrants or whether they have become an irritating formality or a real new barrier to citizenship. (pp. 46-7)

The real test came with the amnesty applicants who became permanent residents and could then apply for citizenship. Presumably, they too would have to pass the English and civics tests whatever the point was. Though amnesty recipients (mostly Mexican) had worked and lived in the United States for an extended period of time, they had mostly done so in segregated conditions. Speaking English was not among the things that a migrant worker and an unauthorized person living in the United States required. Keeping safely on the margins with others in one's same situation could be done entirely in Spanish. This linguistic segregation for Mexican immigrant adults in the workplace is commonplace and documented in studies about agricultural workers (Holmes, 2013; Stephen, 2007) and domestic workers (Hognadeau-Sotelo, 2007).

In 1988, Shannon (the second author of this chapter) had taken an assistant professor position at the University of Colorado Denver when the permanent residency applications began. Teaching Adult English as a Second Language (ESL) teachers in the MA program, she discovered that ESL classes were instituted with the provision that the amnesty recipient had to receive eighty hours of instruction in lieu of the civics test.[6] The federal government had redesigned the testing of English and civics requirement for the particular group of applicants when it was clear that many of the applicants would have failed, making the entire amnesty program a failure. The federal government allotted funds to individual states to remedy the situation. In the case of Colorado, that resulted in the requirement of a certificate that the applicant had taken eighty hours of ESL. Shannon discovered this program by observing in her MA students' classrooms who, several at the time, were teaching in one of these certificate programs.

In the case of one of her students, Shannon found that as a part of the state-funded program he taught a small group of applicants in a church with no pedagogical training nor was he provided with any material beyond a chalkboard. The ages and Spanish literacy levels of the applicants ranged greatly, which made planning and teaching challenging. Most of the students in this small group ended the eighty hours of instruction knowing little more English than when they had begun.[7] The literature on testing and amnesty has no mention of this special program. Shannon, in her advocacy work in the community, had observed individuals and groups prepare for the "regular" test by memorizing a list of one hundred questions about US history and government in English and practicing among themselves. She also accompanied one amnesty applicant to her "interview" for citizenship. The only requirement was the certificate of eighty hours of ESL.

This egregious example of the transcoloniality of power where a whole system of exploitation of workers leads to making a sham of the naturalization process is illustrative of how language became beside the point in testing when the US economy needed workers regardless of language.[8] But it did grant permanent residency and citizenship to thousands of people. And these people were men and women providing for their families including their own children. It is to the children that we now turn.

Transcoloniality and Language in US Schools

The indignities put upon Mexican and Chicano[9] laborers have been ideologically replicated in the schooling of their children. Due in no small part to their linguistic background, these students have been racialized and segregated in American public schools as their parents have been exploited in American fields and factories. Identified by phenotype, surname, and linguistic profile, these students were relegated to *Mexican schools*, marked by inferior facilities and curriculum where students received, at best, "the illusion of schooling" (Donato, 2003; Donato and Hanson, 2012). Various legal victories put an end to the segregation of Mexican and Chicano students by ethnicity[10] but left in place the potential to isolate these students away from a real education due to policies and practices around the education of bilingual students.

The Bilingual Education Act

The Bilingual Education Act (BEA) of 1968 was the first federal legislation to specifically address the needs of students learning English in schools. While providing funding for educational supports and research into bilingual programming, the Act primarily defines emergent bilingual students by their presumed lack of English proficiency and casts their language background as a problem to be solved (Ruiz, 1984). The wording of the BEA makes this position clear:

> One of the *most acute educational problems* in the United States is that which involves millions of children of limited English-speaking ability because they come from environments where the dominant language is other than English; that additional efforts should be made to supplement present attempts *to find adequate and constructive solutions to this unique and perplexing educational situation*; and that the urgent need is for comprehensive and cooperative action now on the local, State, and Federal levels to develop forward-looking approaches to meet the *serious learning difficulties faced by this substantial segment of the Nation's school-age population*. (BEA, 1968, Sec. 702, emphasis our own)

Wiese and García (1998) provide a comprehensive review of the BEA from its inception in 1968 to its final bow in 1994. They indicate how the legislative language moves between assimilationist remedies that replace the other language with English and multicultural approaches that recognize bilingualism as a national asset. This latter approach, however, emphasizes the economic and national security benefits of a multilingual society at the expense of arguments affirming students' cultures (Flores and García, 2017; Petrovic, 2005). This theme will be repeated in separate legislation.

The final reauthorization of the federal BEA came in 1994. At this final point, the act invokes a language-as-resource orientation (Ruiz, 1984) but persists in deficit orientations with reference to the challenges they face in education due to cultural differences, poverty, and issues related to immigration. Wiese and García (1998) point out that neither the original nor subsequent legislation outline what bilingual education would constitute but rather *the class of students* it would target.

While the federal-level legislation about the education of bilingual students was being debated, children of immigrants in US schools became a concern. The US Supreme Court decided *Plyler v. Doe* (1982), a decision that struck down a Texas statute that allowed public school districts to charge tuition or completely deny access to a free public education to children whose parents or who themselves were unauthorized migrants. The court's majority opinion, however, noted that unauthorized residents did not constitute a protected class and that education was not a fundamental right of the students themselves, but rather that "public education has a pivotal role in maintaining the fabric of our society and in sustaining our political and cultural heritage" (Matamuro, 2014, p. 203). In plain terms, Plyler meant that children of unauthorized parents could attend school from kindergarten through high school without reproach, while the adults in their families could very well be working without authorization and in danger of being identified and deported. Again, we see how the transcoloniality of power acts upon Mexicans and Chicanos with legislation that protects the society in which the unauthorized are situated while not giving them rights. We would like to emphasize here that just as the BEA never construed language as a right (Ruiz, 1984), *Plyler* established that the education of undocumented children or of undocumented parents was a benefit for society, not a right that they deserved (Shannon, 1999).

Replacing Instruction with Testing

No Child Left Behind Act of 2001 was federal legislation deciding the educational policies and practices for all children. This legislation did away with the BEA and simultaneously removed reference to "bilingual" in any official way. The Office for Bilingual Education and Language Minority Affairs (OBEMLA) became the Office for English Language Acquisition (OELA). In place of bilingual education, a rigorous testing regime in English was put into place to determine annual progress toward English proficiency. For bilingual students, that has meant testing for content standards and language development measured against an English-monolingual paradigm.

Grinberg and Saavedra (2000) observed during this time that

> contemporary bilingual/ESL education has not advanced a cultural and political critique in a democratic and emancipatory way; instead, it prepares the students it serves to take their places on the lower rungs of the U.S. social hierarchy. (p. 419)

We argue, similarly, that the shift from bilingual education as a way to meet the needs of a special group of students to English-only, test-based approaches continues identifying the problem as residing in the students as the BEA had for twenty-six years and then puts in place testing that has the effect of disciplining and punishing them, a Foucauldian twist of fate.

Critical Consciousness, Teaching for Liberation, and English Language Testing

The final theoretical underpinning of this work is Freire's (2005/1974) notion of critical consciousness. Freire posits that humankind, unlike other species, is able not only to perceive the objective world in its present state but also to place the present into a temporal narrative that considers both causality and future outcomes. By viewing circumstances temporally, humankind is capable of perceiving critically, that is, with an inquisitive lens about the present state of affairs and with the potential to enact change upon present and future conditions. Freire here distinguishes between *adaptation* and *integration*, with the former consisting of human-as-object that is merely adjusted to its condition, while the latter posits a human-as-subject with the "critical capacity to make choices and to transform that reality" (p. 4). Teaching, Freire argues, must foster integration among students such that they are critically engaged with their realities and agentively seeking to improve conditions for themselves and others.

Scholars of bilingual education and ESL teaching have encouraged such a framework in contemporary practice. In work that documented the daily experiences of immigrant students and the "ESL ghetto" of segregated, insipid, and ultimately unhelpful curriculum to which they had been relegated, Valdés (1998, 2001) advances a notion for a critical pedagogy in ESL. Akin to Freirian notions of integration, Valdés advocates for a pedagogy that does more than just prepare students to succeed within current systems, but also to help students perceive the power relations in which their language and their very existences are embedded, and to offer them new ways to understand their lives and opportunities. Such a pedagogy would reject "intellectually impoverished materials" and the teaching "of syllabi based on irrelevant assumptions" (1998, p. 16).

In this vein, Gutiérrez (2008) discusses the pedagogical ecology of a precollegiate summer program for migrant students in Southern California in which students develop conventional academic literacy practices but with a sense of historicity and agency. Gutiérrez specifically describes the learning ecology as one in which "learning is supported and expanded in the language and social practices of the institute's lived curriculum—a curriculum that fuses social, critical, and sociocultural theory with the local, the historical, the present, and the future of migrant communities" (p. 153). Such an arrangement, Gutiérrez argues, creates a *collective Third Space* in which students draw upon their own experiences, histories, and knowledge along with the dialogic guidance of the program's instructors to identify, express, and challenge the tensions and oppression in their lives and others' through joint activity. Analyzing the same summer program, Espinoza (2009) describes a series of inquiring, dialogic exchanges that he characterizes as *educational sanctuary*. Espinoza draws on various conceptualizations of "radical" spaces to frame his observations in the migrant program, characterizing these as "lived spaces in which vernacular collectivities actually breathe, speak, move, interact, make meaning, and critique" (p. 45). Thus, both *collective Third Space* and *educational sanctuary* capture these frameworks of liberation insofar as students' experiences and practices undergird a challenging curriculum that engages them in learning for their own sake and for that of a more just world.

Our own prior work has similarly highlighted opportunities for such counter-hegemonic moves. Shannon (1995, 1995b, 1999) provides insights from one bilingual classroom that disrupted hegemonic English by elevating the status of Spanish in general and students' language practices in particular within the curriculum. The teacher, Mrs. D, did so by positioning students as communicative experts and their linguistic resources as assets that helped them learn content, assist other students, and nurture respect and deeper relationships with family and community. Moreover, Mrs. D expressly rejected the social hierarchies that existed outside her classroom, insisting that equality was a central principle for students and their language practices. Meanwhile, Poza (2016, 2017, 2018) documents experiences for students and one teacher in a fifth-grade bilingual classroom in Northern California. Through ethnographic interviews with the teacher and classroom observations, the work describes a teacher, *Maestro*, mindful of the constraining impulse of tests insofar as the impetus to raise scores and rates of English proficiency reclassification results in students being removed from Spanish instruction for English remediation (Poza, 2016). Ultimately, however, *Maestro* is compelled to let students leverage their bilingual repertoires for purposeful and strategic uses across registers drawing on students' own communicative experiences and competencies (Poza, 2017, 2018). All of these cases exemplify Freire's notion of integration insofar as teachers and students engage dialogically, exalt and leverage familiar histories and language practices, and openly call into question the standards to which they are called to conform as well as the social hierarchies undergirding them.

The affordances of day-to-day classroom practice relative to highly structured standardized tests do not negate the potential for principles of critical consciousness to inform English language testing. Assessment itself can seek to understand English language development within the contexts of students' bi/

multilingualism. For instance, Gorter and Cenoz (2017) review literature on multilingualism in assessment and describe several approaches to the matter. One approach norms students' scores based on their linguistic profiles (Gathercole et al., 2013), and thus students' language development is evaluated relative to that of peers who share their exposure to the target language rather than relying exclusively on a monolingual paradigm. Another approach the authors highlight by Cenoz, Arocena, and Gorter (2013) evaluates students' skills in each of three languages (Spanish, English, and Basque) to obtain individual language scores as well as aggregate bilingual and multilingual scores. In noting that there were no significant differences in bilingual and multilingual scores despite notable difference in individual language scores for Spanish L1 and Basque L1 users, the researchers note that measurement of students' complete repertoires gives a much better view of their linguistic capabilities and affirms the value of their non-English languages. The authors also point to the Language Passport used as part of the European Language Portfolio wherein students self-assess their competencies across languages in their repertoire. Finally, the authors describe a series of works in which translanguaging perspectives (allowances for multilingualism within the assessment either in the prompts or responses) can improve English language testing through both the inclusion of multilingual tasks in assessments and in the production of tests more closely aligned to the actual language practices of multilinguals. This last approach, unlike the earlier strategies that still measure languages in isolation even if doing so at the same time as other languages in students' repertoires, better reflects the concept of a singular linguistic repertoire that proponents of translanguaging perspectives advance.

Conclusion

The uplifting visions of education for Mexican and Chicano students described above, along with many others in that vein, point a way forward despite the raciolinguistic perspectives underlying omnipresent English language testing and its hegemonic push toward white, English-monolingual normativity. English language testing is likely a mainstay in American education for the foreseeable future, but teachers can resist its permeation into their curriculum and relationships with students through adoption of the instructional and assessment philosophies and practice described above. To do so, teachers must provide students access to meaningful yet challenging content rather than diluted materials or extended language practice in isolation. They must affirm, nurture, and expand students' linguistic and academic repertoires rather than treat their prior knowledge and background as deficits to overcome or repertoires to be restricted. Finally, they must themselves call into question the prevalent power relations in language and in language teaching (Flores, 2013) to encourage their students to do so as well.

Notes

1 English proficiency testing in the United States is conducted primarily through two consortium-generated tests: the ACCESS for ELLs 2.0 test developed by WIDA is used in thirty-nine states and territories, including most southwestern states except California and Arizona, which developed their own standards and tests. The ELPA 21 (English Language Proficiency Assessment for the 21st Century) consortium developed separate standards and tests in use in eleven states, mainly in the Southeast and Midwest. Both tests assess language by modality (listening, speaking, reading, writing) and using linear growth trajectories with monolingual paradigms of proficiency (for a more detailed examination of the WIDA ACCESS test in use, see King and Bigelow, 2018).
2 The notion of *languaging* emerges in various literatures to take into account the encounters of languages through colonialization, slavery, and forced migration through the world in "modern" times. We acknowledge the important and extensive work that has been accomplished and is developing in the United States in particular with the related phenomenon of *translanguaging* that we turn to later in the chapter.
3 Mexico had gained its independence from Spain in 1821.
4 Griswold del Castillo (1990) points out that among this number were "a large number of Hispanicized and nomadic Indians" (p. 62).
5 Congress wanted the onus to be not only on the worker but also on business itself. Therefore, IRCA contained provisions that outlawed the hiring of unauthorized workers.
6 Kunnan (2009) reviews the evolution of the language and civics testing for citizenship and shows how it was never clear if the civics test was also a test of English. He cites Etzioni (2007) who concluded, "The test hinders those who do not speak English and favors immigrants from English-speaking countries and persons who can afford extensive English education prior to their arrival, or once they are in the U.S." (p. 43).
7 Congress had to act in order to avoid rendering the whole amnesty program useless. An English as a Second Language (ESL) program was begun with federal dollars funneled to the state level.

8   In order to make a case for the how language is beside the point for testing in the United States, we are circumventing the political and economic forces that have determined how workers come to the United States, including the years in which men came on a seasonal basis (The Bracero Program 1942–64), to the dismantling of that program which did not stop the workers from coming but encouraged their families to join them as the border crossings were too risky and kept families separated for long periods of time. (See Galarza, 1978, for a detailed account.)

9   We refer to Mexicans in the US Southwest here as Mexicans and Chicanos for those who identify as such and to include anyone who resides in the US Southwest or has moved from there to other areas of the United States who are of Mexican origin. We do not intend to ignore other Latinx individuals or communities who are from other parts of Latin America. The cases and examples are about Mexicans and Chicanos specifically or as an example of indexicality (Bucholtz and Hall, 2004); that all Latinx-looking or sounding individuals are Mexican regardless of whether or not is the case.

10 See, for example, *Alvarez v. Lemon Grove*, 1931; *Delgado v. Bastrop*, 1948; *Gonzales v. Sheely*, 1951; and *Mendez v. Westminster*, 1946.

References

Alim, H. S., Rickford, J. R., and Ball, A. F. (2016). *Raciolinguistics: How Language Shapes Our Ideas About Race*. New York, NY: Oxford University Press.

Alvarez v. Lemon Grove School District, Civil Action No. 66625. Superior Court, San Diego County, CA. March 30, 1931.

Atkinson, D. (Ed.). (2011). *Alternative Approaches to Second Language Acquisition*. New York, NY: Routledge.

Bilingual Education Act, Pub.L. No. (90–247), 81 Stat.816 (1968).

Bilingual Education Act, Pub.L. No. (103–382), (1994).

Bucholtz, M. and Hall, K. (2004). Language and identity. In A. Duranti (Ed.), *A Companion to Linguistic Anthropology* (pp. 369–94). Malden, MA: Blackwell Publishing.

Bushnell, M. (2003). Teachers in the schoolhouse panopticon: Complicity and resistance. *Education and Urban Society*, 35(3), 251–72.

California Department of Education (2013). California English Language Development Test alignment and transition to the English Language Proficiency Assessments for California, Presentation given at the fourteenth annual accountability leadership institute for English learners and immigrant students. December 10, 2013. Burlingame, CA.

Callahan, R., Wilkinson, L., and Muller, C. (2010). Academic achievement and course taking among language minority youth in US schools: Effects of ESL placement. *Educational Evaluation and Policy Analysis, 32*(1), 84–117.

Cenoz, J., Arocena, E., and Gorter, D. (2013). Multilingual students and their writing skills in Basque, Spanish and English. In V. C. M. Gathercole (Ed.), *Bilingual Assessment: Issues* (pp. 186–205). Bristol: Multilingual Matters.

Conway, C. (2010). *The US-Mexican War: A Binational Reader*. Indianapolis, IN: Hackett.

Cumming, A. (2008). Assessing oral and literate abilities. In E. Shohamy and N. Hornberger (Eds.), *Encyclopedia of Language and Education: Language Testing and Assessment* (pp. 3–18). New York, NY: Springer.

Dabach, D. (2014). "I am not a shelter!" Stigma and social boundaries in teachers' accounts of students' experience in separate "sheltered" English learner classrooms. *Journal of Education for Students Placed at Risk, 19*(2), 98–124.

Delgado v. Bastrop Independent School District, 388 W.D. Texas (1948).

Donato, R. (2003). Sugar beets, segregation and schools: Mexican Americans in a Northern Colorado Community, 1920-1960. *Journal of Latinos and Education, 2*(2), 69–88.

Donato, R. and Hanson, J. S. (2012). Legally white, socially "Mexican": Mexican Americans and the Politics of De Jure and De Facto Segregation in the American Southwest. *Harvard Educational Review, 82*(2), 202–25.

Escamilla, K., Mahon, E., Riley-Bernal, H., and Rutledge, D. (2003). High-stakes testing, Latinos, and English language learners: Lessons from Colorado. *Bilingual Research Journal, 27*(1), 25–49.

Espinoza, M. (2009). A case study of the production of educational sanctuary in one migrant classroom. *Pedagogies: An International Journal, 4*(1), 44–62.

Flores, N. (2013). Silencing the subaltern: Nation-state/colonial governmentality and bilingual education in the United States. *Critical Inquiry in Language Studies, 10*(4), 263–87.

Flores, N. and García, O. (2017). A critical review of bilingual education in the United States: From basements and pride to boutiques and profit. *Annual Review of Applied Linguistics, 37*, 14–29.

Flores, N. and Rosa, J. (2015). Undoing appropriateness: Raciolinguistic ideologies and language diversity in education. *Harvard Educational Review, 85*(2), 149–71.

Foucault, M. (1975). *Discipline and Punish* (A. Sheridan, trans.) New York, NY: Vintage.

Fregoso Bailón, R. O. and Shannon, S. M. (2016, April). The coloniality of power and transcoloniality extended to Latino bilingual children in the U.S. Paper presented at the annual meeting of the American Educational Research Association (AERA). Washington, DC.

Fregoso Bailón, R. O. and Shannon, S. M. (2019). *Poemas Bilingües: La Patria Grande Latinamericana y el Gran México en letras de estudiantes Mexicanos* [Bilingual

Poems: The Great Latin American Homeland and the Great Mexico in the words of Mexican students]. *Journal of Bilingual Education Research & Instruction*, *20*(1), 36–51.

Freire, P. (2005/1974). *Education for Critical Consciousness*. New York: Continuum. (Original work published 1974).

Galarza, E. (1978). *Merchants of Labor: The Mexican Bracero Story; An Account of the Managed Migration of Mexican Farm Workers in California 1942–1960* (3d ed.). Santa Barbara, CA: McNally & Loftin.

García, O. (2009). Racializing the language practices of US Latinos: Impact on their education. In J. A. Cobas, J. Duany, and J. R. Feagin (Eds.), *How the United States racializes Latinos: White Hegemony and Its Consequences* (pp. 101–15). Boulder, CO: Paradigm Publishers.

García, O. (2009b). *Bilingual Education in the 21st Century: A Global Perspective*. West Sussex: Wiley & Sons.

García Bedolla, L. and Rodriguez, R. (2011). Classifying California's English Learners: Is the CELDT too blunt an instrument? *UC Berkeley*: Center for Latino Policy Research. Retrieved from https://escholarship.org/uc/item/2m74v93d

Gonzales v. Sheely, 96 F. Supp. 1004 (D. Ariz. 1951).

Gathercole, V. C. M., Thomas, E. M., Roberts, E., Hughes, C., and Hughes, E. (2013). Why assessment needs to take exposure into account: Vocabulary and grammatical abilities in bilingual children. In V. C. M. Gathercole (Ed.), *Issues in the Assessment of Bilinguals* (pp. 20–55). Bristol: Multilingual Matters.

Gorter, D. and Cenoz, J. (2017). Language education policy and multilingual assessment. *Language and Education*, *31*(3), 231–48.

Grinberg, J. and Saavedra, E. R. (2000). The constitution of bilingual/ESL education as a disciplinary practice: Genealogical explorations. *Review of Educational Research*, *70*(4), 419–41.

Griswold del Castillo, R. (1990). *The Treaty of Guadalupe Hidalgo: A Legacy of Conflict*. Norman, OK: University of Oklahoma Press.

Gutiérrez, K. D. (2008). Developing a sociocritical literacy in the third space. *Reading Research Quarterly*, *43*(2), 148–64.

Holmes, S. (2013). *Fresh Fruit, Broken Bodies: Migrant Farmworkers in the United States*. Berkeley, CA: University of California Press.

Hondagneu-Sotelo, P. (2007). *Domestica: Immigrant Workers Cleaning and Caring in the Shadows of Affluence, with a New Preface*. Berkeley, CA: University of California Press.

Irvine, J. (1989). When talk isn't cheap: Language and political economy. *American Ethnologist*, *16*(2), 248–26.

Kanno, Y. and Kangas, S. E. N. (2014). "I'm not going to be, like, for the AP": English language learners access to advanced college-preparatory courses in high school. *American Education Research Journal*, *51*(5), 848–78.

King, K. and Bigelow, M. (2018). The language policy of placement tests for newcomer English learners. *Educational Policy*, *32*(7), 936–68.

Koopman, C. (2013). *Genealogy as Critique: Foucault and the Problems of Modernity*. Bloomington, IN: Indiana University Press.

Kroskrity, P. V. (2004). Language ideologies. In A. Duranti (Ed.), *A Companion to Linguistic Anthropology* (pp. 496–517). Malden, MA: Blackwell Publishing.

Kunnan, A. J. (2009). Testing for citizenship: The US naturalization test. *Language Assessment Quarterly*, *6*(1), 89–97.

Leung, C. and Scarino, A. (2016). Reconceptualizing the nature of goals and outcomes in language/s education. *The Modern Language Journal* 100 (Supplement 2016), 81–95.

López, A., Turkan, S., and Guzmán-Orth, D. (2017). *Conceptualizing the Use of Translanguaging in Initial Content Assessments for Newly Arrived Emergent Bilingual Students*. Princeton, NJ: Educational Testing Service.

Macías, R. F. (2014). Spanish as the second national language of the United States: Fact, future, fiction, or hope? *Review of Research in Education*, *38*(1), 33–57.

Mendez v. Westminister School Dist., 64 F. Supp. 544 (S.D. Cal. 1946).

Menken, K. (2006). Teaching to the test: How No Child Left Behind impacts language policy, curriculum, and instruction for English language learners. *Bilingual Research Journal*, *30*(2), 521–46.

Menken, K. (2008). *English Learners Left Behind: Standardized Testing as Language Policy* (Vol. 65). Bristol: Multilingual Matters.

Menken, K. and Solorza, C. (2014). No child left bilingual: Accountability and the elimination of bilingual education programs in New York City schools. *Educational Policy*, *28*(1), 96–125.

Mignolo, W. D. (1996). Linguistic maps, literary geographies, and cultural landscapes: Languages, languaging, and (trans) nationalism. *Modern Language Quarterly*, *57*(2), 181–97.

Mignolo, W. D. (2000). *Local Histories/Global Designs: Coloniality, Subaltern Knowledge, and Border Thinking*. Princeton, NJ: Princeton University Press.

Motomura, H. (2014). *Immigration Outside the Law*. New York, NY: Oxford University Press.

National Center for Education Statistics. (2018). English language learners in public schools. Retrieved from https://nces.ed.gov/programs/coe/indicator_cgf.asp

Office of Civil Rights. (2016). Resolution agreement: Arizona Department of Education. OCR case number 08-06-4006. Retrieved from https://www.justice.gov/crt/file/850411/download

Petrovic, J. E. (2005). The conservative restoration and neoliberal defenses of bilingual education. *Language Policy*, *4*(4), 395–416.

Poza, L. E. (2016). "Puro spelling and grammar": Conceptualizations of language and the marginalization of emergent bilinguals. *Penn GSE Perspectives on Urban Education*, *13*(1), 20–41.

Poza, L. E. (2017). "Where the true power resides": Teacher dispositions and the translanguaging classroom. Paper presented at the annual meeting of the Literacy Research Association. Tampa, FL. December 1, 2017.

Poza, L. E. (2018). The language of ciencia: Translanguaging and learning in a bilingual science classroom. *International Journal of Bilingual Education and Bilingualism*, 21(1), 1–19.

Plyler v. Doe, 457 U.S. 202, 102 S. Ct. 2382, 72 L. Ed. 2d 786 (1982).

Quijano, A. (2000a). Coloniality of power and Eurocentrism in Latin America. *International Sociology*, 15(2), 215–32.

Quijano, A. (2000b). *Colonialidad del poder y clasificación social* [Coloniality of power and social classification] (our translation, article is in English.)[Special issue: Festchrift for Immanuel Wallerstein–Part I]. *Journal of World-Systems Research*, VI(2), 342–86.

Rosa, J. and Flores, N. (2017). Unsettling race and language: Toward a raciolinguistic perspective. *Language in Society*, 46(5), 621–47.

Ruiz, R. (1984). Orientations in language planning. *NABE Journal*, 8(2), 15–34.

San Miguel, Jr., G. and Valenica, R. (1998). From the Treaty of Guadalupe Hidalgo to Hopwood: The educational plight of Mexican Americans in the Southwest. *Harvard Educational Review*, 68(3), 353–413.

Schildkraut, D. J. (2003). American identity and attitudes toward official-English policies. *Political Psychology*, 24(3), 469–99.

Shannon, S. M. (1995a). The hegemony of English: A case study of one bilingual classroom as a site of resistance. *Linguistics and Education*, 7(3), 175–200.

Shannon, S. M. (1995b). The culture of the classroom: Socialization in an urban bilingual classroom. *The Urban Review*, 27(4), 321–45.

Shannon, S. M. (1999). Language rights or language privileges? *TESOL Journal*, 8(3), 23–28.

Shohamy, E. (2006). *Language Policy: Hidden Agendas and New Approaches*. London: Routledge.

Shohamy, E. (2011). Assessing multilingual competencies: Adopting construct valid assessment policies. *The Modern Language Journal*, 95(3), 418–29.

Shohamy, E. (2014). *The Power of Tests: A Critical Perspective on the Uses of Language Tests*. London: Routledge.

Stephen, L. (2007). *Transborder Lives: Indigenous Oaxacans in Mexico, California, and Oregon*. Durham, NC: Duke University Press.

Thompson, K. D. (2015). Questioning the Long-Term English Learner label: How categorization can blind us to students' abilities. *Teachers College Record*, 117(12), 1–50.

Umansky, I. M. (2016). Leveled and exclusionary tracking: English learners' access to academic content in middle school. *American Educational Research Journal*, 53(6), 1792–1833.

Valdés, G. (1998). The world outside and inside schools: Language and immigrant children. *Educational Researcher*, 27(6), 4–18.

Valdés, G. (2001). *Learning and Not Learning English: Latino Students in American Schools*. New York, NY: Teachers College Press.

Valdés, G. and Figueroa, R. A. (1994). *Second Language Learning: Bilingualism and Testing: A Special Case of Bias*. Westport, CT: Ablex Publishing.

Valdés, G., Poza, L., and Brooks, M. D. (2014). Educating students who do not speak the societal language: The social construction of language learner categories. *Profession*. Retrieved from https://profession.mla.hcommons.org/2014/10/09/educating-students-who-do-not-speak-the-societal-language

Webb, P. T., Briscoe, F. M., and Mussman, M. P. (2009). Preparing teachers for the neoliberal panopticon. *Educational Foundations*, 23(3–4), 3–18.

White, M. J., Bean, F. D., and Espenshade, T. J. (1990). The U.S. 1986 Immigration Reform and Control Act and undocumented migration to the United States, *Population Research and Policy Review*, 9(2): 93–116.

Wiese, A. and García, E. E. (1998). The Bilingual Education Act: Language minority students and equal educational opportunity. *Bilingual Research Journal*, 22(1), 1–18.

Wiley, T. G. (2014). Diversity, super-diversity, and monolingual language ideology in the United States: Tolerance or intolerance? *Review of Research in Education*, 38(1), 1–32.

Woolard, K. A. and Schieffelin, B. B. (1994). Language ideology. *Annual Review of Anthropology*, 23(1), 55–82.

4

Language Testing in Service-Learning: A Critical Approach to Socially Situated Language in Use

Netta Avineri and James Perren

Introduction

This chapter introduces a critical framework for language testing in service-learning that highlights the socially situated nature of language in use. Service-learning is a pedagogy that integrates student learning, reflection, curricular concepts, service in communities, and partnership with community organizations. This approach is increasingly being used in ESL/EFL settings and TESOL/TFL teacher training programs. We first discuss trends in assessment that provide relevant frameworks for language testing in service-learning, including assessment of communicative language, pragmatics, interculturality, authenticity, washback, and social considerations. We provide an overview of the pedagogy of service-learning and how it is being integrated into ESL/EFL and TESOL/TFL programs, then sharing one in-depth example each of an ESL service-learning program and a TESOL/TFL service-learning program. Finally, the chapter provides a range of pedagogical implications that follow from this treatment of the relevant literature and case studies, particularly focusing on content-based and task-based instruction. This approach is therefore at the nexus between second language acquisition (SLA) research and theory on the one hand and teacher training and classroom praxis on the other.

Overall, this chapter argues that a socially situated approach to language in use incorporates the following seven features:

1. Sensitivity to context (assessment is relational, not individual)
2. Recognition of ideologies and power dynamics
3. Students' identities, positionality, and agency

4. Community partnerships
5. Balancing standardization with the particulars of a given context
6. Combining a battery of assessment types (qualitative and quantitative)
7. Cultural validity (del Rosario Basterra, Trumbull, and Solano-Flores, 2011)

Through the discussion of both literature and case studies, we will highlight these different features in order to demonstrate their importance to reconceptualizing a critical language assessment within civic engagement and community partnerships.

Service-Learning: One Approach to Civic Engagement

Service-learning is a pedagogy that integrates student learning, reflection, curricular concepts, service in communities, and partnership with community organizations (Butin, 2003; Giles and Eyler, 1994). Service-learning is frequently seen as drawing from Dewey's educational and social philosophy to include "learning from experience, reflective activity, citizenship, community, and democracy" (Giles and Eyler, 1994). Whereas *traditional service-learning* integrates a community component, a classroom component, reflection, learning to serve, and serving to learn, *critical service-learning* complements these with a social change orientation, working to redistribute power and developing authentic relationships (Mitchell, 2008). Examples include community service-learning and Spanish heritage language education (Leeman, Rabin, and Roman-Mendoza, 2011), teacher education and inclusive teaching (Carrington et al., 2015), and critical race theory and critical race pedagogy and TESOL service-learning (TSL). Critical service-learning focuses on root causes for social issues, considering micro-, meso-, and macro-level forces. Language students involved in critical service-learning courses require a socially situated approach to language learning and assessment, one that can meaningfully address issues of social change, power redistribution, and authentic relationship building over time while also acknowledging students' own positionality and identities (Avineri, 2015). These service-learning approaches connect with other critically oriented perspectives in education (e.g., Freire, 1972; Giroux, 1988; McLaren, 2014), decolonizing teacher education and critical interculturality (Martin, Pirbhai-Illich, and Pete, 2017) and critical ethnography (Reyes Cruz, 2008) by including multiple stakeholders in service-learning and civic endeavors. Service-learning is related to critical education perspectives by active and continuous attempts to educate students about agency and empowerment to have an impact on themselves and society in tangible outcomes (praxis and learning). Service-learning is somewhat distinct from critical education perspectives by having the community be the classroom with the "service" aspect being as political as it is in critical education perspectives (but focusing on civic duty as social justice that leads to enhanced community and developing relationships).

Effective service-learning pedagogy in domestic and international contexts (cf. Bringle, Hatcher, and Jones, 2012) is based on a foundation of community-university partnerships (Holland, 2001; Stoecker and Tryon, 2009). The significance of mutuality, collaboration, cooperation, communication, and relationship building have all been highlighted as central to effective partnerships. We argue that a key aspect of building sustainable partnerships is the cultivation of critical empathy (DeStigter, 1999), a recognition that there are limits to one's own perspectives such that inviting others' narratives is critical to building meaningful relationships. A socially situated approach to language assessment would consider how language and intercultural learning can be central to students' engagement with broader societal issues and inequities. This would bring the focus of the assessment beyond an individual student's proficiency to a recognition of students' ongoing, dynamic engagement in diverse contexts and communities.

Socially Situated Assessment of Language and Interculturality

Recent research on language assessment has focused on the socially situated nature of discourse and interaction (Davidson and Lynch, 2008; Fulcher and Davidson, 2007). Foci have included the assessment of pragmatics and authentic language use, highlighting the "multilingual, multicultural, and multicontextual" (Taguchi and Roever, 2017) nature of language in use. Cohen (2008) discusses the perspectives of learners and the importance of teacher preparation in the creation and assessment of pragmatics-focused materials. Ishihara and Cohen (2010) provide language educators with tools to teach "socially and culturally appropriate language for effective communication," including topics such as classroom-based assessments, instructional components, speech act strategies, treatment of learner errors, and SLA theories. Classroom-based assessments and the importance of learner agency and self-assessments are discussed in Eslami and Mirzaei (2012).

Examples of pragmatics assessments in the classroom/instructed setting are tasks focused on speech acts (Beltrán-Palanques, 2016; Cohen, 2014), oral role plays (Bailey and Curtis, 2015; Cohen, 2014), written discourse as if spoken (Cohen, 2014), multiple-choice, short-answer responses (Cohen, 2014), discourse completion tests (multiple choice in Beltrán-Palanques, 2016; Nemati, Rezaee, and Hajmalek, 2014), retrospective verbal reports (Beltrán-Palanques, 2016), elicitation (Liu, 2006), interlanguage pragmatic test items (Liu, 2006), oral proficiency interviews (Kasper and Ross, 2007), and authentic listening tasks (Buck, 2001). One can consider language assessment in the context of service-learning courses to be testing for language for specific purposes (LSP) (Bailey and Curtis, 2015). As Douglas (2000, p. 1) notes, testing for LSP is "a special case of communicative language testing, since both are based on a theoretical construct of contextualized communicative language ability" (Douglas, 2000, p. 1). As noted in the seven features we have identified, context here is central to assessing students' language abilities.

In these examples, the question of being "realistic" (Cohen, 2014) is central to authentic assessment, as is the "authenticity of task and interaction between language knowledge and specific purpose content knowledge" (Douglas, 2000, p. 2). "Realistic" language in assessment is connected with language as it is used in "real-life situations." In addition, one can consider teachers' own linguistic and cultural backgrounds as they relate to rating (Cohen, 2014; del Rosario Basterra, Trumbull, and Solano-Flores, 2011; Leung and Lewkowicz, 2006). The importance of feedback and washback (Bailey, 1996; Bailey and Masuhara, 2013; Brown and Hudson, 1998) is central to a socially situated language assessment, to recognize the complexity of both in-class and community-based interactions. This is the case for "selected-response assessments (including true-false, matching, and multiple-choice assessments); constructed-response assessments (including fill-in, short-answer, and performance assessments); and personal-response assessments (including conference, portfolio, and self- or peer assessments)" (Brown and Hudson, 1998, p. 653).

Recently, there have been compelling critiques of previous approaches to pragmatics assessments. For example, Roever (2011) focuses on sociopragmatic and pragmalinguistic abilities, critiquing an emphasis on speech acts, interlanguage pragmatics, and native-speaker ideals. Instead, he argues for a "discursive re-orientation of pragmatics tests" (p. 463). Ross and Kasper (2013) recognize the importance of assessment instruments and practices for different constructs, purposes, and contexts, specifically providing a conversation analytic perspective on oral proficiency interviews, with an eye toward communicative language ability and interactional competence. Bardovi-Harlig and Shin (2014) critique Hudson, Brown, and Detmer's (1995) framework for assessing cross-cultural pragmatics (including indirect discourse completion tests, oral language production, self-assessment, and requests, apologies, and refusals) with a focus on speech acts, formulaic/typical expressions, amount of speech used and information given, levels of formality, directness, and politeness. Instead, these authors highlight "task authenticity, their practicality for testing, and potential for broadening construct representation" (p. 26). McNamara (2001) has been a leader in highlighting the social considerations, policy issues, and ethics of language testing and assessment, calling for a move away from positivistic orientations to a recognition of the rich cultural and social aspects of language assessments. He has focused on pragmatic, communicative language, and integrative tests in relation to these social considerations. Though the field of pragmatics acknowledges the use of language in context, it has not traditionally focused on broader social issues or a critical, discourse-oriented perspective to language use.

Therefore, in this chapter, we focus on the complexity of interactions during service-learning in-class discussions as well as encounters with community members and consider different approaches to assessment in these contexts. This would involve bringing language assessments outside of the traditional classroom environment and recognizing and assessing the complexity of real-life interactions with community members. This approach would focus not only on traditional speech acts or pragmatics orientations and could perhaps include pair and group assessments (Leung and Lewkowicz, 2006). In addition, this shift in focus could provide students with language and intercultural knowledge, skills, and attitudes to recognize issues of inequity and build toward social justice.

Intimately connected to language learners' pragmatic and social awareness is development of interculturality. Scholars in intercultural studies as well as applied linguistics (e.g., Dervin, 2010; Hua, 2015; Kramsch, 2001; Liddicoat and Scarino, 2013; Piller, 2007; Scarino, 2009; Sercu, 2010) have considered the knowledge, skills, and attitudes necessary for students' intercultural development. Byram (1997) proposed the framework of intercultural communicative competence to include linguistic competence, sociolinguistic competence, discourse competence, and intercultural competence. Deardorff (2011) presents a broader framework for intercultural competence that includes a process orientation, knowledge, skills, and attitudes, and internal and external outcomes. Fantini (2009) and Byram, Gribkova, and Starkey (2002) highlight the rich connections between language learning and intercultural learning. Some scholars also discuss the roles of culture and intercultural learning in foreign language and study abroad contexts (Schulz, 2007; Sinicrope, Norris, and Watanabe, 2007). And interculturality has been to shown to be central to students' ability to engage in service-learning encounters (Avineri, 2015). Considering the rich discussions of the relationships between intercultural learning and language learning, it would seem that there would be a range of assessments in this area (for an exception, see discussion of P-SAP below). However, this kind of socially situated language assessment is still lacking.

Nevertheless, there are a number of large-scale assessments of intercultural learning that are used by educational institutions,[1] which could provide some frameworks for a language assessment that is sensitive to diverse contexts. These various assessments consider a range of intercultural knowledge, skills, and attitudes. However, a focus on language and interaction (as theorized in applied linguistics) can rarely be found in these assessments of learning in intercultural circles.[2] There are some considerations of "communication," "interaction," "expression," and "interpretation" in these assessments. Byram and Feng (2005) and Dervin and Hahl (2015) note that portfolios may be a fruitful avenue for intercultural learning assessment. Liddicoat and Scarino (2013) use SLA theories to consider the roles of task creation and interaction in relation to intercultural learning. However, an in-depth examination of the various roles that language can play in intercultural learning (and vice versa) could be further developed (e.g., Sercu, 2010). A socially situated language assessment in relation to service-learning could be one avenue to explore these relationships more deeply.

Assessment in TESOL/TFL Service-Learning for ESL/EFL Learners

The topic of assessment as part of TSL has been explored by a number of scholars (Askildson, Kelley, and Mick, 2013; Bickel et al., 2013; Crossman and Kite, 2007; Grassi, Hanley, and Liston, 2004; Perren, 2013; Perren, Grove, and Thornton, 2013; Purmensky, 2009; Wurr, 1999). One of the most common standard practices in TSL is students' written reflections being used for both evidence of key social topics being learned and also for the assessment of language proficiency (Crossman and Kite, 2007; Purmensky, 2009; Wurr, 1999, 2002). Wurr (1999) implemented rating scales to measure rhetorical writing gains during a service-learning writing class, focused on assessment of student writing and analysis of persuasive writing of samples collected at the end of the term.

Purmensky (2009) provides an educational model that can be implemented in various content areas through the alignment of service-learning experiences with the national TESOL content standards. Purmensky's publication presents assessment methods for learning outcomes and pedagogical success using both informal and formal assessment. Hamstra (2010) investigated student writing with service-learning through analysis of paragraphs and essays before, during, and after field experiences. Students also completed attitude surveys about writing and self-assessments of their writing skills.

Other reports combine assessment of written reflections with additional elements such as vocabulary, reading, and oral communication (Perren, 2013; Perren et al., 2013). Grassi, Hanley, and Liston (2004) note favorable connections between the impact of service-learning on K-12 ESL learners and their academic achievement as documented through standardized state assessment of reading, writing, and mathematics. Finally, technology use in service-learning assessment is a developing area in the field, including computer-based testing (Perren, 2013; Perren et al., 2013), online social networking sites (e.g., Facebook) and videoconferencing software (e.g., Skype) (Bickel et al., 2013; Purmensky, 2015), and digital mentoring (Purmensky, 2009, 2015). This group of studies demonstrate that assessment is at the forefront of key foundational elements of service-learning, as found in the eleven Essential Elements (EE) of Service-Learning (National Service-Learning Cooperative, 1998). One component that appears to be absent in this presentation of assessment practices, however, is a focus on sociocultural elements of assessment, as viewed through the lens of identity development.

Service-learning scholarship in TESOL involving English language learners (ELLs) has provided some evidence of the ways in which language learners benefit from volunteering in the community, including positive outcomes in social, cognitive, and affective domains. In the social domain, learning about the target culture (Heuser, 1999; Steinke, 2009) is perhaps most prevalent and is supported by the social turn in language learning theories. As argued by Perren (2013), agency, identity, and opposition are frequently manifested in service-learning projects, all of which are present and repeated throughout the literature of community service-learning. Avineri (2015, 2019 in press) also highlights the role of situated identities and multiple knowledges in her conceptualization of "nested interculturality," which foregrounds the layered nature of interactions in service-learning encounters as well as the dual nature of these nests (i.e., spaces of both growth and risk). In terms of agency and identity, positive outcomes of community service-learning are a recurring theme in the literature. On the subject of community and agency, Bickel et al. (2013) found that social media can transform the way individuals who learn ESL think about themselves as agents of social change, even when the instructors and students are in different hemispheres of the globe. In this case, Web 2.0 technologies critically underpin the interaction that could not otherwise effectively take place. Identity and opposition are constructs present in DePew (2011) and Bickel et al. (2013), both of which reported a heightened or highlighted sense of agency in terms of how learners learned about their power to change and be agents of change in their various fields of practice, be in their impoverished communities (Brazil) or vis-à-vis school authorities (teachers) that challenge their knowledge of their multiliterate sensibilities. DePew (2011) reports that social media is an opportunity for students to perform "multiliterate practices" and "make sophisticated choices about their literacy experiences" (p. 56). Thus, social media offers students a way to resist prescribed practices, such as with orthography, punctuation, and even grammar. Online media spaces, "where individuals are literally prompted to define themselves" (DePew, 2011, p. 57), are not defined by not knowing the rules and discourse norms of the standard dialect. In essence, DePew (2011) recognizes the power of social media to "transform discursive practices and reposition the power of the media" (p. 56). Nevertheless, it is still unclear how assessment practices in stated programs can provide evidence of how measurement of identity can be orchestrated in conjunction with traditional assessment practices in service-learning through the use of written reflections; in short, how assessment practices for TSL can leverage critical test authenticity (Leung and Lewkowicz, 2006). Only a few such reports have presented research findings related to this topic. With these observations in mind, a socially situated approach to language assessment for ESL and EFL service-learning projects, programs, and contexts can explore the possibilities for resolving problematic language testing and assessment issues such as the claim that "performance tests that strive to be highly authentic are often extremely complex" (Leung and Lewkowicz, 2006, p. 216). One recommendation is to implement an assessment of individual or group problem solving as in the Problem Solving Analysis Protocol (P-SAP), a written problem-solving protocol for assessing problem-solving skills for easy integration in normal class activities by changing the issue as needed to match the content of the course (Steinke and Fitch, 2003). This specific recommendation for using the P-SAP test would address the issue of foregrounding construct validity and what it is that we are intending to focus on or measure for assessment of language in use (Leung and Lewkowicz, 2006). There are also possibilities of using testing practices such as pair and group testing (TSL classroom activities and field experiences often use both) to assess or measure language use in context, which would also allow for the assessment of *both* language and key content areas of social justice and civic engagement.

Assessment in Service-Learning TESOL Teacher Education

Socially situated language assessment related to the combination of service-learning, second language learning and assessment, and teacher education is important because of the growing implementation of TSL (Perren and Wurr, 2015). A number of studies have reported on the importance of assessment as a key factor in a particular context for TESOL teacher training (Fitzgerald, 2009; Lindahl et al., 2018; Murtiningsih, 2015; Purmensky, 2015). Several identified themes and trends in this subset of literature include meeting the needs of a modified national curriculum (Murtiningsih, 2015), assessment in digital mentoring (Purmensky, 2015), and teaching cultural and linguistic diversity (Fitzgerald, 2009; Lindahl et al., 2018).

In her case study of a school's service-learning program, Murtiningsih (2015) indicates that assessment of reflective writing was a key concern for students and the teacher educator because students maintained high expectations for earning high service-learning scores in the credit-bearing courses. The researcher notes the challenges with this main assessment tool for teacher candidates, due to their and the teacher educators' limited knowledge on writing narrative reflection journals. Murtiningsih points out that "this may be caused by the Indonesian culture that encourages very little to be reflective" (Murtiningsih, 2015, pp. 536–37). This issue could also coincide with the idea that test "authenticity is a matter of perception" (Leung and Lewkowicz, 2006, p. 215). By reasonable extension, the reflections might not have been valued by the teacher candidates as authentic uses of language in this context.

Another study examining service-learning in TESOL teacher education illustrates an online ESL tutoring project linking ten preservice TESOL teachers with ten "at-risk" ELLs in local middle schools (Purmensky, 2015). The primary connection to assessment is the use of reflections, but additional observations are noted by the author concerning modifying assessment based on program and student need. This specific point is related to our understanding of how assessment in TSL can be broadened to better match the socially situated needs of contemporary TESOL programs. The practices undertaken in this project exemplify the necessary adjustments for providing a socially situated assessment approach in TSL to better match the needs of contemporary TESOL programs.

Fitzgerald (2009) describes the implementation of a service-learning curriculum designed to teach university students from across majors about ethnic diversity. The project's preplanning stages are suggested as being highly influential to its beneficial outcome. Furthermore, the reflective writing and tutoring experiences facilitated the integration of inclusion and ethnic diversity into the university even while the tutors lacked racial and ethnic diversity. This project provides an example for how to leverage limited university resources to achieve high community impact with outreach of a significant number of participants. It points to the relevance of a broadened definition of assessment to better match the socially situated needs of contemporary TESOL program by integrating quantification of impact as part of the assessment battery to demonstrate TSL's effectiveness. Quantifying "impact" could be offered through easy-to-use statistics for quick assessment of learning, reporting on program effectiveness, and seeking future funding.

The overall strengths of this sampling of research are that in each of these projects around the globe, there is a growing consensus of standardized key components that facilitate more structured and comprehensive preparation phases. Also, implementation success is linked to recognizing the service-learning pedagogy demands and organizing resources to better serve the needs of all involved, including the community and the institution of learning. This points to the Honnet and Poulsen (1989) Wingspread "Principles for Good Practice" in service-learning that indicated the need for potential specific standardization processes for second and foreign language program implementation, especially for globally dominant languages such as English that carry connotations of hegemonic political and economic practices (Lindahl et al., 2018). The overall weaknesses of these group of studies are that not all of these studies point to the necessity of including the community partner and community interpretations of assessment and how that information can be gathered and systematically included in the overall assessment battery as part of the implementation of service-learning pedagogy. This approach to collaborative assessment with community partners integrates various perspectives and expertise, with both possibilities and limitations. We see in the Lindahl et al. (2018) report and the Murtinigsih (2015) study that the authors clearly identified the importance of including the community partner's voice more fully (Stoecker and Tryon, 2009) to prepare for future successful service-learning program implementation. This is one aspect of TSL programming that might be missing from the literature to date. Next steps for assessment research in TSL could address lack of program success based on exclusion of community partner perspectives on assessment. Other gaps in the research base could include examining multiple impacts gained from numerous stakeholders in the service-learning process (Driscoll, Holand, Gelmon, and Kerrigan, 1996), more accurate determination of problem sources (Hollis, 2004) utilizing a closely linked problem-based assessment (such as the P-SAP), and connections to international service-learning (Rubin and Matthews, 2013). These suggestions all point to our proposed model of a socially situated approach to language assessment for TSL.

A Critical Service-Learning Course for Japanese International Students in California

Beginning in 2016, Dr. Netta Avineri (the first author of this chapter) codeveloped the curriculum for a critical service-learning course for Japanese ESL students at California State University, Monterey Bay, called "Hunger and Homelessness in the Salad Bowl of the World." Each semester, the program welcomed twenty-five to forty-five students from a Japanese university. The program team included instructors, student assistants, a coordinator, and various offices on-campus. The administrators focused on three interconnected learning outcomes: service-learning, language learning, and interculturality learning. The three sets of learning outcomes were intentionally distinguished from one another to ensure sufficient focus on each, while also allowing for exploration of connection points among them. There are three phases to the curriculum: what, so what, and now what. In the "what" phase, students were exposed to core concepts relevant to understanding hunger and homelessness in the Monterey County region, including privilege, marginalization, poverty, diversity, and identity. In the "so what" phase, students began to connect these concepts to the particular issues that are the focus of the course, such as food security, housing, and homelessness, as well as their experiences at their service sites. In the "now what" phase, students considered next steps in addressing issues of hunger and homelessness and engaging in social action more broadly. The sites were local community partners of the institution focused on hunger and homelessness, including day centers, food banks, churches serving homeless populations, and women's shelters.

Given the complex nature of the course, there were a range of socially situated and integrated assignments and assessments that addressed to varying degrees the learning outcomes in the course, all of which are completed in the context of community partnerships (feature 4 identified at the beginning of the chapter). These included community exploration assignments, ongoing reflections, reading responses, vocabulary journals, role-play activities, and individual and group presentations, which together provided a composite picture of the students' language and intercultural development over time. This approach dovetails with feature 6 identified at the beginning of this chapter (combining a battery of assessment types: qualitative and quantitative). The community exploration assignment completed in the first weeks of the course allowed students to observe and ask questions about the communities they would engage with, providing opportunities for critical thinking about "preflection." Ongoing reflections during the what, so what, and now what phases of the course connected students' experiences with course content (e.g., diversity, privilege, systemic social change), providing an integrated approach to language learning, service-learning, and intercultural learning goals. Role-play activities allowed the instructor to provide scenarios of interactions at students' service sites, giving students the chance to demonstrate their language and intercultural learning. Reading responses, vocabulary journals, and individual and group presentations, while considered more traditional assessments, also provided integrated opportunities for formative and summative assessments of multiple learning goals in the three different areas.

These assignments provided students with multiple opportunities for assessment of pragmatics (in class and at their sites); feedback and washback; reflection on their own positionality, identities, and cultures (feature 3—students' identities, positionality, and agency; feature 7—cultural validity); and a recognition of relevant social issues (feature 5—balancing standardization with the particulars of a given context), ideologies, and power dynamics (feature 2). Within the curriculum, students had the opportunity to explore micro- and macro-level issues related to hunger and homelessness, including interpersonal interactions as well as broader sociopolitical trends (feature 1—sensitivity to context). The assessments go further than this as well by integrating the complexity of ongoing interactions with community members and community organizations as well as the language and intercultural learning necessary for in-depth consideration of social issues in the United States.

Alliant TESOL Program Service-Learning Integration

A number of service-learning practices have been integrated into TESOL programs at both the MA and doctoral program levels at Alliant International

University, where James Perren (the second author of this chapter) teaches, since the fall semester, 2015. The following items reflect specific elements in a programmatic effort to include service-learning in both teacher preparation and research-focused courses. Perren (a TESOL faculty member) has been extensively involved in service-learning activities and professional development and brought his interest to the TESOL program through the development and implementation of a doctoral-level service-learning course and organizing service-learning opportunities for faculty and students. A doctoral-level service-learning course introduced TESOL students to service-learning as a viable pedagogical approach for TESOL professionals and to familiarize doctoral students with another avenue for research that can be conducted in relation to community engagement and social justice issues. Graduate students wrote about their service experiences and classroom interactions about course content through repeated written reflections using National Service-Learning Clearinghouse prompts and recorded their learning in teacher e-Portfolios. Service-learning events are held each semester, open to all TESOL students and faculty to participate in and advertised through local venues and are organized as a means of giving back to the community.

The Alliant TESOL faculty also have regular formal discussions regarding the official doctoral program comprehensive exam and the master's degree practicum project to assess the program reliability and validity and whether it requires revisions. One change in progress is adding a service-learning project option to the practicum project. The faculty have also instituted a professional development requirement, one option for which is a service-learning activity selected in consultation with the TESOL faculty. The most recent addition to this list is the creation during the 2018 summer of the Alliant International University Community English School.

To exemplify how the programs described in this chapter address the concerns identified in the literature related specifically to both socially situated language assessment and critical assessment of interculturality, a closer examination of TESOL teacher training at Alliant International University is warranted. A first example is found within the seminar course for doctoral students in which the students are first provided with an introduction to related concepts and foundational readings such as Dewey (1938), Furco (2003), and others as preparation for subsequent assignments and educational experiences.[3]

The main assignments for the doctoral seminar course are the original TSL literature review assignment and then the organization, implementation, and evaluation of an actual (authentic) service-learning experience for the class as field work outside the four walls of the classroom such as a beach, park, or river cleanup or a meal service at a local homeless center. The literature review assignment initially provides students with foundational literature that includes classical pieces from education, applied linguistics, and service-learning fields. Subsequently, students are guided through the process of systematic comparison and synthesis of empirical studies in TSL in which case many research projects students read about and analyze take place in different parts of the world, often providing them with a geographic and cultural connection. They are strongly encouraged and guided through the process of tailoring their own research questions through the literature review writing process toward an individual area of interest in TSL. Next, the creation of an authentic service-learning experience as a main assignment (in teams of two or three) provides students with an in-depth and hands-on experience. They become highly involved and responsible for the selection of community partners and related important social issues to them personally and as a team (cf. Askildson et al., 2013). Reflection is used during both reading and writing phases in these two main assignments and is continuous and systematic throughout the course. Both of these key assignments allow for multiple and systematic reflection on their own background, identity, and cultures; there is also a direct correspondence to several features of the proposed socially situated approach to language in use in this chapter: ideologies and power dynamics (feature 2); students' identities, positionality, and agency (feature 3); and recognizing relevant social issues— balancing standardization with the particulars of a given context (feature 5). These regular engagements in the community are interspersed with reflective writing as formal assessments. These written assignments become components of a student e-Portfolio (performance assessment) due near the completion of the course and are expected to contain multiple reflections and a final reflective report. In total, these systematic educational activities and assessment practices directly relate to the previously mentioned literature concerning the need for pragmatic-focused and socially situated, context-sensitive instructional practices and assessment (McNamara, 2001) directed at TESOL educators particularly (Cohen, 2014). Integrating these educational practices aligns closely with feature 6 in which a battery of assessment types is aggregated for learning assessment.

As a second illustration, independent nonacademic activities are planned with current and former TESOL graduate students as well as invited California TESOL (CATESOL) San Diego Chapter members. During these extracurricular activities there is no formal assessment completed, yet several features of the proposed socially situated approach are applicable. In terms of feature 2 (recognition of ideologies and power dynamics), the predeparture and on-site field work reading materials are shared during these activities. Event participants are directed to numerous resources such as websites, publications, documents, etc., that are repositories of information about TSL syllabi, lesson planning, assessment, and community partner relationship development. Feature 3, students' identities, positionality, and agency, is also relevant. All participants are encouraged to initiate tasks related to field work experiences, which require leadership and collaborative skills characteristic of the MA: TESOL teacher training dispositions. A third feature demonstrating relevance is feature 4, community partnerships. The importance of community partners' needs and completing tasks to their specifications is a critical discussion and analysis component as a post-field work phase and thus an essential and standard practice.

Implications of Socially Situated Language Assessment for Language Education

In this section, we highlight some of the ways that a socially situated language assessment can meaningfully connect with diverse and innovative approaches to language education. Our intention is to have scholars and practitioners explore pedagogical implications of the theoretical and practical issues we have raised throughout the chapter.

Content-Based Instruction

This chapter's focus on a socially situated language assessment has implications for content-based instruction (Cammarata, 2016; Lyster, 2007; Tedick and Wesley, 2015; Troyan, Cammarata, and Martel, 2017), if one considers the "content" in this case to be service and community engagement. In content-based language teaching, there is an "expectation that students can learn—and teachers can teach—both academic subject matter content and a new language at the same time" (Lightbown, 2014, p. 6). Lyster (2007) introduces a counterbalanced approach to integrating content and language; and the balancing act is also highlighted in Bailey and Curtis's (2015) discussion of content-based assessment. The Sheltered Instruction Observation Protocol (SIOP) (Echevarria, Vogt, and Short, 2017) provides one model for integrating content and language. A socially situated language assessment to content-based instruction would involve an individual's language proficiency and also their dynamic ability to shift their language use based on context and circumstance. In critical service-learning, it also involves language and intercultural skills necessary to understand and respond to societal issues. Meaningfully integrating these various elements would provide students with deep opportunities for learning at multiple levels (e.g., "collateral learning"; see Dewey, 1938) and would allow instructors to create learning experiences that move beyond the classroom. However, this would also necessitate in-depth teacher training focused on discrete concepts such as service-learning, content-based instruction, and intercultural learning and also a discussion of the balancing acts involved in connecting these different pieces within one assignment and across a unit or curriculum. This is a complex but exciting area for exploration.

Task-Based Language Teaching and Service-Learning in TESOL

One prominent methodological approach to highlight in consideration of a socially situated language assessment approach is task-based language teaching (TBLT) and centers on authentic language use. "Subsumed under the rubric of CLT" (Brown and Lee, 2015, p. 44), teachers using TBLT direct students to perform meaningful tasks using the target language. Assessment of TBLT is based on task outcome and the appropriate completion of real-world tasks. This is a suitable entry point for TSL since TBLT can be implemented for influencing target language fluency as well as student confidence. TBLT has been used to prioritize the communicative nature of the language classroom allowing for a direct connection between classroom activities and real-life situations.

One useful characterization of a "task" is that it possesses the following: meaning is primary, there is a communication problem to solve, there is a relationship to comparable real-world activities, task completion has some priority, the assessment of the task is in terms of outcome (Skehan, 1998, p. 98). A useful distinction is outlined between target tasks (beyond the classroom) and pedagogical tasks (classroom activities) (Brown and Lee, 2015). This two-part analysis of tasks further supports the overlap between TBLT and TSL. The pedagogical soundness in development and sequence of tasks is contingent on a teacher taking into account several key communicative elements such as assessment. Finally, it has been suggested that combining TBLT would allow students to engage in meaningful action, learn important content, and reach curriculum objectives (Miller, 2016). Project-based learning (PBL) matches well with service-learning as both focus on authenticity and meaningful work.

Conclusion

This chapter provides a conceptual framework for socially situated language assessment in service-learning, based on research and literature across a range of fields. This interdisciplinary approach is central to meaningful language assessment for students engaged in community-based work. The reader can determine which of the seven features listed in the introduction are relevant to prioritize within a given context and group of learners. Our goal in this chapter is to present theoretical conceptualizations of pertinent issues in our field (e.g., ideology, power, identity, dominance) while also providing accessible, concretized, practical, hands-on approaches to those issues in classrooms and communities. This approach is therefore at the nexus between SLA research and theory on the one hand and teacher training and classroom praxis on the other. A socially situated language assessment, while based on theoretical frameworks, should therefore be based on what educators and students need and want as well as the questions and dilemmas they face. If we are to prioritize local instances of theory, then we must also recognize the power dynamics inherent in academic research about classroom and community praxis. This chapter seeks to apply these theoretical and ideological concerns to the classroom as one step toward more equitable educational environments and just societies more broadly.

Notes

1. These include the Intercultural Effectiveness Scale (http://intercultural.org/ies.html), Intercultural Development Inventory (https://idiinventory.com/), Intercultural Edge (https://icedge.com/), GlobeSmart Profile (http://www.aperianglobal.com/product/globesmart-forhigher-education), AAC & U Value Rubrics (https://www.aacu.org/value/rubrics?CFID=357689&CFTOKEN=44930763), and IASKSS+ (The Intercultural Attitudes, Skills, and Knowledge Short Scale PLUS).
2. The possible relationships between ICC assessment and language were examined in a directed study I (Avineri) oversaw by a Middlebury Institute of International Studies at Monterey student Jeanine Kosinski. I thank her for highlighting these issues, which I have then adapted for the purposes of this chapter.
3. At this point it is worth mentioning that the ratio of international graduate students to domestic native English language speakers is constantly fluctuating in this program. Currently, there are at least 75 percent international speakers of English

enrolled in the graduate programs at this institution. The importance of mentioning this is that the educational approach applied in this setting is to train teachers who will ultimately teach other language teachers and so they will also provide authentic context-based, socially situated teacher training activities and research activities to improve and expand on their current skill level when working with English language learners. Many of the instructional ideas presented to these teacher/researcher candidates can also be extended and or modified to meet the need of their future learners of English as a second or foreign language. Thus, many of the activities practiced in this graduate program are equally effective in providing professional training for English language teachers and authentic language opportunity practice for the same individuals.

References

Askildson, L. R., Kelly, A. C., and Mick, C. S. (2013). Developing multiple literacies in academic English through service—learning and community engagement. *TESOL Journal*, *4*(3), 402–38.
Avineri, N. (2015). Nested interculturality, multiple knowledges, and situated identities through service-learning in language education. In J. M. Perren and A. J. Wurr (Eds.), *Learning the Language of Global Citizenship: Strengthening Service-Learning in TESOL* (pp. 197–223). Champaign, IL: Common Ground Publishers.
Avineri, N. (2019, in press). "Nested interculturality": Dispositions and practices for navigating tensions in immersion experiences. In D. Martin and E. Smolcic (Eds.), *Redefining Competence Through Cultural Immersion: Teacher Preparation for Linguistic and Culturally Diverse Classrooms*. London: Palgrave Macmillan.
Bailey, K. M. (1996). Working for washback: A review of the washback concept in language testing. *Language Testing*, *13*(3), 257–79.
Bailey, K. M. and Curtis, A. (2015). *Learning about Language Assessment: Dilemmas, Decisions, and Directions* (2nd ed.). Boston, MA: National Geographic Learning.
Bailey, M. and Masuhara, H. (2013). Language testing washback: The role of materials. In B. Tomlinson (Ed.), *Applied Linguistics and Materials Development* (pp. 303–18). New York, NY: Bloomsbury Publishing.
Bardovi-Harlig, K. and Shin, S. Y. (2014). Expanding traditional testing measures with tasks from L2 pragmatics research. *Iranian Journal of Language Testing*, *4*(1), 26–49.
Beltrán-Palanques, V. (2016). Assessing pragmatics: DCTs and retrospective verbal reports. In A. Pareja-Lora, C. Calle-Martínez, and P. Rodríguez-Arancón (Eds.), *New Perspectives on Teaching and Working with Languages in the Digital Era* (pp. 303–12). Dublin: Research-publishing.net.

Bickel, B., Shin, J. K., Taylor, J., Faust, H., and Penniston, T. (2013). Learning English internationally while engaging communities locally: Online EFL supporting community learning for young leaders. *TESOL Journal, 4*(3), 439–62.

Bringle, R. G., Hatcher, J. A., and Jones, S. G. (Eds.) (2012). *International Service Learning: Conceptual Frameworks and Research*. Sterling, VA: Stylus Publishing, LLC.

Brown, H. D. and Lee, H. (2015). *Teaching by Principles: An Interactive Approach to Language Pedagogy*. White Plains, NY: Pearson Education.

Brown, J. D., and Hudson, T. (1998). The alternatives in language assessment. *TESOL Quarterly, 32*(4), 653–75.

Buck, G. (2001). *Assessing Listening*. Cambridge: Cambridge University Press.

Butin, D. W. (2003). Of what use is it? Multiple conceptualizations of service learning within education. *Teachers College Record, 105*(9), 1674–92.

Byram, M. (1997). *Teaching and Assessing Intercultural Communicative Competence*. Bristol, PA: Multilingual Matters.

Byram, M. and Feng, A. (2005). Teaching and researching intercultural competence. In E. Hinkel (Ed.), *Handbook of Research in Second Language Teaching and Learning* (pp. 911–30). Mahwah, NJ: Lawrence Erlbaum.

Byram, M., Gribkova, B., and Starkey, H. (2002). *Developing the Intercultural Dimension in Language Teaching: A Practical Introduction for Teachers*. Strasbourg: Council of Europe.

Cammarata, L. (2016). *Content-based Foreign Language Teaching: Curriculum and Pedagogy for Developing Advanced Thinking and Literacy Skills*. New York, NY: Routledge.

Carrington, S., Mercer, K. L., Iyer, R., and Selva, G. (2015). The impact of transformative learning in a critical service-learning program on teacher development: Building a foundation for inclusive teaching. *Reflective Practice, 16*(1), 61–72.

Crossman, J. M. and Kite, S. L. (2007). Their perspectives: ESL students' reflections on collaborative community service learning. *Business Communication Quarterly, 70*(2), 147–65.

Cohen, A. D. (2008). Teaching and assessing L2 pragmatics: What can we expect from learners? *Language Teaching, 41*(2), 213–35.

Cohen, A. D. (2014). *Strategies in Learning and Using a Second Language* (2nd ed.). London: Routledge.

Davidson, F. and Lynch, B. K. (2008). *Testcraft: A Teacher's Guide to Writing and Using Language Test Specifications*. New Haven, CT: Yale University Press.

Deardorff, D. K. (2011). Assessing intercultural competence. *New Directions for Institutional Research*, 2011(149), 65–79.

del Rosario Basterra, M., Trumbull, E., and Solano-Flores, G. (Eds.) (2011). *Cultural Validity in Assessment: Addressing Linguistic and Cultural Diversity*. New York, NY: Routledge.

DePew, K. E. (2011). Social media at academia's periphery: Studying multilingual developmental writers' Facebook composing strategies. *Reading Matrix: An International Online Journal*, 11(1), 54–75.

Dervin, F. (2010). Assessing intercultural competence in language learning and teaching: A critical review of current efforts. In F. Dervin and E. Suomela-Salmi (Eds.), *New Approaches to Assessment in Higher Education* (pp. 155–72). New York, NY: Peter Lang.

Dervin, F. and Hahl, K. (2015). Developing a portfolio of intercultural competences in teacher education: The case of a Finnish international programme. *Scandinavian Journal of Educational Research*, 59(1), 95–109.

DeStigter, T. (1999). Public displays of affection: Political community through critical empathy. *Research in the Teaching of English*, 33(3), 235–44.

Dewey, J. (1938). *Experience and Education*. New York, NY: Collier Books.

Douglas, D. (2000). *Assessing Language for Specific Purposes*. Cambridge: Cambridge University Press.

Driscoll, A., Holland, B., Gelmon, S. and Kerrigan, S. (1996). An assessment model for service-learning: Comprehensive case studies of impact on faculty, students, community, and institution. *Michigan Journal of Community Service Learning*, 3, 66–71.

Echevarria, J., Vogt, M., and Short, D. (2017). *Making Content Comprehensible for English Language Learners: The SIOP Model*. London: Pearson Publishers.

Eslami, Z. R. and Mirzaei, A. (2012). Assessment of second language pragmatics. In C. Coombe, P. Davidson, B. O'Sullivan, and S. Stoynoff (Eds.), *The Cambridge Guide to Second Language Assessment* (pp. 198–208). Cambridge: Cambridge University Press.

Fantini, A. E. (2009). Assessing intercultural competence. In D. K. Deardorff (Ed.), *The SAGE Handbook of Intercultural Competence* (pp. 456–76). Thousand Oaks, CA: Sage.

Fitzgerald, C. (2009). Language and community: Using service learning to reconfigure the multicultural classroom. *Language and Education*, 23(3), 217–31.

Freire, P. (1972). *Pedagogy of the Oppressed*. New York, NY: Herder and Herder.

Fulcher, G. and Davidson, F. (2007). *Language Testing and Assessment*. London: Routledge.

Furco, A. (2003). Service learning: A balanced approach to experiential education. In *Introduction to Service-Learning Toolkit* (pp. 11–14). Providence, RI: Campus Compact.

Giles, Jr., D. E. and Eyler, J. (1994). The theoretical roots of service-learning in John Dewey: Toward a theory of service-learning. *Michigan Journal of Community Service Learning*, 1(1), 7.

Giroux, H. A. (1988). *Teachers as Intellectuals: Toward a Critical Pedagogy of Learning*. Granby, MA: Bergin & Garvey.

Grassi, E., Hanley, D., and Liston, D. (2004). Service-learning: An innovative approach for second language learners. *Journal of Experiential Education*, 27(1), 87–110.

Hamstra, M. D. P. (2010). *The Impact of Service-Learning On Second Language Writing Skills.* Master of Arts Thesis, Indiana University, Indianapolis.

Heuser, L. (1999). Service-learning as a pedagogy to promote the content, cross-cultural, and language learning of ESL students. *TESL Canada Journal, 17*(1), 54–71.

Holland, B. A. (2001). A comprehensive model for assessing service-learning and community-university partnerships. *New Directions for Higher Education,* 2001(114), 51–60.

Hollis, S. A. (2004). Blaming me, blaming you: Assessing service learning and participants' tendency to blame the victim. *Sociological Spectrum, 24*(5), 575–600.

Honnet, E. P. and Poulsen, S. J. (1989). *Principles of Good Practice for Combining Service and Learning.* Racine, WI: The Johnson Foundation.

Hua, Z. (Ed.) (2015). *Research Methods in Intercultural Communication: A Practical Guide.* Chichester: John Wiley & Sons.

Hudson, T., Brown, J. D., and Detmer, E. (1995). *Developing Prototypic Measures of Cross-Cultural Pragmatics* (Vol. 7). Manoa, HI: University of Hawai'i Press.

Ishihara, N. and Cohen, A. D. (2010). *Teaching and Learning Pragmatics: Where Language and Culture Meet.* New York, NY: Routledge.

Kasper, G. and Ross, S. J. (2007). Multiple questions in oral proficiency interviews. *Journal of Pragmatics, 39*(11), 2045–70.

Kramsch, C. (2001). Intercultural communication. In R. Carter and D. Nunan (Eds.), *The Cambridge Guide to Teaching English to Speakers of other Languages* (pp. 201–6). Cambridge: Cambridge University Press.

Leeman, J., Rabin, L., and Roman-Mendoza, E. (2011). Critical pedagogy beyond the classroom walls: Community service-learning and Spanish heritage language education. *Heritage Language Journal, 8*(3), 1–22.

Leung, C. and Lewkowicz, M. (2006). Expanding horizons and unresolved conundrums: Language testing and assessment. *TESOL Quarterly, 4*(1), 211–34.

Liddicoat, A. J. and Scarino, A. (2013). *Intercultural Language Teaching and Learning.* Chichester: John Wiley & Sons.

Lightbown, P. M. (2014). *Focus on Content-based Language Teaching—Oxford Key Concepts for the Language Classroom.* Oxford: Oxford University Press.

Lindahl, K. M., Tomas, Z., Farrelly, R., and Krulatz, A. (2018). The value of service-learning in L2 teacher preparation: Engaging in diverse contexts. In T. D. Meidl and M. M. S. Dowell (Eds.), *Handbook of Research on Service-Learning Initiatives in Teacher Education Programs* (pp. 103–24). Hershey, PA: IGI Global.

Liu, J. (2006). Assessing EFL learners' interlanguage pragmatic knowledge: Implications for testers and teachers. *Reflections on English Language Teaching, 5*(1), 1–22.

Lyster, R. (2007). *Learning and Teaching Languages Through Content: A Counterbalanced Approach.* Amsterdam, Netherlands: John Benjamins.

Martin, F., Pirbhai-Illich, F., and Pete, S. (2017). Beyond culturally responsive pedagogy: Decolonizing teacher education. In F. Pirbhai-Illich, S. Pete, and F. Martin (Eds.), *Culturally Responsive Pedagogy* (pp. 235–55). Cham: Palgrave Macmillan.

McLaren, P. (2014). *Life in Schools: An Introduction to Critical Pedagogy in the Foundations of Education* (6th ed.). Herndon, VA: Paradigm Publishers.

McNamara, T. (2001). Language assessment as social practice: Challenges for research. *Language Testing, 18*(4), 333–49.

Miller, A. (November 15, 2016). Tips for combining project-based and service-learning. Edutopia. Retrieved from https://www.edutopia.org/article/tips-combining-project-based-and-service-learning-andrew-miller

Mitchell, T. D. (2008). Traditional vs. critical service-learning: Engaging the literature to differentiate two models. *Michigan Journal of Community Service Learning, 14*(2), 50–65.

Murtiningsih, S. R. (2015). Reframing service-learning in curriculum reform in TESOL teacher education in Indonesia. In J. M. Perren and A. J. Wurr (Eds.), *Learning the Language of Global Citizenship: Service-Learning in Applied Linguistics* (pp. 523–48). Champaign, IL: Common Ground Publishing.

National Service-Learning Cooperative (1998). *Essential Elements of Service Learning.* St. Paul, MN: National Service-Learning Cooperative.

Nemati, M., Rezaee, A. A., and Mahdi Hajmalek, M. (2014). Assessing pragmatics through MDCTs: A Case of Iranian EFL Learners. *Iranian Journal of Applied Language Studies, 6*(2), 59–80.

Perren, J. (2013). Strategies steps to successful service-learning in TESOL: From critical to practical. *TESOL Journal, 4*(3), 487–513.

Perren, J., Grove, N., and Thornton, J. (2013). Three empowering curricular innovations for service-learning in ESL programs. *TESOL Journal, 4*(3), 463–86.

Perren, J. M. and Wurr, A. J. (Eds.) (2015). *Learning the Language of Global Citizenship: Service-Learning in Applied Linguistics.* Champaign, IL: Common Ground Publishing.

Piller, I. (2007). Linguistics and intercultural communication. *Language and Linguistics Compass, 1*(3), 208–26.

Purmensky, K. L. (2009). *Service-Learning for Diverse Communities: Critical Pedagogy and Mentoring English Language Learners.* Charlotte, NC: Information Age Publishing.

Purmensky, K. L. (2015). Bridging the gap for English learners: Service-learning digital mentorship for school success. In J. M. Perren and A. J. Wurr (Eds.), *Learning the Language of Global Citizenship: Service-Learning in Applied Linguistics* (pp. 569–98). Champaign, IL: Common Ground Publishing.

Reyes Cruz, M. (2008). What if I just cite Graciela? Working toward decolonizing knowledge through a critical ethnography. *Qualitative Inquiry, 14*(4), 651–58.

Roever, C. (2011). Testing of second language pragmatics: Past and future. *Language Testing, 28*(4), 463–81.

Ross, S. and Kasper, G. (Eds.) (2013). *Assessing Second Language Pragmatics.* New York, NY: Palgrave MacMillan.

Rubin, D. L. and Matthews, P. H. (2013). Learning outcomes assessment: Extrapolating from study abroad to international service-learning. *Journal of Higher Education Outreach and Engagement, 17*(2), 67–86.

Scarino, A. (2009). Assessing intercultural capability in learning languages: Some issues and considerations. *Language Teaching, 42*(1), 67–80.

Schulz, R. A. (2007). The challenge of assessing cultural understanding in the context of foreign language instruction. *Foreign Language Annals, 40*(1), 9–26.

Sercu, L. (2010). Assessing intercultural competence: More questions than answers. In A. Paran and L. Sercu (Eds.), *Testing the Untestable in Language Education* (pp. 17–34). Tonawando, NY: Multilingual Matters.

Sinicrope, C., Norris, J., and Watanabe, Y. (2007). Understanding and assessing intercultural competence: A summary of theory, research, and practice. *Second Language Studies, 26,* 1–58.

Skehan, P. (1998). Task-based instruction. In W. Grabe (Ed.), *Annual Review of Applied Linguistics (1998)* (pp. 268–86). New York, NY: Cambridge University Press.

Steinke, M. H. (2009). Learning English by helping others: Implementing service learning into the ESOL classroom. *The Journal for Civic Commitment, 12.* Retrieved from http://ccncce.org/articles/learning-english-by-helping-others-implementing-service-learning-into-the-esol-classroom

Steinke, P. and Fitch, P. (2003). Using written protocols to measure service-learning outcomes. In J. Eyler and S. H. Billig (Eds.), *Deconstructing Service-Learning: Research Exploring Context, Participation and Impacts* (pp. 171–94). Greenwich, CT: Information Age Publishing.

Stoecker, R. and Tryon, E. (Eds.) (2009). *The Unheard Voices: Community Organizations and Service Learning.* Philadelphia, PA: Temple University Press.

Taguchi, N. and Roever, C. (2017). *Second Language Pragmatics.* Oxford: Oxford University Press.

Tedick, D. and Wesley, P. (2015). A review of research on content-based foreign/second language education in US K-12 contexts. *Language, Culture and Curriculum, 28,* 25–40.

Troyan, F. J., Cammarata, L., and Martel, J. (2017). Integration PCK: Modeling the knowledge (s) underlying a world language teacher's implementation of CBI. *Foreign Language Annals, 50*(2), 458–76.

Wurr, A. J. (1999). A pilot study of the impact of service-learning in college composition on native and non-native speakers of English. *Academic Exchange Quarterly, 3*(4), 54–61.

Wurr, A. J. (2002). Service-learning and student writing. In S. H. Billig and A. Furco (Eds.), *Service Learning Through a Multidisciplinary Lens* (pp. 103–21). Greenwich, CT: Information Age Publishing.

5

Moving beyond Deficit Positioning of Linguistically Diverse Test Takers: Bi/Multilingualism and the Essence of Validity

Jamie L. Schissel

Introduction

This chapter begins with the assumption that understanding who the test taker is and the consequences that a test taker faces are an integral aspect of English language testing. This perspective reflects a use-oriented testing approach, which foregrounds the experiences of test takers in conjunction with the sociopolitical climates in which the testing occurs (Shohamy, 2001).

A general definition of a test taker guides most test development processes, and the Standards for Psychological and Educational Testing (henceforth, the *Standards*; AERA, APA, and NCME, 2014) serves as the modeling document for such definitions. The *Standards* are testing standards developed by the three major research associations: American Educational Research Association, the American Psychological Association, and the National Council on Measurement in Education. Since 1966, the *Standards* and subsequent revisions have served as the gold standard in providing guidance on testing—in particular for English language testing—at a global level. Yet these guidelines use a definition of a language-minoritized bilingual as an English language learner that begins with deficit framing of these individuals (Schissel, 2019). The *Standards* are not alone in viewing language-minoritized bilinguals through a deficit lens, as educational policies in the United States have long been noted as doing the same (García, Kleifgen, and Falchi, 2008). To understand the impact and origins of this deficit framing, this chapter presents how it is intertwined with approaches to validity for this group of individuals, in particular, the concept of construct-irrelevant variance and the development of test accommodations, and how this deficit view can be traced genealogically throughout histories and legacies of settler colonialism and white supremacy.

To break this pattern of deficit positioning, I aim to amplify calls made for essential shifts in testing that are reflective of and responsive to the sociopolitical contexts in which they operate (e.g., Shohamy, 2001, 2011). For shifts in approaches to validity specifically, I point to the work of Solano-Flores (2011) on cultural validity and McNamara's (2012) discussions around values within validity. This is followed by examples of the concrete ways these shifts are being taken up with ongoing work using heteroglossic approaches to testing. Heteroglossic views and ideologies of language proficiency—as was first explored in the work of Bakhtin (1981)—have been theorized by Blackledge and Creese (2010) as the dynamic, fluid communication among multilingual interlocutors as unremarkably normal, as part of the natural language ecology of a community.

Defining the Test Taker

Placing the definition of the test taker in the forefront of this chapter is reflective of use-oriented approaches to testing. In a use-oriented testing view, Shohamy (2001) describes testing as "embedded in educational, social, and political contexts" (p. 4). This view of testing "is concerned with what happens to the test takers who take the tests . . . the ethicality and fairness of the tests, the long- and short-term consequences that tests have on education and society" (p. 4). Importantly, use-oriented testing emphasizes who the test takers are and their experiences. In test development for language-minoritized bilinguals, the definition of the test taker often begins with the *Standards*. This definition is used for other forms of testing as well (e.g., content area assessments), which is particularly relevant with respect to the discussion of construct-irrelevant variance that follows. The individuals I refer to as language-minoritized bilinguals in this chapter can also be understood as those who the *Standards* refer to as English language learners. The full definition from the *Standards* is as follows:

> English language learner (ELL): An individual who is not yet proficient in English. An ELL may be an individual whose first language is not English, a language minority individual just beginning to learn English, or an individual who has to develop considerable proficiency in English. Related terms include

English learner (EL), limited English proficient (LEP), English as a second language (ESL), and culturally and linguistically diverse. (AERA, APA, and NCME, 2014, p. 218)

The first line of the definition, *not yet proficient in English*, indexes how these individuals are perceived by other individuals, tests, institutions, or policies to not possess English language proficiency based on monolingual constructs and ideologies of proficiency. That is to say, they are not seen as possessing or knowing a type of English, which is typically associated with monolingual, standardized language ideals (Poza and Valdés, 2016; Schissel, 2019; Valdés and Figueroa, 1994; Valdés, Poza, and Brooks, 2014). And like other ways in which bilingualism has been removed from educational policies in the United States (Hornberger, 2006), this definition of English language learner erases the bi/multilingualism of these individuals, presenting notions of English language proficiency as separate from bi/multilingualism. In doing so, this definition presents English proficiency as a binary category, where an individual is either English proficient or not (Abedi and Linquanti, 2012), and these two resulting categories present a reductionist conceptualization of language proficiency (Leung and Scarino, 2016).

The term and definition of English language learner in the *Standards* is closely connected with K-12 educational policies in the United States. The *Bilingual Education Act* of 1968, for example, is the first federal policy for these students and referred to language-minoritized bilinguals as limited English-speaking-ability students and has also been argued to be reflective of deficit positioning of language-minoritized bilinguals (Wright, 2005). Subsequent name changes leading up to English language learner (e.g., limited English proficient) have continued under the same deficit perspectives largely because they have not addressed the monolingual ideologies that undergird this terminology. The term English language learner in the *Standards* is emblematic of this tension, as the term seems to be focusing on what the learner is doing—learning English—yet the definition emphasizes what they are not, that is, a perceived knower or possessor of English. Thus, approaches to testing that incorporate this perspective are set up to be inadequate in creating more equitable testing approaches because they continue to operate within monolingual ideological frameworks that are incongruent with the semiotic and linguistic practices of language-minoritized bilinguals. These continued issues are intertwined with histories and legacies of settler colonialism and white supremacy connected to views of objectivity in testing and monolingual linguistic standards.

Genealogical Historical Approaches to Validity

In discussing deficit positioning of language-minoritized bilinguals, I use a genealogical approach to make the case that deficit framing is reflective of settler colonialism and white supremacy, which are intertwined with approaches to validity. A genealogical historical lens serves as an impetus to make meaningful, lasting change in the testing of language-minoritized bilinguals. This approach thoughtfully engages with troubling histories in order to actively work toward equitable change by critically examining the value of and values reflected in testing. For the sake of space, I focus on the United States, while noting that settler colonialism and white supremacy are not restricted to this region alone.

Settler Colonialism and White Supremacy

Settler colonial contexts, in contrast with (post)colonialism, are characterized by the continued operation of unequal power relationships because of the ongoing presence of colonizers and their descendants. The contrast between these two views of colonialism is summed up by Veracini (2017) as such to provide a detailed view of settler colonialism:

> Settler colonialism is a relationship. It is related to colonialism but also inherently distinct from it. As a system defined by unequal relationships (like colonialism) where an exogenous collective aim to locally and permanently replace indigenous ones (unlike colonialism), settler colonialism has no geographical, cultural or chronological bounds. It is culturally nonspecific. . . . It can happen at any time, and everyone is a settler if they are part of a collective and sovereign displacement that moves to stay, that moves to establish a permanent homeland by way of displacement. (p. 4)

In the United States, Hixson (2017) describes settler colonialism as subjugation and (forced) assimilation of Native American communities as well as the internal colonization of African Americans, Asian Americans, Latinos, and other racialized groups. In expanding on these views of settler colonialism in connection with white supremacy, both coexist with a value frame that privileges the notion of objectivity, which in turn is manifested within testing practices. This argument is derived from previous scholarship critiquing power and testing (Foucault, 1977; Shohamy, 2001) and scientific racism (Chase, 1977). Stern (2015) has defined scientific racism as the use of evidence presented as objective to substantiate racist claims and the actions taken. Her foundational work, for example, illustrated how Mexican Americans, Mexican immigrants, and Native Americans were disproportionately subjected to forced sterilization in California from 1909 to 1979 and how people such as medical professionals, psychologists, and legal officials used tests and test scores to support these decisions.

The links between settler colonialism and white supremacy exist outside of testing as well. With respect to whiteness throughout the history of the United States, there has been a shifting definition of who is considered to be white, with the gradual acceptance of Italian, Irish, and Polish immigrants (Roediger, 2005). Irish immigrants, for example, were initially seen as uncivilized, impoverished, and compared to and depicted as African Americans in cartoons and other illustrations. Ignatiev (1995) explored in detail how Irish immigrants become accepted as white by becoming brutally oppressive against African Americans. In aligning themselves with whiteness through the oppression and displacement of African Americans, the case of Irish immigrants illustrates the interconnectedness of settler colonialism and white supremacy.

For language-minoritized bilinguals, race and language[1] either alternately or combined serve to separate these individuals from settler colonizing white supremacists. The ways in which race and language have been used sometimes interchangeably to perpetuate deficit perspectives of language-minoritized bilinguals have been taken up with scholarship in *raciolinguistic ideologies*. Flores and Rosa (2015) explain that

> *raciolinguistic ideologies* . . . conflate certain racialized bodies with linguistic deficiency unrelated to any objective linguistic practices. That is, raciolinguistic ideologies produce racialized speaking subjects who are constructed as linguistically deviant even when engaging in linguistic practices positioned as normative or innovative when produced by privileged white subjects. (p. 150)

In connecting legacies of genealogical histories of settler colonialism with race and language, Rosa (2016) describes how Latino high school students' bilingual language skills were misconstrued as *languagelessness*, or to refer back to the *Standards* definition, these students were seen as not yet proficient in English *and* Spanish. Such deficit perspectives of language-minoritized bilinguals have been circulating for decades, with tests often being leveraged to provide evidence to restrict language-minoritized bilinguals' access to various educational opportunities. For researchers who argued language-minoritized bilinguals had inherited low intelligence due to patterned poor performance on intelligence tests, Hakuta explained that researchers viewed these children as "deficient in both languages" (Anastasi and Cordova, 1953; as cited in Hakuta, 1986, p. 32). Over the years, language-minoritized bilinguals have continued to disproportionally not perform as well as their perceived monolingual English peers on intelligent tests, content tests, and language proficiency tests. Such positioning of language-minoritized bilinguals as being *semilingual* or having limited bilingualism (Cummins, 1979, 1981) has been critiqued as a (gross) mischaracterization of bilingualism (Edelsky et al., 1983; Martin-Jones and Romaine, 1986) that has continued legacies in categories such as referring to language-minoritized bilinguals as *non-nons* (MacSwan, 2000).

Rosa (2016) summarized how even having an awareness of the issues with test scores and educational programs did not impact this view of students' languagelessness. He explained that one high school administrator said that "[English] language proficiency assessments underestimated students' language abilities; similarly, prolonged stays in bilingual education programs prevented students from learning at grade level" (p. 170). Questioning test scores and the programs available to language-minoritized bilinguals often remains in the shadow of the attention paid to low scores of language-minoritized bilinguals on tests.

The ubiquitous differences in test performance between language-minoritized bilinguals and their peers—often referred to as the achievement gap—have been noted since early work on standardized testing has begun. Discussions around differences in performances are often dismissed as a representation of existing inequities. Schissel (2019) has built upon previous scholarship that looked at the flaws in approaches of testing language-minoritized bilinguals (Shohamy, 2011; Valdés and Figueroa, 1994) by also including the social consequences for language-minoritized bilinguals based on their test performance. Schissel (2019) has argued that the history of social consequences of testing illustrates how language-minoritized bilinguals have faced repeated, often severe, consequences, which illustrates how tests have exacerbated existing and introduced new inequities in conjunction with legacies of settler colonialism and white supremacy. Similarly, in commenting on the histories of discrimination connecting race and language-minoritized bilinguals with testing, Menken (2008) argues that

> the testing movement has historically been tied to racism and linguicism, rising in response to the record rates of immigration to this country. Tests are presented to the public as objective and their power is largely unquestioned, yet historically they have served to legitimize the marginalization of racial and ethnic minorities. (p. 19)

To unpack how mechanisms connected within testing linked with reproductions of inequities, the next section explores approaches to validity that can be seen as contributing to these issues.

Histories of Validity

Histories of the development of test validity often focus on the development of the concept or the methods associated with validity without a discussion of the sociopolitical context in which these ideas have been developed (i.e., Sireci, 2009). Though these histories provide useful information, an examination inclusive of the sociopolitical context offers information that can specifically work toward addressing the legacies of inequities seen in modern testing practices.

Early forms of testing were used to make links between language/ethnicity/race and test performance, and then these test scores were used to make generalized claims about different groups. For example, in some of the first published discussions about approaches to validity with the testing of language-minoritized bilinguals using the Army Beta intelligence test in the late 1910s, Brigham (1923) wrote about whether the test was measuring what it was intended to measure or if it was capturing something unintended, a "typical American" factor:

> If our results reflect another factor independent of intelligence, which might be designated "the better adaptation of the more thoroughly Americanized group to the situation of the examination," we have no means of controlling this factor. Ultimately, the validity of our conclusion from this study rests on the validity of the alpha, beta, and the individual examinations. . . . If the tests used some mysterious type of situation that was "typically American," we are indeed fortunate, for this is America, and the purpose of our inquiry is that of obtaining a measure of the character of our immigration. (pp. 95–96)

Brigham ultimately accepted that the scores from the test could be trusted and connected the test scores with theories of innate or inherited intelligence to claim that immigrants from non-Nordic regions were born with lower intelligence. Brigham and many of his contemporaries used test scores as evidence that support their views aligning with the eugenics movement. In invoking validity of the testing instrument to support claims that certain groups had inherently lower intelligence, the scientific racism employed by Brigham and his contemporaries reflected and contributed to public sentiments that were supportive of US policies that enforced racial discrimination such as segregation, interracial marriage bans, and race-based naturalization policies.

During the 1930s and 1940s, most scholars who were involved in the eugenics movement or who were espousing explicitly racist claims retracted their statements. However, in renouncing their affiliations scholars did not address the gravity of the impact of their work. Henry Goddard, who introduced the first translated version of the Binet-Simon intelligence scale from French into English (the basis for the modern-day Stanford-Binet test), is an example of such resistance to acknowledging the harm that his work was associated with. Zenderland (1998) summarized how Goddard shifted his views on eugenics, and how he acknowledged that his previous conclusions about the links between race and intelligence were "probably negligible" (Goddard, 1928; as cited in Zenderland, 1998, p. 326). Yet he remained silent on the impact and implications of his work. Zenderland explained,

> In Goddard's brave new world, social as well as genetic engineering would produce both a better society and a more intelligent man. . . . [Yet,] Goddard remained completely unconscious both of his own deep class biases and of the dangerous potential for political totalitarianism within his technocratic, eugenic utopia. (p. 330)

Throughout his life, Goddard never directly addressed some of the most egregious links between his work and the gross negative social consequences that many others called into question.

In presenting this historical context, I aim to highlight how the very idea of validity can be viewed as coming from a particular epistemological framework that views that intelligence, and other factors, can be objectively assessed. Connected to this framework is the eugenics movement, with genetics as the simple, albeit racist, explanation of lower test scores. Also connected, cultural racism attributed test-score differences to environmental factors. As the biological argument waned with the decline of eugenics in the 1930s, the cultural argument rose to prominence and is still a primary discourse within educational circles. Across both perspectives are notions of objectivity that are used to substantiate harmful actions against language-minoritized bilinguals and other minoritized persons. These actions have served to sustain hierarchical power structures of settler colonialism and white supremacy.

Throughout this time there was resistance to such scientific racist approaches, notably by one of the few Mexican American, bilingual scholars involved in these debates: George Sánchez. Being one of the few Mexican American, bilingual scholars was in large part to the racist intellectual debates around testing that would render him, and other bilingual and language-minoritized scholars, left out of these major discussions and debates. In questioning the validity claims of an assessment developed based on norms that excluded language-minoritized bilinguals, Sánchez (1934) wrote,

> As long as the tests do not at least sample in equal degree a state of saturation that is equal for the "norm children" and the particular bilingual child it cannot be assumed that the test is a valid one for that child. (p. 771)

His concerns are echoed in critics of tests today, where scholars are calling for tests to work for the benefit of language-minoritized bilinguals (Otheguy, García, and Reid, 2015; Shohamy, 2011). Currently, one common approach to creating testing practices for language-minoritized bilinguals are test accommodations that aim to reduce construct-irrelevant variance due to language. Yet as described in the next sections, these approaches fall short of their goal because they are constrained by the histories that they are connected to.

Construct-Irrelevant Variance and Test Accommodations

Samuel Messick's (1980, 1989, 1994) work on validity has looked at ways to understand the social consequences of testing within approaches to validity. Of this work, one aspect of validity that has been directly applied to developing or adapting tests for language-minoritized bilinguals is the concept of construct-irrelevant variance. Construct-irrelevant variance is extraneous, uncontrolled attributes that affect test performance. Construct-irrelevant variance has become particularly relevant for adapting content academic performance tests (e.g., mathematics, science) for language-minoritized bilinguals. Presently, the most prevalent and expanding method in work on content tests for language-minoritized bilinguals in the United States is using test accommodations (Abedi, 2017; Rivera and Collum, 2006). Test accommodations are changes to the test administration (e.g., small group), test response (e.g., transcription), or the test itself (e.g., bilingual test forms) that aim to reduce construct-irrelevant variance due to language proficiency or cultural background for language-minoritized bilinguals while not changing the construct that is intended to be measured.

Despite the intentions behind developing test accommodations to reduce construct-irrelevant variance, accommodations have remained largely ineffective in meeting this goal. A meta-analysis by Kieffer, Rivera, and Francis (2012) found limited support for simplified English, English glossaries, giving the test in the language that matches the medium of instruction, and extended or untimed tests. Pennock-Roman and Rivera (2007) found some support of accommodations when test takers' English language proficiency level is taken into account. These failures in creating more equitable approaches through test accommodations can be in part attributed to the fact that "test items are generally not developed with test accommodations in mind" (Faulkner-Bond and Forte, 2015, p. 406). Researchers who have worked in the development of test accommodations also caution against their widespread use, because accommodations "are not a solution to the larger issues of promoting the academic skills of ELLs [English language learners/language-minoritized bilinguals]" (Kieffer, Rivera, and Francis, 2009, p. 1190). Yet because currently, test accommodations present an option where there are few, they are used in all fifty states and are being further developed with each new content area test, making it more difficult to shift away for this practice as it becomes more developed and entrenched.

The limited evidence on test accommodations as a means of reducing construct-irrelevant variance is not sufficient to warrant any claim of erasing or even minimizing the impact of bilingualism on test results. And by failing to address how test accommodations perpetuate monolingual constructs and ideologies of proficiency steeped in histories of settler colonialism and white supremacy, they are also ill-equipped to reduce inequities in test performance for language-minoritized bilinguals. Thus, this genealogical lens highlights how test accommodations are a tool that operates under the guise of promoting equity that rather further adds to the marginalization of language-minoritized bilinguals, in particular, because it also restricts the development of alternative efforts.

To further understand why accommodations cannot succeed as tools to promote equity in the testing of language-minoritized bilinguals, I refer back to the definition of an English language learner from the *Standards* and the concept of construct-irrelevant variance. First, there are the issues with the definition's erasure of bilingualism or to put it another way, incomplete picture of language-minoritized bilinguals with respect to language. This erasure is failing to recognize the full humanity of language-minoritized bilinguals when it does not recognize their full linguistic repertoires.

Attempts or efforts to reduce construct-irrelevant variance also serve to erase language abilities. Rather than challenging deficit perspectives of language-minoritized bilinguals, test accommodations toe the line, so to speak, furthering approaches to testing that have functioned to oppress language-minoritized bilinguals (Schissel, 2019). The act of providing an accommodation, then, can be seen as partially—if not completely—blinds a language-minoritized bilingual (Shohamy, 2011). Even test accommodations that work to integrate multilingualism in their approach are susceptible to perpetuating inequities because the approach continues to work within a paradigm that is characterized by these unaddressed and underlying flaws.

Yet there are other approaches to cultural validity and values in testing that are working from asset-based framing of language-minoritized bilinguals through heteroglossic approaches. This shift is dramatic but necessary in order to break the repeated pattern of exacerbated existing and introducing new inequities.

Essential Shifts

Moving past the issues raised in the previous sections is possible. To do so, those working with assessments can (1) address histories and legacies of deficit perspectives of language-minoritized bilinguals and monolingual ideologies underlying constructs steeped in settler colonialism and white supremacy and (2) posit new directions based on asset-based perspectives and heteroglossic theories and ideologies about language.

Cultural Validity and Values

Solano-Flores (2011) and Solano-Flores and Nelson-Barber (2001) have argued for cultural validity in testing that positions cultural and linguistic diversity as integral to test design. The title of this chapter in part is inspired by their work, where they state that culture and bi/multilingualism are "the essence of validity" (Solano-Flores, 2011, p. 3) rather than a source of measurement error. Solano-Flores's (2011) foundational work on cultural validity presents a dramatic, essential shift in how tests can be developed for language-minoritized bilinguals. He begins with a sociopolitical orientation as inherent to understanding validity:

> Viewing tests as cultural artifacts enables us to appreciate that, to a great extent, the ways in which students interpret test items and respond to them are mediated by cultural factors that do not have to do necessarily with the knowledge assessed. This is a matter of validity—scores obtained by students on a test should not be due to factors other than those that the test is intended to measure. (p. 3)

In seeing that cultural factors, including language, cannot easily be excluded from traditional testing approaches, he instead argues for their inclusion in testing, making cultural diversity, broadly defined, as intrinsic to the test design.

His approach views the test taker more not only holistically but also with a humanizing perspective that sees the test taker as a complicated human being. This may seem a bit obvious of a position to take about test takers—that they are humans who cannot be thought of as devoid of culture—but it has been largely absent, ignored, explained away, or sought to be controlled in testing circles.

To make these changes, he was careful to address the fact that these efforts currently exist within the field of testing.

> Test developers take different sorts of actions intended to address different aspects of cultural and linguistic diversity. Indeed, in these days, it is virtually impossible to imagine a test that has not gone through some kind of internal or external scrutiny intended to address potential cultural or linguistic bias at some point of its development. Yet it is extremely difficult to determine when some of those actions are effective and when they simply address *superficial* aspects of culture and language or underestimate their complexities. (p. 4, emphasis added)

Though they are not aligned with the same critiques of test accommodations presented above, his views point to simplistic or reductionist approaches to employing methods that seek to develop tests specifically for language-minoritized bilinguals. Test accommodations, for example, may be seen as addressing culture and language superficially.

McNamara (2012) similarly has written about the relationship between validity and sociopolitical contexts. He has reflected on how poststructuralist approaches reveal these connections:

> Although psychometrics can help us interpret the score as a manifestation of a particular construct, the construct itself, not the score as such, is an expression of social values that are necessarily open to interpretation of a different kind. Poststructuralism opens up not single but multiple readings of the meanings of scores, not in the psychometric sense, but in the social and political sense. (p. 574)

The implications of values within testing emphasizes the importance of understanding that tests, and in particular tests scores, are intertwined with values, meaning that tests and test scores ultimately reflect the value systems that contributed to the development of tests. McNamara also connects his ideas about values with Messick's work on validity, in particular the role that social values are "recognized in the discussion of validity by Messick (1989), who argues that one aspect of test validation is the articulation and justification of the value implications of test constructs" (p. 572). McNamara's argument here and his concession that test scores interpretations can be ambiguous moves away from entrenched views of objectivity in measurement and testing.

McNamara's work highlights the situatedness of test-score interpretations, and the need to understand how they are connected to sociopolitical values systems, which can create opportunities to actively confront settler colonialism and white supremacy. In looking at some of the issues that arise when trying to measure language proficiency, he discusses the importance of understanding the ideologies that are represented in the definitions used within tests:

> Poststructuralist readings of test constructs can reveal a tension between the overt meaning of the construct, for example "language proficiency," and its covert meaning, in terms of the values or ideologies it represents. Another way of putting this is that the interpretations of individuals encoded in test scores can be made in reference to multiple constructs; test scores are not necessarily, or even usually, the manifestation of a single cultural value. In this sense, a test score is a sign open to various readings, and hence to dispute; tests are often sites of competition or struggle over values. (p. 572)

Overall, in incorporating values within an understanding of validity, McNamara has introduced methods to name and confront the values connected with values of objectivity or scientific racism that are reflective of white supremacy, settler colonialism, and monolingual ideologies that continue to contribute to deficit framing of language-minoritized bilinguals. His work opens up spaces in the test development and, importantly, in the interpretation of scores to engage with the historical sociopolitical contexts that inform them. These different approaches address some of the ways in which the essence of validity presents essential shifts away from histories steeped in scientific racism to equitable approaches that begin with asset-based framing of language-minoritized bilinguals. The final section presents some efforts that have been taken up to create tests reflective of these shifts.

Heteroglossic Approaches to Testing

Language testing researchers have been adopting heteroglossic perspectives that view the bi/multilingualism of the test taker as integral to test design, development, and interpretation. In leading these new approaches that extend beyond the paradigms aligned with the *Standards*' definition of an English language learner and efforts to reduce construct-irrelevant variance, they have begun to develop approaches that may be able to introduce essential shifts in testing practices. The findings of research in this area offer promising insights into the new directions for testing that could actively confront the legacies of settler colonialism and white supremacy. The studies presented here represent how these approaches have been applied across different sociopolitical contexts in different regions of the world. Each example illustrates a different heteroglossic approach to assessment, and shows shifts in testing that affirm language-minoritized bilinguals' full linguistic repertoires.

Schissel, Leung, López-Gopar, and Davis (2018) used a heteroglossic approach with an English classroom-based language assessment in their participatory action research study with preservice English language teachers (n = 39) in Oaxaca, Mexico. They collaborated with the classroom teacher to select contextually relevant topics focused on type 2 diabetes and litter management into a reading and writing assessment in alignment with the learning objectives on course syllabuses. Preservice teachers completed one task, which was intentionally designed to engage in their English and Spanish competencies with readings, and one that engaged only their English reading competencies. Both tasks prompted the teachers to write a response in English. For example, for the first task about type II diabetes, they needed to read one text in Spanish, one in English, and also to understand a table reporting statistical data about type II diabetes worldwide. Each of the readings, including the reading in Spanish, had the information necessary for completing the writing task. The analyses indicated that the test takers performed better on the English/Spanish task than the English-only task at a level of statistical significance. Specifically, the findings served to counter views that multilingualism is irrelevant to the capacity to perform in the target language, with particular implications for the assessment of learners' higher-order thinking skills. This study's findings suggest that integrating bi/multilingual approaches with task-based assessment can support the general principle that bilinguals tend to perform better on assessments when their full linguistic repertoire is utilized.

In two elementary schools in the United States, Ascenzi-Moreno (2018) worked with three teachers to create responsive adaptations of formative assessments that viewed bi/multilingualism of the students as integral in understanding their learning in language arts classes. Ascenzi-Moreno describes how the assessment process fully embraced students' bi/multilingualism as a resource and was "primarily a pedagogical endeavor rooted in a robust understanding of students' unique language practices" (p. 365). What the teacher accomplished in this approach was to work with her students to gain more information about *what* and *how* the students were learning. In learning more about the students through assessment practices that were attuned to the students' full linguistic repertoires, this approach illustrates, in particular, the benefits of using a flexible assessment approach. In contrast with test accommodations, her study posits that making these changes do not follow a set formula. Rather, the approach develops from teachers' involved investigations of not only the assessment process but also explorations of who their students are.

Heugh et al. (2017) demonstrate how student's multilingualism can be integrated into large-scale, high-stakes testing using longitudinal data from system-wide tests in South Africa. They draw attention to over a century of bi/multilingual educational policies, practices, and tests and the sociopolitical contexts that have made this possible. Their findings illustrate how large-scale assessments, in conjunction with system-wide supports, can be used to address issues around equity in testing. They conclude that these approaches to assessment aid in students' learning and increased access to other opportunities predicated on their performances on these tests.

Across these different studies is an active engagement with the sociopolitical contexts in which testing is taking place and dynamic conceptualizations of the linguistic resources that the test taker brings to the testing situation.

Summary Thoughts

This chapter uses a genealogical historical lens to explore how testing interacts with the sociopolitical contexts in which they operate. After unpacking the deficit positioning of language-minoritized bilinguals in the *Standards*, histories of settler colonialism and white supremacy were explored in general and with respect to validity in the testing of language-minoritized bilinguals. The chapter then explored recent efforts related to reducing construct-irrelevant variance due to language with test accommodations. In light of these underlying and un(der)addressed issues, I argued that current approaches to assessment for language-minoritized bilinguals were inherently inequitable. Identifying and confronting legacies of settler colonialism and white supremacy are essential to offer new ways forward that actively address historic sociopolitical issues in these previous approaches. Both cultural validity and investigating values in testing support efforts to develop assessments that can be uniquely developed for language-minoritized bilinguals in ways that are explicitly meant to be anti-discriminatory. The examples of assessment approaches taking a heteroglossic view are possibly taking steps in this direction. Overall, the chapter set forth to lay the groundwork for essential shifts in English language testing that see bi/multilingualism as the essence of validity.

Note

1 Intersections with class, gender, sexual orientation, disability status, religion, and other identities are not included because of the focus on race and language in this overview, and thus the omission of these identities is meant to heighten the focus of the examination on race and language but not diminish their impacts as well.

References

AERA, APA, and NCME (2014). *The Standards for Educational and Psychological Testing*. American Educational Research Association, Washington.

Abedi, J. (2017). Utilizing accommodations in assessment. In *Language Testing and Assessment* (pp. 303–22). New York City: Springer.

Abedi, J. and Linquanti, R. (2012). Issues and opportunities in strengthening large scale assessment systems for ELLs. In *Understanding Language Conference*, Stanford University, CA.

Ascenzi-Moreno, L. (2018). Translanguaging and responsive assessment adaptations: Emergent bilingual readers through the lens of possibility. *Language Arts*, 95(6), 355–69.

Bakhtin, M. M. (1981). *The Dialogical Imagination*, edited and translated C. Emerson and M. Holquist. Austin: University of Texas Press.

Blackledge, A. and Creese, A. (2010). *Multilingualism: A Critical Perspective*. Bloomsbury Publishing.

Brigham, C. C. (1923). *A Study of American Intelligence*. Princeton, NJ: Princeton University Press.

Chase, A. (1977). *The Legacy of Malthus: The Social Cost of Scientific Racism*. New York: Alfred A. Knopf.

Cummins, J. (1979). Linguistic interdependence and the educational development of bilingual children. *Review of Educational Research*, 49(2), 222–51.

Cummins, J. (1981). The role of primary language development in promoting educational success for language minority students. In California State Department of Education (Ed.), *Schooling and Language Minority Students: A Theoretical Framework* (pp. 3–49). Los Angeles: Evaluation, Dissemination and Assessment Center, California State University.

Edelsky, C., Hudelson, S., Flores, B., Barkin, F., Altwerger, B., and Jilbert, K. (1983). Semilingualism and language deficit. *Applied Linguistics*, 4(1), 1–22.

Faulkner-Bond, M. and Forte, E. (2015). English learners and accountability: The promise, pitfalls, and peculiarity of assessing language minorities via large-scale assessment. In C. S. Wells, M. Faulkner-Bond, and E. Hambleton (Eds.), *Educational Measurement: From Foundations to Future* (pp. 395–415). New York City: Guildford Press.

Flores, N. and Rosa, J. (2015). Undoing appropriateness: Raciolinguistic ideologies and language diversity in education. *Harvard Educational Review*, 85(2), 149–71.

Foucault, M. (1977). *Discipline and Punish: The Birth of the Prison* (A. Sheridan, trans.). Allen Lane. (Originally published as Surveiller et Punir: Naissance de la Prison. E´ditions Gallimard, 1975.)

García, O., Kleifgen, J. A., and Falchi, L. (2008). From English language learners to emergent bilinguals. Equity Matters. Research Review No. 1. Campaign for Educational Equity, Teachers College, Columbia University.

Hakuta, K. (1986). *The Mirror of Language: The Debate on Bilingualism*. New York: Basic Books.

Heugh, K., Prinsloo, C., Makgamatha, M., Diedericks, G., and Winnaar, L. (2017). Multilingualism (s) and system-wide assessment: A southern perspective. *Language and Education*, 31(3), 197–216.

Hixson, W. L. (2017). Adaptation, resistance and representation in the modern US settler state. In E. Cavanagh and L. Veracini (Eds.), *The Routledge Handbook of the History of Settler Colonialism* (pp. 169–84). Milton Park: Taylor & Francis.

Hornberger, N. H. (2006). Nichols to NCLB: Local and global perspectives on U.S. language education policy. In O. García, T. Skutnabb-Kangas, and M. Torres-Guzmán (Eds.), *Imagining Multilingual Schools: Languages in Education and Glocalization* (pp. 223–37). Clevedon: Multilingual Matters.

Ignatiev, N. (1995). *How the Irish Became White*. New York: Routledge.

Kieffer, M. J., Rivera, M., and Francis, D. J. (2012). *Practical Guidelines for the Education of English Language Learners: Research-Based Recommendations for the use of Accommodations in Large-Scale Assessments*. Portsmouth, NH: RMC Research Corporation, Center on Instruction.

Kieffer, M. J., Lesaux, N. K., Rivera, M. and Francis, D. J. (2009). Accommodations for English language learners taking large-scale assessments: A meta-analysis on effectiveness and validity. *Review of Educational Research*, 79(3), 1168–1201.

Leung, C. and Scarino, A. (2016). Reconceptualizing the nature of goals and outcomes in language/s education. *The Modern Language Journal*, 100(S1), 81–95.

MacSwan, J. (2000). The threshold hypothesis, semilingualism, and other contributions to a deficit view of linguistic minorities. *Hispanic Journal of Behavioral Sciences*, 22(1), 3–45.

Martin-Jones, M. and Romaine, S. (1986). Semilingualism: A halfbaked theory of communicative competence. *Applied Linguistics*, 7(1), 26–38.

McNamara, T. (2012). Poststructuralism and its challenges for applied linguistics. *Applied Linguistics*, 33(5), 473–82.

Menken, K. (2008). *English Learners Left Behind: Standardized Testing as Language Policy*. Clevedon: Multilingual Matters.

Messick, S. (1980). Test validity and the ethics of assessment. *American Psychologist*, 35(11), 1012.

Messick, S. (1989). Validity. In R. L. Linn (Ed.), *Educational Measurement* (3rd ed.), (pp. 13–103). London: Collier Mcmillan.

Messick, S. (1994). The interplay of evidence and consequences in the validation of performance assessments. *Educational Researcher*, 23(2), 13–23.

Otheguy, R., García, O., and Reid, W. (2015). Clarifying translanguaging and deconstructing named languages: A perspective from linguistics. *Applied Linguistics Review*, 6(3), 281–307.

Pennock-Roman, M. and Rivera, C. (2007). Test validity and mean effects of test accommodations for ELLs and non-ELLs: A meta-analysis. Washington, DC: Center for Equity and Excellence in Education, George Washington University.

Poza, L. E. and Valdés, G. (2016). Assessing English language proficiency in the United States. In E. Shohamy, I. Or, and S. May (Eds.), *Language Testing and Assessment. Encyclopedia of Language and Education* (3rd ed.), (pp. 1–14). Cham: Springer.

Rivera, C. and Collum, E. (2006). *State Assessment Policy and Practice for English Language Learners: A National Perspective*. Mahwah, NJ: Lawrence Erlbaum Associates, Publishers.

Roediger, D. R. (2005). *Working Toward Whiteness: How America's Immigrants Became White: The Strange Journey from Ellis Island to the Suburbs*. Basic Books (AZ).

Rosa, J. D. (2016). Standardization, racialization, languagelessness: Raciolinguistic ideologies across communicative contexts. *Journal of Linguistic Anthropology*, 26(2), 162–83.

Sánchez, G. I. (1934). Bilingualism and mental measures. A word of caution. *Journal of Applied Psychology*, 18(6), 765.

Schissel, J. L. (2019). *Social Consequences of Testing for Language-Minoritized Bilinguals in the United States*. Bristol: Multilingual Matters.

Schissel, J. L., Leung, C., López-Gopar, M., and Davis, J. R. (2018). Multilingual learners in language assessment: Assessment design for linguistically diverse communities. *Language and Education*, 32(2), 167–82.

Shohamy, E. (2001). *The Power of Tests: A Critical Perspective on the uses of Language Tests*. Harlow: Longman.

Shohamy, E. (2011). Assessing multilingual competencies: Adopting construct valid assessment policies. *The Modern Language Journal*, 95(3), 417–29.

Sireci, S. G. (2009). Packing and unpacking sources of validity evidence. In S. G. Sireci, *The Concept of Validity: Revisions, New Directions and Applications* (pp. 19–37). Charlotte, NC: Information Age Publishing.

Solano-Flores, G. (2011). Assessing the cultural validity of assessment practices: An introduction. In M. del Rosario Basterra, E. Trumbull, and G. Solano-Flores (Eds.), *Cultural Validity in Assessment: Addressing Linguistic and Cultural Diversity* (pp. 3–21), New York: Routledge.

Solano-Flores, G. and Nelson-Barber, S. (2001). On the cultural validity of science assessments. *Journal of Research in Science Teaching, 38*(5), 553–73.

Stern, A. M. (2015). *Eugenic Nation: Faults and Frontiers of Better Breeding in Modern America*. Berkeley: University of California Press.

Valdés, G. and Figueroa, R. A. (1994). *Bilingualism and Testing: A Special Case of Bias*. Ablex Publishing.

Valdés, G., Poza, L., and Brooks, M. D. (2014). Educating students who do not speak the societal language: The social construction of language learner categories. Profession. Retrieved from https://profession.mla.hcommons.org/2014/10/09/educating-students-who-do-not-speak-the-societal-language

Veracini, L. (2017). Introduction: Settler colonialism as a distinct mode of domination. In E. Cavanagh and L. Veracini (Eds.), *The Routledge Handbook of the History of Settler Colonialism* (pp. 1–8). Milton Park: Taylor & Francis.

Wright, W. (2005). *Evolution of Federal Policy and Implications of No Child Left Behind for Language Minority Students*. Tempe, AZ: Educational Policy Studies Laboratory.

Zenderland, L. (1998). *Measuring Minds*. Cambridge: Cambridge University Press.

Part Two

The Politics of Testing in the Non-English-Speaking World

6

The Coloniality of English Language Testing

Ruanni Tupas

Introduction

This chapter tackles the coloniality of language testing. It argues that certain aspects and practices of language testing reflect social structures and values that conflict with the experiences of those doing the tests. Those experiences are still shaped by a history of colonialism and imperialism that continues to shape the present. Critical dimensions of language testing—for example, its role in perpetuating social and educational inequalities—have been raised forcefully by a number of scholars for at least two decades now, but investigations into the coloniality of English language testing have thus far received much less attention in applied linguistics, educational research, and related fields. "For the most part," according to Shahjahan (2013), "critical scholarship on higher education policy continues to ignore colonial experiences" (p. 676).

This chapter mobilizes two complementary definitions of *coloniality* that will be crucial for understanding the role of language testing in the global and local maintenance and reconstitution of unequal structures and practices of knowledge production deriving from colonial history. First, coloniality refers to "an imperial logic of domination that derives from colonial and imperial experiences" (Shahjahan, 2013, p. 677). Second, it refers to "mechanisms of settler colonialism and colonial administration, structures which continue to shape our contemporary institutions, global practices, and individual livelihoods" (Hsu, 2015, p. 126). Through the lens of coloniality, this chapter views language testing both as a control mechanism that follows an imperial pattern of domination and as an enactment of such a control lived through the practices and livelihoods of communities and individuals around the world. Language testing is a globally shaped local practice, both politically and culturally hegemonic but, at the same time, not completely closed to "resistive" practices and policies (Acheraïou, 2011, p. 150).

This chapter maps out and examines the multilayered politics of language testing in the context of a US development aid English Language Teaching (ELT) project in the Philippines, which, as will be unpacked later, was actually deployed as part of the US global anti-terrorism campaign in the aftermath of the 9/11 attacks. Called JEEP—Jobs Enabling English Programme—it essentially aimed at students in Mindanao that has been plagued by decades-old armed Muslim separatism and by high incidence of violence and poverty. However, the expressed purpose of JEEP was to help students improve their English proficiency in order to become more competitive in the job market and, thus, would help break the cycle of poverty in their respective communities. JEEP has been subjected to some critical scrutiny, for example, its embeddedness in neoliberal discourses and practices (Tabiola and Lorente, 2017) as well its overall complicity with the structures and practices of neocolonialism in the Philippines (Tupas and Tabiola, 2017). However, in this chapter the discussion is focused on the geopolitical dimension of language testing deployed in the project and how it substantiates the claim that coloniality is "*still* the most general form of domination in the world today" (Quijano, 2007, p. 170, italics supplied). Language testing in this project is avowedly and unapologetically native-speakerist (Holliday, 2006), using a professional vocabulary that describes levels in English language proficiency as a progression of language development toward the native-speaker ideal in communication. The deployment of language testing instruments and technical vocabulary—mainly through the use of a software developed in the United States and facilitated through the mechanism of development aid—is devoid of contextualization because the software is intended as a culture-free ELT material that can be used in any educational setting around the world. Native-speakerist ideologies and practices, and the use of decontextualized and homogenizing materials, including the crucial placement tests, are geopolitical realizations of JEEP as a development aid project. To put it in another way, JEEP, along with its language testing component, activates and affirms conditions of coloniality in the Philippines.

Several scholars (Alatis and Straehle, 2006; Davies, 1996; Spolsky, 2004) have strongly objected to the claim that there are links between language testing and imperialism designs (Phillipson, 1992, 2007), arguing that there is no conspiracy involved, as though Western powers and their allies are engaged in some grand plot to control the world. They argue that the demand for particular languages (most notably English) arises mainly from rational and pragmatic choices made by parents and students who wish to fulfill their goals in life. This chapter chooses not to frame the issue of language teaching and testing in terms of such simple binaries, preferring instead to surface the entanglements of language teaching institutions, knowledges, ideologies, and practices with the enduring mechanisms and conditions of coloniality (Kumaravadivelu, 2016; Macedo, 2017; Pennycook, 2007). Complicities of different stakeholders in language teaching in the making and perpetuation of unequal structures of global power and knowledge production are real, but it is by exposing and interrogating the complex network of such relations (mediated, for example, by the geopolitical mechanism of development aid) that we can, in fact, find spaces of intervention and make positive changes in society through the practice of language teaching. This does not mean, however, that the paper discounts the messiness and complexity of language testing practices, ignoring the agency of individuals involved in such practices. As mentioned earlier in this chapter, it acknowledges "resistive" practices and actions of people and institutions (Acheraïou, 2011, p. 150), which deny particular hegemonic policies and institutions' complete domination. The purpose of this chapter is to highlight the structural dimensions of language testing, which are linked in intricate ways with the enduring structures of coloniality.

Coloniality as Lens

One of the major pitfalls of postcolonial theorizing in applied linguistics, sociolinguistics, and, in fact, in most of the humanities and social sciences has been to sidestep, de-emphasize, or ignore the enduring impact of colonialism on the lives of the colonized as well as on the shape and structures of institutions and social relations in "new" independent nations (Kumaravadivelu, 2016; Tupas, 2004). The postcolonial celebration of subjugated peoples writing back to the empire (Ashcroft et al., 1989) has been premature (Dirlik, 1994). There is theoretical ground and political wisdom for excavating the silenced voices of the oppressed or the colonized as these would prove that the colonial project was never complete and successful since people also resisted or transformed it on their own terms. Local populations survived despite the rapacity and harshness of colonialism because they creatively or strategically carved out spaces of resistance or negotiation, thus allowing us to see the subjugated people not simply as dupes of colonialism, passively embracing the ideologies and practices imposed upon them by their foreign rulers, but also as agentive (active) participants in the making and reconstitution of the colonial process, both in terms of creating their own conditions and in continuing to engage with and resist the conditions being imposed on them (Canagarajah, 1999; Kachru, 1996).

However, the theoretical consequence of such a view has been to overly focus on the agency of the colonized at the expense of investigations into the structuring conditions of individual people's lives. As argued by Quijano (2007), nominal political independence does not mean cultural, economic, and ideological independence as well. Colonialism "as an explicit political order" (p. 170) may have been destroyed, but it remains the "main framework" (p. 170) of current "modes of exploitation and domination between peoples" (p. 170). Grosfoguel (2011) also adds, "The mythology of the 'decolonization of the world' obscures the continuities between the colonial past and current global colonial/racial hierarchies and contributes to the invisibility of 'coloniality' today" (p. 14).

What we are experiencing now are conditions of coloniality that have survived colonialism (Maldonado-Torres, 2007, p. 243). This theoretical lens does not in any way preclude any examination of postcolonial agencies and practices; in fact, this is intrinsic to a framework of coloniality. It is unhelpful to swing back to determinist perspectives on global power and domination, but it is certainly also unconstructive to turn a blind eye to the structuring conditions within which the dominated assert or express agentive possibilities not only to survive but also to score victories against imperial rule. In other words, the lens of coloniality also helps recuperate resistive practices and knowledges derived from subjugated people's engagement with oppressive mechanisms of power and relations but always with the view that such recuperation is implicated in global colonial matrices of power (Ndlovu-Gatsheni, 2013). In the context of ELT, Pennycook (2007) asserts that such resistive practices and knowledges "always need to be understood in the context of the very real and continuing neo-colonial power of English" (p. 22). A decolonizing option, after all, should be the political agenda of the lens of coloniality where the subaltern or the dominated do not only speak and write but, most especially, *act* against such matrices of power (Kumaravadivelu, 2016, p. 82). The binary between structure and agency, or domination and resistance, does not serve to explain the politics of the exercise of global power today. They should be conceptualized together in order not to relegate perspectives on structure and domination "to the postcolonial theoretical hinterlands" (Acheraïou, 2011, p. 150) by crucially engaging in the fundamental understanding of global power relations as grounded in an imperialist logic of domination.

Therefore, it is not enough to acknowledge the colonial beginnings or histories of English language teaching, learning, testing, and/or use and then choose to gloss over these colonial questions because the colonized have also demonstrated individual agency, and the erstwhile colonized communities are no longer beholden to their colonial past. People imagine that mechanisms like standardized testing can still be used for a socially beneficial purpose, as though the history of such mechanisms can simply be discounted. But that history still shapes the attitudes and practices that characterize such mechanisms operating today. English has two faces, according to Kachru (1997): one is the face of the colonial past, and the other is the face of the postcolonial present. This chapter rather argues that we need to foreground the entanglements of the past and present, and we can do it through the lens of coloniality.

In language education, including English language testing in schools and in society at large, substantial work has been done to show the disastrous impact of tests on students and minority speakers who take institutionalized tests as part of citizenship and other institutional requirements (Kunnan, 2009; Shohamy, 2017). However, locating language testing regimes within conditions of coloniality has not yet been systematically explored in a consistent way, although there are a few who raise critical voices in this area (Pepper, 2006; Shajahan, 2013). In the world today, the "forces of domination seem to be getting even more entrenched" (Kumaravadivelu, 2016, p. 72); thus, it is worthwhile to examine the enduring imperial mechanisms of control and power in education, foremost of which is language testing.

A Geopolitics of English Language Testing

Language testing is not just an educational issue but also a geopolitical one. It is embedded in overlapping layers of power relations with multiple ideological, cultural, political, and economic mechanisms mobilized to sustain or reconstitute such relations. In the case of the ELT project in Mindanao, which will be the subject of discussion in this section, such mechanisms include colonially mediated US-Philippine historical ties, for example, through development aid projects, joint US-Philippine military exercises, and the anti-terrorism drive; language policy and English-only school policies; ELT methodologies; and (technologically mediated) teaching materials. Language testing is not detached from these mechanisms of power and knowledge distribution but is, in fact, actively engaged in the organization and operation of these mechanisms.

Development Aid and the Global War on Terror (GWOT) in Mindanao

"Since the U.S. incursions into Afghanistan and Iraq," according to Stuebner and Hirsch (2010), "scholars, strategists, and policymakers seem interested in discovering how to fight smarter or, preferably, how to win without fighting" (p. 129). "One of the best places to look for such a case study of fighting and winning 'smart' is in Mindanao in the southern Philippines" (p. 129). Mindanao is where most Muslim Filipinos live, constituting 11 percent of the national population and 20 percent of the population of the region (Laudencia, 2017). It is home to decades-old Muslim separatist conflicts, recently reframed after 9/11 as the US-led global war on terror (GWOT), although these conflicts actually have historical roots in agrarian injustice at the turn of the twentieth century when the region was pacified through American colonial rule (Vellema et al., 2011). The Spanish, who came before the Americans, did not succeed in placing Mindanao under their rule. Through military might and subtle forms of pacification (called *benevolent assimilation* [Miller, 1982]) not only did the United States become far more successful in integrating the region into the colonial economic system, it also succeeded in exploiting the region's vast natural resources by co-opting local elites who served as mediators in conflicts between their subjects and the American rulers (Vellema et al., 2011). The recent involvement of the US military in Mindanao justified on grounds of fighting growing terrorism around the world can actually be seen as a seamless continuation of more than a century of American presence and intervention in the Philippines. In fact, recent US involvement in security in the Philippines has been based on a treaty promulgated around seven decades ago—the Mutual Defense Treaty of 1951 (Laudencia, 2017). At the beginning of American colonial rule, one of the cornerstone policies of the colonial government was the pacification of Muslims and other non-Christian people of the region (Vellema et al., 2011). On the other hand, one important political mechanism that has been crucial in facilitating American military operations in Mindanao in recent years has been the US Agency for International Development's (USAID's) Growth with Equity in Mindanao (GEM) program. This is where we see development aid—which is political through and through (Carothers and De Gramont, 2013)—as a mechanism in the sustenance of colonially mediated geopolitical relations.

The GEM program has five general components, namely (1) infrastructure development, (2) business development, (3) workforce preparation, (4) governance improvement, and (5) former combatant reintegration. The program, in short, is a comprehensive approach to economic and peace development in Mindanao (Stuebner and Hirsch, 2010):

> USAID/GEM is accepted into conflict affected communities by wary residents because it is a civilian development program carried out by noncombatant civilians. It has developed into a comprehensive, multidisciplinary program that addresses a wide range of livelihood, infrastructure, education, and governance needs, complementing strategic objectives by helping stabilize communities and focusing stakeholder attention on economic growth and not insurgency. (p. 132)

This, in essence, is the geopolitical context of the Job Enabling English Proficiency (JEEP) Project that is listed as one of the subcomponents of workforce preparation under the GEM program. JEEP was launched in 2009 and then introduced in several partner universities in Mindanao with the explicit aim of helping students of the region "secure and retain jobs in highly-favored sectors which require proficiency in English, such as international nursing and allied health, call center and other Business Processing Outsourcing (BPO) employment in these areas" (Berowa, 2012, p. 130). In other words, there is an interplay of discourses surrounding JEEP: the more explicit one has to do with the pragmatic aspect of English language learning and the more subtle one implicates its geopolitical dimensions. The pragmatic discourse isolates JEEP from its colonial and geopolitical moorings, but if they are viewed as interlocking discourses, what emerges is a complex picture of unequal US-Philippine relations where the United States invests heavily in Mindanao on terms that serve its national interests rather than those of the Philippines. It is for these reasons that the introduction of technologically mediated language testing instruments—perceived by both students and teachers as new and innovative (Berowa, 2012; Tupas and Tabiola, 2017)—must be deeply scrutinized in terms of how they act as concrete mechanisms in mobilizing practices and ideologies of coloniality sited within the geopolitical entanglements of the Philippines with the United States and its GWOT through the mediation of development aid.

The Native-Speaker Goal

The language testing component of JEEP is crucial in the implementation of the project because the whole idea of JEEP is computer-assisted language learning or CALL. Critical to JEEP is the learning of General English and teachers use of a software that requires students to log on and go through a multilevel series of lessons on, say, speaking or listening. A student is placed on a particular level and stays on the same level unless he or she achieves a score that qualifies him or her to move to the next. According to the software developer, "If a student has difficulty in skill areas that are assumed for the next level of the course, the test will stop and place the student at the lower level" (DynEd International, Inc., 2006, p. 4). Even though the series of placement tests is not meant to capture the overall proficiency of students it "should [at least] provide a good indication" (p. 14). The placement levels begin at Level 0.0, which is described as Beginner or False Beginner, with an accompanying Level 0.5 described as being able to "speak and understand a few phrases in English" (p. 14). Students who begin at Level 0.0 would then move up through several levels (Low Intermediate, Intermediate, High Intermediate Advanced, and Advanced) until they reach 4.0 that is defined as "Fluent non-native," and the highest level, 5.0, "*Educated* native speaker" (p. 14, italics as original).

One popular English language course used in JEEP classrooms is *New Dynamic English* that is comprised of eight modules organized progressively according to the different levels described above. Its key features include Voice Record and Speech Recognition Exercises, Listening Comprehension & Grammar-based Exercises, and, of course, Placement Tests (DynEd International, Inc., 2014). According to some teachers who were involved in the project, students using the software engage in a lot of repeating of sounds, words, sentences, and stock phrases that they would record into the software (Tupas and Tabiola, 2017). One particular teacher describes the impact of the exercises and placement tests on what exactly happens in the classroom:

> Try to repeat again and then listen to your own recording and then record it again because it is through speaking that you get that knowledge that the knowledge retains more. Yeah. I think that's the reason why there's you know repeating. And although there's repeating because we cannot be good communicators at one instance. Like this speaking this sentence. So you need to you know repeat this sentence again and again. That is for you to be also a practice of your speaking skills. Speaking skills you need to you're able to listen to your own speech so can assess "ay kapangit diay nako paminawon or kabati" [ah I sound awful] so the good thing with that is that before you speak to a group of people you have already heard yourself speaking. So you record it until it becomes pleasing to hear or to listen so "yun" [that's it]. That's the reason why we have recording we have repeating basically for speaking purposes and for the retain [*sic*] of information. (p. 5)

The main goal of repetition is, of course, to speak like an educated native speaker, which is "pleasing to hear." Given the fact that students are first language speakers of Philippine languages, the placement tests are such that the highest level can never be achieved despite the students' constant repetition work because they will never be educated *and* native speakers. Using the words of Kramsch (1998), the placement tests define the students "in terms of what they are *not*, or at least *not yet*" (p. 28, italics as original), "[o]r," adds Cook (1999), "*not ever*" (p. 189, italics as original). Yet, as another teacher describes it, what students need to do is "copy the virtual native speaker" (p. 5) and by getting closer speaking like one, he or she progresses to the next level.

Several dimensions of the JEEP classroom have already been examined such as its physical setup where students are placed into individual cubicles engaged in individual learning, its English-only policy, neoliberal discourses that underpin the rationalization of the project, as well as several teachers' own experience facilitating JEEP classrooms (Tupas and Tabiola, 2017; Tabiola and Lorente, 2017) and students' willingness to learn English (Berowa, 2012). Zeroing now on its testing component such as the placement tests described above, we identify three key features of these tests.

Three Key Features and Their Colonial Genesis

The first, of course, is its avowedly—and certainly outdated—native-speaker ideal. "What counts as native speaker competence is now a moot point even in so-called native English-speaking environments" (Jenkins and Leung, 2017, p. 109). This is because as English has globalized, it has also pluralized in such a way that speakers require multidialectal competence in English or knowledge and use of pluralities of English when communicating with other speakers of English (Canagarajah, 2006). Yet, the JEEP project through the use of software developed in the United States remains complicit with monolingualist and native-speakerist ideologies when it assumes the native speaker as the ideal goal of language learning. The second is the central role of technology in the placement tests that subtly promote the homogenization of English language learning. There are "extension classroom activities" (DynEd International, Inc., 2006, p. 16) (although teachers interviewed about their participation in JEEP report no time to engage in these extension activities [Tabiola, 2015; Tupas and Tabiola, 2017]) as well as opportunities to customize "the study path for each student or class" by relying on consolidated test results to decide which aspects of language learning students must focus on.

However, these activities and opportunities to customize do not in any way alter the premise that any improvement must be oriented toward the native speaker ideal, especially if students must continue to use the same exercises and placement tests in order to unlock the software to allow them to move to the next level of lessons. This brings us to the third feature that is its decontextualized and universalizing nature. The software is also used elsewhere in the world, regardless of cultural and educational differences and expectations (see Baş, 2010; Bingham and Larson, 2006; Brown, Campbell, and Weatherford, 2008). It has been used in China, France, Malaysia, Korea, Myanmar, and Turkey, and while teachers and students welcome its use, "it tends to be quite formulaic in the patterning of its instructional sequences, from unit to unit" (Baş, 2010, p. 16). Most students in these countries who use the software are bilingual or multilingual speakers, but there is no provision for cultural appropriation through the software. The placement tests are uniform across all cultural contexts and, of course, all users must listen to and engage with the same American native speakers in the software. Thus, aside from the use of the native speaker as the goal of language learning (which does not reflect the sociolinguistic and cultural realities of English language use in the world today), the software and its placement tests more specifically gloss over culturally shaped content, classroom practices, and student and teacher identities. In other words, they carry with them a "universalizing imperialist" ethos (Gough, 2002, p. 176) that renders the learning of English homogeneous and uniform across different contexts.

These key features of the exercises and tests in the software are native-speakerist, homogenizing, and universalizing approaches to the learning and teaching of English. They have been, in many scholarly works (Kumaravadivelu, 2006; Pennycook, 2007; Phillipson, 1992), shown to be at the core of the colonial ideological construction of English language teaching, which have thus contributed to the marginalization and devaluation of local linguistic repertoires, expertise, and pedagogies in the teaching of English. In the case of the Philippines, for example, such marginalization and devaluation are traceable to colonial processes and discourses that emerged out of American imperial rule in the country (Hsu, 2015; Tupas, 2004, 2015) when, after its forcible entry through the bloody Philippine-American War of 1899–1902, it institutionalized the policy of benevolent assimilation (Miller, 1982), which essentially meant the subjugation of local people through subtle means.

The key mechanism of benevolent assimilation was education and, more specifically, the imposition of English as the sole medium of instruction (Constantino, 1970), which has remained practically unchallenged in a significant way until, perhaps, 1974 when the bilingual education policy was instituted. Nevertheless, while this policy stipulated that English would be limited to the teaching of only mathematics and science, and all other courses would be taught in the national language ("Filipino," but which was then called "Pilipino"), the symbolic power of English has in fact solidified further through post–Second World War US-led globalization where English increasingly became critical in multinational and corporate profit-making, interstate relations, use of technology, and people-to-people communication. Ideologies and practices associated with the symbolic power of English—for example, the supremacy of American Standard English or what Bautista (2000) calls the "standard of standards" in the Philippines (p. 17), English-only policies in school as homogenizing practices, and the reliance on teaching methods that disregard the usefulness of local languages in the classroom (Cook, 2001)—endure in current articulations and practices of the teaching and learning of English. It is in this context that "the coloniality of the English language is undeniable" (Kumaravadivelu, 2016, p. 13).

Nevertheless, the coloniality of language testing in the JEEP project cannot simply be explained by the durability of native-speakerist, homogenizing, and universalizing practices and ideologies associated with and shaped by the use of a software, without surfacing the mediating and critical role of JEEP as a development aid project. In other words, we need to recognize that there are concrete mechanisms—such as development aid in the service of another nation's GWOT—which serve as geopolitical conduits through which such practices and ideologies continue to be propagated in recipient countries' language policy and educational regimes. In this interplay between colonially shaped practices and ideologies of English teaching and learning, US-Philippine relations, development aid, and GWOT, we see how language testing practices and ideologies built into the JEEP project are not simply located in a network of multilayered discourses and global/local politics. Rather, they themselves mobilize and enact imperial structures of relations. In the case of the Philippines and the United States, such structures or relations have been historically shaped by their intertwined but unequal colonial experience. Such mobilization and enactment have been enabled by present-day development aid as a colonial project (Slater and Bell, 2002).

Conclusion

Language testing in essence can never be completely "objective." It is always sited in a network of geopolitical, social, cultural, educational, and economic interests, even if the avowed intentions or aims are well-meaning. Language testing practices and ideologies must be liberated from "the prison of coloniality" (Quijano, 2007, p. 178), although transformative and resistive options are intricately woven into structural constraints in the light of the fact that the operationalization of such practices and ideologies is shaped and conditioned by powerful forces of domination much larger than the individual. Kumaravadivelu (2016) is poignant and frank here: "celebrations of sterile forms of resistance can only lull the marginalized into a false sense of liberation. It would be naïve to think that the passive tactics of the weak can deter the aggressive strategies of the strong" (p. 75). How can educational institutions and teachers located in flash points of conflict and economic poverty resist and alter conditions of coloniality when their opening up to much needed development aid and their general approval of native-speakerist, homogenous, and universalizing approaches to teaching and learning of English follow the imperial logic of domination in the first place?

Nevertheless—and precisely because of the overwhelming weight of domination on teachers, students, and schools that are themselves at the receiving end of such domination—the imperative to *act* against matrices of power (Kumaravadivelu, 2016) has never been more urgent and compelling. Thus, the initiative must come from the teachers, students, and schools themselves. The role of teachers especially is crucial here because, as far as their work in the classroom is concerned, the use of the software by itself is already a foregone conclusion. How does a teacher navigate the language of the placement tests when the native speaker as ideal norm is built into the software itself?

The assumption in this imperative to act, of course, is that teachers are already critically aware of the disempowering use of colonial vocabulary in which they participate in their perpetuation, foremost of which is the use of "native" and "non-native" categories in one's teaching and learning. If teachers and local education administrators are powerless in making decisions on whether JEEP should be inserted into their curricula, they can within their power conceptualize and conduct workshops and other learning opportunities. These activities should sensitize all those involved in the local implementation of the project to the sociolinguistic and cultural implications of embracing an ELT development aid project that uses a software developed elsewhere. Scholars clearly argue that this is not enough in attempting to act against structures of inequality and marginalization in the field (Kumaravadivelu, 2016; Tupas, 2004). However, this is a necessary starting point. One thing that teachers can do in the classroom, for example, if they are critically engaged in conversations about the ethical, ideological, cultural, and political problems with constructs like the "native" or the "non-native speaker" is to completely disregard "5.0 *Educated* native speaker" as the ultimate goal of English language learning that is prescribed through the JEEP-prescribed software.

Students must be relieved of the burden of aspiring to become educated native speakers because their participation in the use of colonial vocabulary in English language teaching and learning unnecessarily places them in positions of marginality and weakness. Repetition and automaticity in the use of exercises and placement tests in the software should not hide the fact that the educated native-speaker goal is completely unrealistic and unattainable. In fact, teachers may even decide not to play the vocabulary game further by renaming "4.0 Fluent non-native" into another that erases the underlying "deficit" assumption (Cook, 1999) of the placement label. Students, despite being "fluent," are defined by what they are not, that is, they are not native speakers. There are alternative achievable goals in English language learning and teaching, for example, Rampton's (1990) *expert speaker* that draws attention to the notion of competence not on terms of the native speaker but on terms of expert use of English in authentic and everyday contexts of communication in the world today. This strategic unframing and reframing of the placement tests away from the native-speaker ideal should be discussed with students. Thus, an alternative vocabulary demands expert use of English from *all* users of English—including the so-called native speakers—and the shared responsibility of making sure that communication is successful. The point here is to liberate oneself from the bondage of coloniality and, in this specific case, from the negative influence of a colonial (native-speakerist) professional vocabulary that defines much of our work as English language teachers.

Unfortunately, as we move beyond teachers' agency and capacity to act, as well as beyond the classroom, resistive possibilities become even more complex and challenging. It requires a government and institutions that are able to renegotiate the terms of discussion, but how is it possible to do this when much needed foreign aid for "development" might be lost? It looks like, at least on the level of coloniality of language testing, one key battleground remains the school, which can unpack for teachers the colonial vocabulary of tests, and English language teaching and learning in general. Teachers' professional development is crucial here, especially if it targets teacher ideology (Trueba and Bartolomé, 2000) as a key feature in helping teachers find their professional identity: "the need for clarity of political beliefs, practices, and commitments is as important as the actual pedagogical strategies used in instruction" (p. 278). Teachers may then be in a better position to scrutinize the JEEP project, the software and its placement tests, and their deep cultural, geopolitical, social, economic, and historical entanglements with global, national, and local affairs.

If the JEEP project defines the role of the teachers as facilitators of knowledge—which essentially means facilitators of knowledge produced outside the realms of their own cultural realities and experience—teachers may then reclaim the role of producers of knowledge alongside their students, vis-à-vis the colonial knowledge regimes that have produced it. Ultimately, teachers should seize upon these little opportunities and spaces of empowerment and use them to help students—through multilingual role plays and dialogues, self-assessments of multicompetence, direct and critical engagements with harmful concepts such as the native-speaker ideal, and development of alternative conceptions of expertise—become *expert users of English*.

References

Acheraïou, A. (2011). *Questioning Hybridity, Postcolonialism and Globalization*. London: Palgrave Macmillan.

Alatis, J. and Straehle, C. A. (2006). The universe of English. Imperialism, chauvinism, and paranoia. In K. Bolton and B. Kachru (Eds.), *World Englishes: Critical Concepts in Linguistics*, vol. 5 (pp. 250–70). London and New York: Routledge.

Ashcroft, B., Griffiths, G., and Tiffin, H. (1989). *The Empire Writes Back: Theory and Practice in Post-Colonial Criticism*. London and New York: Routledge.

Baş, G. (2010). Evaluation of DynED courses used in elementary schools from the views of teachers in Turkey. *Journal of Language and Linguistic Studies*, 6(1), 14–39.

Berowa, A. M. (2012). Factors affecting job Enabling English Proficiency (JEEP) Program: Students' willingness to communicate in English. *The Asian Conference on Language Learning 2012 Official Conference Proceedings* (pp. 124–38). Osaka, Japan.

Bingham, S. and Larson, E. (2006). Using CALL as the major element of study for a university English class in Japan. *JALT CALL Journal*, 2(3), 39–52.

Brown, I., Campbell, A. P., and Weatherford, Y. (2008). Using DynEd and ALC with low-level university freshmen. *The JALT CALL Journal*, 4(3), 37–53.

Canagarajah, A. S. (1999). *Resisting Linguistic Imperialism in English Teaching*. Oxford: Oxford University Press.

Canagarajah, S. (2006). Changing communicative needs, revised assessment objectives: Testing English as an international language. *Language Assessment Quarterly: An International Journal*, 3(3), 229–42.

Carothers, T. and De Gramont, D. (2013). *Development Aid Confronts Politics: The Almost Revolution*. Washington DC: Carnegie Endowment for International Peace.

Constantino, R. (1970). The mis-education of the Filipino. *Journal of Contemporary Asia*, *30*(3), 428–44.

Cook, V. (1999). Going beyond the native speaker in language teaching. *TESOL Quarterly*, *33*(2), 185–209.

Cook, V. (2001). Using the first language in the classroom. *The Canadian Modern Language Review*, *57*(3), 402–23.

Davies, A. (1996). Ironising the myth of linguicism. *Journal of Multilingual and Multicultural Development*, *17*(6), 485–96.

Dirlik, A. (1994). The postcolonial aura: Third World criticism in the age of global capitalism. *Critical Inquiry*, *20*(2), 328–56.

DynEd International, Inc. (2006). Teacher's guide for DynEd placement tests. Retrieved October 4, 2018 from https://www.msu.edu/course/esl/094/DynEdOLD/doc/pte.pdf

DynEd International, Inc. (2014). New dynamic English. Retrieved October 4, 2018, September 17, 2014 from https://www.dyned.com/us/products/newdynamicenglish

Gough, N. (2002). The long arm(s) of globalization: Transnational imaginaries in curriculum work. In William E. Doll and N. Gough (Eds.), *Curriculum Visions* (pp. 167–78). New York: Peter Lang.

Grosfoguel, R. (2011). Decolonizing post-colonial studies and paradigms of political-economy: Transmodernity, decolonial thinking, and global coloniality. *TRANSMODERNITY: Journal of Peripheral Cultural Production of the Luso-Hispanic World*, *1*(1), 1–37.

Holliday, A. (2006). Native-speakerism. *ELT Journal*, *60*(4), 385–87.

Hsu, F. (2015). The coloniality of neoliberal English: The enduring structures of American colonial English instruction in the Philippines and Puerto Rico. *L2 Journal*, *7*(3), 123–45.

Jenkins, J. and Leung, C. (2017). Assessing English as a lingua franca. In E. Shohamy (Ed.), *Language Testing and Assessment* (pp. 103–17). Cham: Springer International Publishing AG.

Kachru, B. B. (1996). World Englishes: Agony and ecstasy. *Journal of Aesthetic Education*, *30*(2), 135–55.

Kachru, B. B. (1997). English as an Asian language. In M. L. S. Bautista (Ed.), *English Is an Asian Language: The Philippines Context* (pp. 1–23). Sydney: The Macquarie Library Pty. Ltd.

Kramsch, C. (1998). The privilege of the intercultural speaker. In M. Byram and M. Fleming (Eds.), *Language Learning in Intercultural Perspective: Approaches Through Drama and Ethnography* (pp. 16–31). Cambridge: Cambridge University Press.

Kumaravadivelu, B. (2006). Dangerous liaison: Globalization, empire and TESOL. In J. Edge (Ed.), *(Re-)locating TESOL in an Age of Empire* (pp. 1–26). London: Palgrave Macmillan.

Kumaravadivelu, B. (2016). The decolonial option in English teaching: Can the subaltern act? *TESOL Quarterly*, *50*(1), 66–85.

Kunnan, A. J. (2009). Testing for citizenship: The U.S. naturalization test. *Language Assessment Quarterly*, 6(1), 89–97.

Laudencia, E. H. R. (2017). *Politics of Aid in Conflict Areas: Case of Mindanao, Philippines*. MA Thesis, Seoul National University.

Macedo, D. (2017). Imperialist desires in English-Only language policy. *The CATESOL Journal*, 29(1), 81–110.

Maldonado-Torres, N. (2007). On the coloniality of being: Contributions to the development of a concept. *Cultural Studies*, 21(2–3), 240–70.

Miller, S. C. (1982). *Benevolent Assimilation: The American Conquest of the Philippines, 1899–1903*. New Heaven: Yale University Press.

Ndlovu-Gatsheni, S. J. (2013). The entrapment of Africa within the global colonial matrices of power: Eurocentrism, coloniality, and deimperialization in the twenty-first century. *Journal of Developing Societies*, 29(4), 331–53.

Pennycook, A. (2007). ELT and colonialism. In J. Cummins and C. Davidson (Eds.), *International Handbook of English Language Teaching* (pp. 13–24). Boston, MA: Springer.

Pepper, M. (2006). No corporation left behind: How a century of illegitimate testing has been used to justify internal colonialism. *Monthly Review*, November, 38–47.

Phillipson, R. (1992). *Linguistic Imperialism*. Oxford: Oxford University Press.

Phillipson, R. (2007). Linguistic imperialism: A conspiracy, or a conspiracy of silence? *Language Policy*, 6(3–4), 377–83.

Quijano, A. (2007). Coloniality and modernity/rationality. *Cultural Studies*, 21(2–3), 168–78.

Rampton, B. (1990). Displacing the "native speaker": Expertise, affiliation and inheritance. *ELT Journal*, 44, 97–101.

Shajahan, R. A. (2013). Coloniality and a global testing regime in higher education: Unpacking the OECD's AHELO initiative. *Journal of Education Policy*, 28(5), 676–94.

Shohamy, E. (2017). Critical language testing. In E. Shohamy, I. G. Or, and S. May (Eds.), *Language Testing and Assessment* (3rd ed.), (pp. 441–54). Cham: Springer.

Slater, D. and Bell, M. (2002). Aid and the geopolitics of the post-colonial: Critical reflections on New Labour's overseas development strategy. *Development and Change*, 33(2), 335–60.

Spolsky, B. (2004). *Language Policy*. Cambridge: Cambridge University Press.

Stuebner, W. A. and Hirsch, R. (2010). Mindanao: A community-based approach to counterinsurgency. *PRISM*, 1(3), 129–38.

Tabiola, H. (2015). *Uncovering Ideology in an ELT Aid: The Case of a Recipient Tertiary Institution in the Southern Philippine*. MA Thesis, Ateneo de Manila University.

Tabiola, H. and Lorente, B. (2017). Neoliberalism in ELT aid: Interrogating a USAID ELT project in southern Philippines. In M. C. Flubacher and A. Del Percio (Eds.), *Language, Education and Neoliberalism: Critical Studies in Sociolinguistics* (pp. 122–39). Bristol: Multilingual Matters.

Trueba, E. and Bartolomé, L. (2000). Beyond the politics of schools and the rhetoric of fashionable pedagogies: The significance of teacher ideology. In E. Trueba and L. Bartolomé (Eds.), *Immigrant Voices: In Search of Educational Equity* (pp. 277–92). Lanham: Rowman & Littlefield.

Tupas, R. (2004). The politics of Philippine English: Neocolonialism, global politics, and the problem of postcolonialism. *World Englishes, 23*(1), 47–58.

Tupas, R. (2015). Inequalities of multilingualism: Challenges to mother tongue-based multilingual education. *Language and Education, 29*(2), 112–24.

Tupas, R. and Tabiola, H. (2017). Language policy and development aid: A critical analysis of an ELT project. *Current Issues in Language Planning, 18*(4), 407–21.

Vellema, S., Borras, S. M. J., and Lara, F. J. (2011). The agrarian roots of contemporary violent conflict in Mindanao, Southern Philippines. *Journal of Agrarian Change, 11*(3), 298–320.

Reforming Foreign Language Teaching Policy in Japan: The Politics of "Standardization"

Masaki Oda

Introduction

This chapter discusses cases in which standardized tests and their scores are used to legitimate implementation of language policies in education. I will focus on the significance of these standardized tests in several contexts, particularly those that appear in newspapers, in the production of news stories. In addition, I investigate how these stories in combination with different layers of gatekeeping processes influence the formulation of learners' beliefs about learning foreign languages including English and their subsequent attitudes and actions (cf. Oda, 2014).

The Ministry of Education, Culture, Sports, Science and Technology of Japan (MEXT) conducts a survey on English language education in Japanese schools every year since 2012, and it publishes a report in the following year. When *Heisei 27 nendo Eigo Kyouiku Jisshi Jyokyo Chosa* [A survey on the Status of English Language Education 2015] was published in April 2016 (MEXT, 2016), for example, most major newspapers reported this survey to the general public as it is an important topic many people are interested in. Some of the headlines are presented below:

中高生の英語力、国の目標に届かず [Proficiency of English among secondary students has not reached the goal set by the government.] (*Yomiuri* (Japanese), April 4, 2016)

英語力、高校は群馬、中学は千葉が1位、都道府県別データ公表、文科省調査 [Gumma is the highest for upper secondary, while Chiba claims the first place for lower secondary, prefecture by prefecture data have been published for the MEXT survey on English language education.] (*Sankei Shimbun* (Japanese), April 5, 2016)

生徒の英語力、文科省初公表、中学は千葉、高校は群馬が1位 [Survey on English Language education, Published to the public for the first time by MEXT, Chiba is in the first place for lower secondary, Gumma is in the first place for the upper secondary.] (*Nikkei* (Japanese) April 4, 2016)

The 2015 survey was composed of five parts: (1) students' proficiency of English, (2) teachers' proficiency of English, (3) opportunities of using English, (4) involvement of assistant language teachers (ALTs), and (5) utilization of information and communication technology (ICT). Among the five areas, however, the issue of English language proficiency is of mass media interest as you can see from the headlines.

In the articles above, the journalists' attention was paid to (1) students' proficiency of English and (2) teachers' proficiency of English. In the actual survey, the former is based on the students' self-declaration and/or their teachers' perception of whether or not a student has attained a certain level of *Eiken* (Step), one of the most widely used tests for English language proficiency in Japan (*Overview of the Eiken tests*, 2019), while the latter is also based on self-declaration by the teachers on whether or not they have attained the Pre-1st level of *Eiken* or equivalent scores in other standardized tests including *TOEFL* and *TOEIC L&R* tests.

According to the *Overview of the Eiken tests* (2019), the number of examinees has exceeded more than 95 million since its inception. The tests have undergone several revisions. Currently it offers seven levels: 1st, Pre-1st, 2nd, Pre-2nd, 3rd, 4th, and 5th, with the 1st being the highest. They are basically Pass or Fail tests, and if an examinee has attained a required score for each level, she or he will be awarded a certificate of attainment. The *Eiken* levels are also used as a reference to indicate scores in other standardized English tests such as *TOEFL* or *IELTS*, simply because of its popularity among the Japanese general public. On the "research" section of the *Eiken* website, various studies primarily report on the validity of the tests, and a score comparison table among *Eiken*, *TOEFL (PBT and iBT)*, and *Common European Framework of References (CEFR)* is also often reported (http://www.eiken.or.jp/eiken/en/research/). As Eiken has been one of the most widely used tests for English language proficiency in Japan, Japanese mass media often use it as a benchmark for indicating English language proficiency. The scores in other standardized tests such as the *TOEFL iBT* are often supplemented with a description such as "equivalent to *Eiken* level 2," despite the fact that the objectives and constructs of these tests are different from each other.

The survey has been influential in many respects. First, it was conducted and published by MEXT, and thus is the "official" one. Because of this status, it is easy for many journalists to cite it to validate their stories, at least superficially. For many people, these stories appear to be convincing, and thus they are likely to accept them without criticism, because very few, if any, alternatives are provided. In other words, these news stories were produced after going through multiple layers of filters to appear valuable to the readers (Allan, 1999). Second, while the standardized tests, particularly *Eiken* levels, are used as indicators of English language proficiency of both students and teachers, these newspaper articles do not provide sufficient background information on these tests to the readers. Using standardized test scores would be "interpreted by the public as a sign of a serious and meaningful attitude towards education" (Shohamy, 2001, p. 39) and thus is often enough to satisfy the readers, even though the validity of the tests is not necessarily justified.

Standardized Tests as "the" Indicators of Language Proficiency?

As mentioned in the introduction, the newspapers reported the results of the survey, primarily focusing on students' proficiency of English. Among the three articles mentioned earlier, the article in the *Yomiuri* on April 4, 2016, focused on the fact that neither at the upper secondary (ages 15 to 18) nor at the lower secondary (ages 12 to 14) levels, the students' levels of English language proficiency met the expectations of the policy makers. More specifically, only 34.3 percent of the twelfth graders (upper secondary) have attained *Eiken* Pre-2nd level, which is perceived as equivalent to the completion of tenth- to eleventh-grade English, and 36.6 percent have attained *Eiken* level 3, which is equivalent to the completion of ninth-grade (lower secondary) English. Also highlighted were a table that revealed prefecture-by-prefecture averages of the results, which was highlighted in the headline and the percentages of upper and lower secondary school English teachers who had achieved the level equivalent to *Eiken* Pre-1st level (university level) but without any comments.

The article on *Sankei Shimbun* on April 5, 2016, had also focused on the students' English language proficiency as it was in the *Yomiuri* article. However, the article also described the teachers' English language proficiency and questioned the reliability of the survey itself as it had included both the students' self-declaration and their teachers' perception of whether or not a student has attained a certain level of *Eiken* tests.

Finally, the article on *Nikkei* on April 4, 2016, reported as if the survey had been on the students' English language proficiency and compared the rankings among the forty-seven prefectures for both upper secondary and lower secondary levels. While the article noted that *Eiken* Pre-2nd and 3 levels had been based on the respondents' perceptions and thus warned the readers to interpret the results carefully, a large part of the article was dedicated to discussing which prefecture had performed better, accompanied with a table listing average scores for each of the forty-seven prefectures.

We understand from various studies in media discourse (van Ginneken, 1998) that each journalist has a different story she or he wants to write in a given space in order to attract audience. In light of this reality, of interest is how these three articles reported on the survey differently. The article authors also seemed more interested in the fact that standardized tests (including *Eiken* tests) are perceived as a reliable indicator in the survey and the newspapers appear to accept the results of the survey without any criticism. I will, therefore, examine the power of such standardized tests in relation to the beliefs about language proficiency by teachers and students.

University Entrance Examination Reform and Standardized Tests

In July 2017, MEXT announced a proposal of new national university entrance examinations, which would replace the current examination, National Center Test for University Admissions (NCTUA) administered by the National Center for University Entrance Examinations (NCUEE). The examination includes "Foreign Language" that is a required subject for upper secondary schools nationwide. Theoretically, a student can select any foreign language available at his or her school. However, English is the only language available at many schools and thus is the de facto foreign language for students. While the current NCTUA still has options of Chinese, French, German, and Korean, only 997 out of 541,335 examinees (0.18 percent) selected the language other than English in the exam administered in January 2018 according to NCUEE (2018a). The current English examination is comprised of a written test for eighty minutes, which is worth 80 percent of the score, and a listening test for sixty minutes (thirty minutes for listening and thirty minutes for responding), which is worth the remaining 20 percent of the total score (NCUEE, 2018c).

A new proposed examination will be launched in 2020. At the time of writing, the plan is that, instead of NCUEE producing its own English test to replace the current one. Since the announcement of the plan was made in 2017, it has generated overwhelming media attention.

On November 1, 2017, NCUEE issued a call for participation for providers of English standardized tests in the new university entrance examination system. The guidelines issued by the NCUEE (2018b) list various conditions that the test providers are expected to meet. I would like to address the following four conditions placed on the tests themselves:

1. The test has been used by upper secondary students and/or [as a credential of] university admission in Japan.
2. The test can measure four skills (Reading, Writing, Listening, Speaking) in a single test administration, and the provider will be able to present scores for each of four skills.
3. The test is consistent with *Courses of Study for Upper Secondary Schools*, the national curriculum guideline.
4. The test provider has shown the correspondence relationship between the test scores and Common European Framework of Reference for Languages (CEFR) including research findings as evidence and a system to verify it.

After several months of evaluation period, NCUEE announced the list of eight standardized tests that had qualified for the new university entrance examination system on March 26, 2018. These tests included *The Cambridge English Exam Series*, *The Test of English as a Foreign Language (TOEFL)*, *The Test of English for International Communication L & R; S & W (TOEIC)*, *The Global Test of English for Communication. (GTEC)*, *The Test of English for Academic Purposes (TEAP)*, *The Test of English for Academic Purposes Computer Based Test (TEAP CBT)*, *Eiken*, and *The International English Language Testing System (IELTS)*. Since then, the test providers and various sectors in English language teaching industry have aggressively promoted their tests, study aid books, learning materials, and preparation courses by providing the consumers very limited pieces of information. For the consumers, including upper secondary students and their parents, newspaper articles are their main source of information for the new university entrance examinations. Therefore, they eagerly seek information from the limited news resources available to them, despite the fact that the details of the new examination have not been fully decided.

It should also be noted that even though the new university entrance examination system attracts media attention, it is reasonable to assume that the new examination system would affect only a particular groups of upper secondary school graduates who apply for admission to colleges or universities. Estimating from the fact that 54.8 percent of upper secondary school graduates entered colleges/universities in the same year (MEXT, 2017a), and given that the majority of private universities do not require their applicants to take the NCTUA and probably its successor as well, the new examination system is not expected to affect a large portion of upper secondary school graduates.

In 2017, 616,584 students entered four-year universities across Japan. If we look at the type of admission, at least 273,025 (approximately 44.3 percent) students had been accepted into the institutions in the schemes (AO or Commendation admission schemes) that do not normally require paper and pen exams including the existing NCTUA. If we just consider private universities, the rate rises to 51.2 percent (249,398 out of 486,857), according to the report issued by MEXT (2017b). Furthermore, I add that even though the students had been required to take paper and pen exams, they would not have necessarily been the NCUEE examination. Nevertheless, the impact of the proposed change is predicted to be far more impactful for three main reasons. First, it would play a significant influence on what will be taught at English classes at upper secondary schools. The MEXT publishes the *Courses of Study* (COS), the national set of guidelines for school education in Japan. These guidelines, which are available in Japanese, are revised and published approximately every ten years. The schools in Japan, including primary and secondary schools from grades 1 through 12, have to plan their instruction based on the COS. However, provisional English translations of some key documents of the most recent edition are also accessible through the MEXT website. In the most recent revision, two keywords—"Four Skills" and "CEFR (equivalence)"—appear as key concepts in the section of English as a subject (MEXT 2018c). This corresponds with the newspaper discourse of the new NCUEE examinations, which will be discussed in this chapter, suggesting that the planning must have been taken place at the same time. However, it is possible to say that they are closely related with each other. Second, NCUEE examinations have served as an indicator of "ideal" competency to be achieved at the completion of upper secondary schools. Whether or not it is reflective of a particular context, the proficiency defined for English (or any foreign language) test by NCUEE will become a benchmark in determining "realistic" goal of

English language teaching at each school. Third, and perhaps most important, the new university entrance examination system proposed by NCUEE, particularly the use of commercial standardized tests, has been picked up as a topic of newspaper article quite frequently since the plan was announced. Regardless of whether one is going take the examination or not, the repeated appearance of the topic is likely to frame the reader's perception of desired "proficiency" in English with limited information. In light of these developments, in the next section, I will present my analysis of how these standardized tests are illustrated in the context of the new university entrance examination system and their potential impact on secondary schools, and how their implementation might affect readers' attitudes toward learning English.

Language Tests in the News

Since the announcement of the plan to reform the NCTUA, Japanese major newspapers have published numerous articles on the topic. The issue of using commercial standardized test of English alone has been featured in many occasions. As I have discussed above, these articles are likely to serve as a major source of information for the general public, and thus it is worth investigating what the people are exposed to. Some scholars have analyzed newspaper discourse to investigate the roles discourse practices play in shaping the norms of learning and teaching English as a social practice and, consequently, how they influence the formulation of beliefs and subsequent actions. Mirhosseini (2014), for example, investigated the ideological assumption of teaching English in Iran by analyzing advertisements of private language institutes that appeared in a major Iranian newspaper and concluded that "a complex ideology of ELT [English language teaching] emerges that, upon repeated encounters, become naturalized and influence the public opinion about what language education involves" (pp. 13-14). The cases presented in his article address policy changes initiated by government agencies. In other words, these institutions have power to begin with, and they already decided that the new examination system would be implemented. However, I am particularly interested in finding out if the conclusion drawn on the process of the naturalization of ideology among the general public discussed by Mirhosseini also applies to the issues discussed in this chapter.

To this end, I analyzed articles on major Japanese newspapers published between January and March 2018. The period coincides with the time the NCUEE was evaluating which standardized tests would qualify as replacements of the current English test of the NCTUA. In order to select the articles, I used online database systems of the three major newspapers (*Asahi, Mainichi, Yomiuri*) and searched for articles by putting two keywords in Japanese, 入試 [entrance exam] and 民間試験 [exams administered by nongovernment sectors], as these are the words often used to describe English language tests in the new entrance examination system. After the articles with the keywords were identified, only those related to the use of commercial standardized tests were selected for analysis.

A total of seventy-four articles, including twenty-one from *Asahi*, thirty-two from *Yomiuri*, and twenty-one from *Mainichi*, were analyzed. These articles include both those from national and regional editions of these newspapers.

The purpose of the analysis was not to count the frequency of particular keywords that appeared in the newspapers. In fact, the data above are not reliable for quantitative analysis as a number of articles from local editions cite a part of the articles published in the national edition, hence resulting in some level of overlap. Instead, I critically looked at the issues, "Four skills" and "CEFR," highlighted in the articles that discussed the new NCUEE examinations. An attempt was made to find out the process in and through which the definition of "proficiency" was shaped by newspaper discourse, which subsequently contributed to emergent beliefs about learning foreign languages (including English) among the general public.

Next, it should be noted that the questions in university entrance examinations, including those in the current NCTUA, are supposed to reflect what the examinees should have learned at upper secondary schools. Therefore, it is natural that these keywords would effectively display that the new NCUEE examination corresponds with the revised COS discussed earlier (MEXT 2018c), regardless of whether or not "Four skills" and/or "CEFR" were fully understood by the journalists who wrote the articles. The journalists must have believed that it would be "newsworthy" to discuss "Four skills" and "CEFR" in connection with the proposed new NCUEE examination. They reproduce the discourse of dominant ideology, in this case, superficial legitimation of the new NCUEE examination, by having their audience repeatedly exposed to the keywords. As van Dijk (2008) points out, the media including newspaper articles not only reproduce the ideologies of the people and/or institutions with power but also confirm and legitimate the power further when the keywords are routinely appeared in the news on the new NCUEE examination. With this observation in mind, I thought it was worthwhile to look at this mechanism through excerpts from newspaper articles. Finally, as all the articles are in Japanese, English translations are provided by me. I have made my best effort to preserve the meanings of the original message in order to illustrate the problems clearly.

Four Skills

The term "Four skills" appears very frequently in the analyzed articles. As discussed, the term appears as a feature of the new NCUEE examination system.

2020年度から始まる大学入学共通テストは英語の「4技能」を測るため

民間試験を活用する。[The university entrance examination system which Starts in 2020 will utilize commercial standardized test to measure the "four skills" of English.] (*Asahi Shimbun*, February 24, 2018)

...文部科学省の共通テスト実施方針では、24年度からは英語は「聞く、読む、

話す、書く」の4技能を測れる民間試験に全面移行するが... [According to the Implementation policy by MEXT, English test will completely have been transferred to Commercial standardized tests in 2024 in order to measure the "four skills."] (*Yomiuri Shimbun*, March 9, 2018)

As we can see from the excerpts above, the articles report that the rationale behind using commercial standardized tests in the new university entrance examination system is that these tests can measure the "four skills." However, policy makers including MEXT and NCUEE have not provided any clear explanation for why they need to measure the "four skills" in English. Moreover, no information has been available to the general public regarding why "commercial" tests have to be used. Despite these concerns, however, "four skills" appears in the articles to represent innovation in language teaching and thus something desirable to the general public.

While some are critical of utilizing commercial standardized tests to replace current English test in NCTUA discussed earlier, the idea of the "four skills" was never criticized in the articles, despite the fact that the validity of four skills in language teaching has been questioned by some scholars for many years. Holliday (2005), for example, describes the term as "a long standing cultural icon in English-speaking Western TESOL" (p. 43) and warns that the discourse of "four skills" is often interpreted "as the natural, default mechanism for solving curriculum problems" (p. 43). Toh (2016) in his discussion of English in Japanese higher education also points out that university English courses in Japan are "invariably be broken down into Reading, Writing, Speaking and Listening components" (p. 141), which makes it easier for policy makers, schools, as well as textbook publishers to provide a plausible framework for their purposes. Timetables, textbooks, and assessments are generally arranged around the four skills. In other words, everything seems to be set up with very little room for negotiation before the information is presented to the general public. In other words, the general public is exposed to the "four skills" as a default framework for discussing learning English language, without being given any alternatives.

The widespread discourse of "four skills" is illustrated in Abe (2018) who devoted a chapter to the topic in his book on language policy in education in Japan. He highlighted that "four skills" has been interpreted differently at the convenience of policy makers of the time and pointed out that the objective of the "four skills" approach in ELT in Japan is to master each of these skills in a balanced way. This approach has been used to criticize prevailing teaching styles in English language classrooms in Japanese schools where the language is often taught through grammar-translation (pp. 92–93). The "four skills" approach was used by policy makers to promote "communication" over "structure" in the 1990s, which resulted in producing large cohorts of learners without basic skills. This was done by equating communication with oral skills, namely, listening and speaking. As a result, oral skills (listening and speaking) were emphasized at the expense of reading and writing. This new initiative led to the addition of the listening component of English test in the NCTUA in 2006, in partial fulfillment of the demands for increasing oral skill components in ELT.

Relatedly, Abe (2018) notes that "four skills" actually refers to the addition of a speaking component. However, the use of the term was effective enough to make the readers believe that, in the context to university entrance examination, the addition of a speaking component to the testing is necessary, thereby helping policy makers to instantly legitimize their agenda and, subsequently, helping test producers and textbook publishers as well. Crucially, the discourse of the "four skills" also appeared in the article featuring English language teaching at secondary schools.

[最前線]「話す」英語都立高入試に4技能重視広がる

[[Frontline] "Speaking" to be added in the entrance exam of Tokyo Metropolitan Public Upper Secondary School—Emphasis on The four skills is expanding.]   (*Yomiuri*, January 26, 2018)

This headline illustrates the issues discussed above, that is, a confusion between an addition of speaking and the "four skills" as well as the overgeneralization of the discourse of the "four skills" in university entrance examinations to secondary education. The article begins with a description of the three components— Reading, Writing, and Listening—of the new entrance exam of Tokyo Metropolitan Public Upper Secondary Schools. This description is followed by a detailed description of the Speaking component, which is a highlight of the new examination. The writer says that the addition of the Speaking component is a reflection of the proposed adaptation of commercial standardized tests in the university entrance examination.

> …背景には英語教育で4技能重視が強まっていることがある。（Snip）
> 大学入試センター試験に代わって20年度導入される大学入学共通テスト
> では、実用英語検定試験（英検）など4技能を測る民間試験が活用される。

> [The background for [the addition of Speaking component] is an increasing emphasis of the "four skills" in English Language Teaching. (Snip) In the new University Entrance Examination system which will be introduced in 2020 to replace the [current] NCTUA, commercial standardized tests such as *Eiken* will be utilized.] (*Yomiuri*, January 26, 2018)

From the above, it is clear that the addition of speaking components to the entrance exam at secondary level is discussed in connection with the new NCUEE examination system in which commercial standardized tests are used as they are supposed to measure the "four skills." *Eiken*, one of the major English standardized tests in Japan, is cited as an example of the standardized tests in this article that was written on January 26, 2018, despite the fact that the test was not identified as among the qualified standardized tests announced by the NCUEE on March 26, 2018. Finally, the article concluded with the following quotation from an academic:

> 「中学校では4技能が定着してきており、高校入試の4技能は当然の流れと言える。ただ高校だけで4技能のテストを行うのは難しい。東京都教委のように、採点や試験運営のノウハウを持つ民間試験団体の協力を得て、導スを探るのが現実的な選択だ」と話している

> [As the "four skills" is entrenched in lower secondary schools, it is natural that the entrance examinations for the upper secondary school becomes "four skills" exams. Therefore, it is a realistic choice for us to cooperate with commercial

exam organizations who are familiar with scoring and test administration.] (*Yomiuri*, January 26, 2016)

According to van Dijk (2008), the voices of experts often reinforce the messages that appear in articles, especially when readers have limited access to relevant information. Given van Dijk's observation, the excerpt above is likely to appear plausible. Thus, many readers without relevant information would believe that the "four skills" is something good after reading the article. It is evident from the discussion above, however, that we are apparently talking about the "four skills" without knowing what exactly the term is referring to.

Common European Framework of Reference

The Common European Framework of Reference (CEFR) is another term that has appeared very frequently in the articles I have analyzed. It is a framework that "provides a common basis for the elaboration of language syllabus, curriculum guidelines, examinations, textbooks, etc. across Europe" (Council of Europe, 2001, p. 1). In the articles that were analyzed, the CEFR appears as follows:

受験生は文科省が対象と認めた民間試験を高校3年の4月~12月まで2回受験できる。成績は素点と、国際的指標の「CEFR」に基づく初心者「A1」からネーティブに近い「C2」までの6段階の評価が大学に送られる。[Applicants [of universities/colleges] can take a commercial standardized test twice between April and December.

The grade will be given in raw score and a six-point scale grade between "A1," a basic user, and "C2," near native proficiency according to CEFR, an international index, and be sent directly to the institutions.] (*Mainichi*, February 19, 2018)

This article is misleading, however, because it describes CEFR as an international index. In other words, the readers of the newspapers are neither provided sufficient nor correct information. In the proposed new examination system, CEFR levels will be used as a benchmark for comparing the eight commercial standardized tests approved by the NCUEE mentioned earlier. Unlike the idea of "four skills," which seemed to be already a part of routine discourse of MEXT and NCUEE, some articles were critical of the use of the CEFR scale as the benchmark.

ビジネスや留学など目的が異なる複数の試験のスコアを比べられるよう、文科省は各試験の得点が国際基準「CEFR（セファール）」の6段階のレベルのどこに当たるかを示す対照表を作った。だが公平性に懸念の声も上がる。

[MEXT produced a table which enables us to compare scores of tests with different objectives including business and study-abroad based on the six level scale of CEFR, the international standard. However, some questions its fairness.]
(*Asahi*, March 27, 2018)

Significantly, the article questions the fairness of the conversion table, noting specifically that the table was based on the score conversion tables supplied by the testing organizations themselves without verification. On the other hand, CEFR's hypothetical status as the international standard is still alive and strong in the newspaper articles without receiving any criticism. The implementation of foreign language teaching policy in reference to CEFR is not unique to Japan, however. As Shohamy (2019) maintained, governments "adopt the CEFR, no questions asked, and view it as the ultimate definition of language proficiency" (p. 276). From the excerpts presented above, we can assert that the CEFR is in the process of becoming the ultimate definition of language proficiency among the Japanese general public, given its endorsement in the news. The general public, particularly those students who are going to take the new NUCEE entrance examinations as well as their parents, need to understand the theoretical rationale underpinning CEFR, however. Specifically, they should be provided with sufficient information to make a series of key decisions at various stages when they prepare to take (or decide against taking) the new NUCEE examinations.

Dealing with News Stories

In earlier section, I discussed the ways in which news stories are formulated. News stories are produced after going through multiple layers of filters to appear valuable to the readers (Allan, 1999). As far as the newspaper articles I have analyzed are concerned, the news stories successfully corresponded with the policy makers' agenda. In order for the proposed new university entrance examination system to be accepted, particularly by students who are going to take the exam in the next few years as well as their parents, policy makers need to inform them that the new system is better than the existing one. In the case of English in the new entrance examination system, policy makers need to convince the students and their parents that the use of commercial standardized tests will be more beneficial than taking the existing NCTUA produced by the NCUEE.

Looking at the newspaper articles above, the readers were not given sufficient information on some of the crucial items necessary for them to make a fair judgment on whether the proposed new university entrance examination system is beneficial or not. As Shohamy (2006) pointed out, language policies "are mostly manifestations of intentions" (p. 51) of policy makers, in this case, the MEXT or perhaps the NCUEE. The newspaper articles analyzed above suggest that the information in the articles had already been aligned with the policy makers' agenda.

While it is not clear whether the policy makers had any direct or indirect control on the production of the "stories" published in the newspaper articles analyzed in this paper, it is apparent that the articles reflect the policy makers' intentions and reinforce these intentions by the time the information is shared with the readers. The writers of the articles can take advantage of the access to relevant background information surrounding the proposed new university entrance examinations as well as the commercial standardized tests to be used as a part of the new examination system. They can then select what to include in their articles. In other words, they can control the readers' access to information in order for their stories to be aligned with their intentions (van Dijk, 2008).

As discussed, the readers are presented with information through the articles as though the idea of the "four skills" is fait accompli, with the CEFR presented as the international standard. Given the time available for the general public before the new exam system is implemented, most readers often have no choice but to decide on their actions based on the limited amount of information available to them. Furthermore, each of the eight approved commercial standardized English tests has different targets with different purposes. For example, *TOEIC* is designed to measure proficiency in business communication, while *TOEFL* is primarily for measuring the examinees' readiness to begin studying at universities in North America. In addition, *Eiken*, which is among the most popular standardized English examinations in Japan, is basically a pass–fail test, while the scores of *IELTS* are divided into seven different bands. Therefore, it is difficult to compare scores of these standardized English tests and convert them to an index that was originally designed to deal with the diverse languages in Europe.

Most of the news stories analyzed in this study have included the details discussed above, even though these are crucial for the general public to make a decision on how to deal with the new entrance examination. van Dijk (2008) states that in media encounters, such as the cases discussed in this study, "the relative position and power of news actors, and journalists usually determine who may have access to whom" (p. 68). Whether or not the policy makers, including the MEXT and the NCUEE as news actors and the journalists, made any coordination efforts in creating these news stories, the important details discussed in this section have not been presented to the readers. Put simply, we can say from the cases discussed in this chapter that a new policy can be implemented in a short time by constructing stories to align with policy makers' agenda. This is done by deliberately selecting the readers' access to information that would elicit questions and/or protests for the implementation of the new policy.

Conclusion

In this chapter, I have attempted to illustrate the power of the mass media that affects the implementation of new foreign language teaching policies, with special attention given to how standardized tests appear in the media discourse in relation to the policy makers' agenda. When a new policy is proposed, policy makers work hard to implement it smoothly within a limited term. As far as foreign language teaching and learning are concerned, standardized tests scores are often used as an indicator of language proficiency or, as Shohamy (2001) notes, "a sign of a serious and meaningful attitude towards education" (p. 39) to the public. This is further reinforced by repeated uses of terms like "four skills" and "CEFR" by the mass media. These terms in addition to some standardized tests such as *Eiken*, *TOEFL*, or *TOEIC* are familiar to the public, because they always appear in media discourse in association with the topics in foreign language teaching, even though many people in the general public know what each of them exactly is. From the analysis presented in this chapter, it was found that such superficial familiarity of these key terms helps the policy makers' agenda be executed smoothly.

The lack of access to the relevant information often becomes a major determining factor in shaping the final decision. In fact, such cases have been reported in the context of a vote on commercial whaling at an international conference (Takahashi, 1991) and a vote on the Proposition 63: California English Language Amendment in 1986 (Dyste, 1989). In both of the studies, the authors concluded that access of the relevant information had played significant roles in determining voting behaviors. These findings correspond with the cases presented in this chapter. The readers of the newspaper articles have to make their decisions without being aware of the fact that their own beliefs have already been controlled by the media discourse.

Finally, the point Mirhosseini (2014) has made in his paper that "a complex ideology of ELT [English language teaching] emerges that, upon repeated encounters, become naturalized and influence the public opinion about what language education involves" (pp. 13–14) is also valid in the cases presented in this chapter. Repeated encounters of limited concepts and underlying ideologies to support them are effective enough in reinforcing the support for the agenda set by the policy makers. That the policies had already been put in effect by the time the general public became aware of the validity of the news stories they had read made the policies themselves questionable.[1]

Note

1 This work was supported by JSPS KAKENHI Grant Number JP 18K00792.

References

Abe, M. (2018). *Shijo Saiaku no Eigo Seisaku* [The Worst ever ELT policies]. Tokyo: a. Hitsuji Shobo.
Allan, S. (1999). *News Culture*. Buckingham: Open University Press.
Council of Europe. (2001). *Common European Framework of Reference for Languages: Learning, Teaching, Assessment*. Cambridge: Cambridge University Press.
Dyste, C. (1989). Proposition 63: The California English language amendment. *Applied Linguistics, 10*(3), 313–30.
Holliday, A. (2005). *The Struggle to Teaching English as an International Language*. Oxford: Oxford University Press.
Mirhosseini, S. A. (2014). Resisting magic waves: Ideologies of "English Language Teaching" in Iranian newspaper advertisements. *Discourse: Studies in the Cultural Politics of Education*, 1–16. DOI: 10.1080/01596306.2014.918462
MEXT. (2016). *Heisei 27 nendo Eigo Kyouiku Jisshi Jyokyo Chosa* [A survey on the Status of English Language Education 2015]. Tokyo: Author.
MEXT. (2017a). *MEXT Press Release, December 22, 2017*. Tokyo: Author. Retrieved from http://www.mext.go.jp/component/b_menu/other/__icsFiles/afieldfile/2018/02/05/1388639_1.pdf

MEXT. (2017b). *Heisei 29 nendo Kokkoushiritsu Daigaku Nyugakusha Senbatsu Jisshi Jyokyo* [A summary of college/university admission selection in 2017]. Tokyo: Author. Retrieved from http://www.mext.go.jp/b_menu/houdou/29/12/__icsFiles/afieldfile/2017/12/01/1398976_01.pdf

NCUEE. (2018a). *Heisei 29 nendo Daigaku Nyushi Sentaa Shiken Jisshi Kekka no Gaiyo* [A summary of NCTUA in 2017 Academic Year]. Tokyo:Author. Retrieved from http://www.dnc.ac.jp/albums/abm.php?f=abm00009782.pdf&n=2_%E5%AE%9F%E6%96%BD%E7%B5%90%E6%9E%9C%E3%81%AE%E6%A6%82%E8%A6%81.pdf

NCUEE. (2018b). *Daigaku Nyushi Seiseki Teikyo Sisutemu Sanka Yoken* [Requirements for participating in the University Entrance Examination Score Provider System]. Tokyo: Author. Retrieved from https://www.dnc.ac.jp/albums/abm.php?f=abm00011205.pdf&n=1_%E6%88%90%E7%B8%BE%E6%8F%90%E4%BE%9B%E3%82%B7%E3%82%B9%E3%83%86%E3%83%A0%E5%8F%82%E5%8A%A0%E8%A6%81%E4%BB%B6.pdf

NCUEE. (2018c). *Heisei 31 nendo Daigaku Nyushi Sentaa Shiken Shutsudai Kyouka/Kamoku no Shutsudai Houhou To*) [Subjects and Methods of NCTUA in 2019 Academic Year]. Tokyo: Author. Retrieved from https://www.dnc.ac.jp/albums/abm.php?f=abm00033209.pdf&n=31%E3%82%BB%E3%83%B3%E3%82%BF%E3%83%BC%E8%A9%A6%E9%A8%93%E5%AE%9F%E6%96%BD%E8%A6%81%E9%A0%85.pdf

Oda, M. (2014). Reconditioning the conditions for second language learning. In K. Sung and B. Spolsky (Eds.), *Conditions for English Language Teaching and Learning in Asia* (pp. 105–25). New Castle upon Tyne: Cambridge Scholars Publishing.

Overview of the Eiken Tests. (February 2019). Retrieved from http://www.eiken.or.jp/eiken/en/eiken-tests/overview

Shohamy, E. (2001). *The Power of Tests: A Critical Perspective on the uses of Language Tests*. Harlow: Longman.

Shohamy, E. (2006). *Language Policy: Hidden Agendas and New Approaches*. London: Routledge.

Shohamy, E. (2019). Critical language testing and English as a lingua franca: How can one help the other? In K. Murata (Ed.), *English-Medium Instruction from an English as a Lingua Franca Perspective: Exploring the Higher Education Context* (pp. 271–85). London: Routledge.

Takahashi, J. (1991). Kokusai Kaigi ni miru Nihonjin no Ibunka Koushou [Intercultural Negotiation Strategies among the Japanese at International Conferences]. In J. Takahashi, O. Nakayama, K. Midooka, and F. Watanabe (Eds.), *Ibunka e no Sutorateji* [Intercultural Communication Strategies] (pp. 181–201). Tokyo: Kawashima Shoten.

Toh, G. (2016). *English as a Medium of Instruction in Japanese Higher Education: Presumption, Mirage or Bluff*. Basingstoke: Palgrave McMillan.

Van Dijk, T. (2008). *Discourse and Power*. Basingstoke: Palgrave McMillan.

Van Ginneken, J. (1998). *Understanding Global News*. London: Sage Publications.

8

Sociopolitical Factors Surrounding the Rise and Demise of the National English Ability Test (NEAT) in South Korea

Gwan-Hyeok Im, Liying Cheng, and Dongil Shin

Introduction and Context

Language testing is inexorably linked to sociopolitical factors such as policy makers' intentions and public opinions (hereafter, stakeholders' values) in terms of initiating and using a language test (Fulcher, 2009; McNamara and Roever, 2006; Shin and Im, 2011). Traditionally, language testing has been regarded as a scientific inquiry devoid of value. However, ever since Messick (1989) articulated the social aspects of testing (i.e., value implications and consequences) in test validity, researchers have begun to pay attention to the perspective that language testing is interrelated with sociopolitical factors (Shin and Im, 2011; Shohamy, 1998, 2001, 2007; Spolsky, 2000). Despite the shift in research focus, to date there have been few empirical studies that have examined the sociopolitical factors of language testing. As McNamara (2005) pointed out, "all language testing is potentially political" (p. 368), so there is a critical need to look at how sociopolitical factors have been associated with language testing.

In order to build upon empirical studies on sociopolitical factors, this chapter explores standardized testing in South Korea (hereafter Korea), specifically the National English Ability Test (hereafter NEAT). In Korea, there had been public discourses about "ideal" English speakers and the issue that learners who have been taught English in educational settings cannot fluently speak even one English word to English-speaking people. These discourses had been corroborated by the government and news media in Korea since 2006. The discourse event of "TOEFL crisis"[1] (Shin, 2012) also stimulated the interests in a homegrown test of English, as the media critically reported about frustrated

TOEFL test takers in Korea. The new Presidential Transition Committee 2008 for president-elect Myungbak Lee announced the innovative agendas on English education, including the development of a newly government-led English proficiency test, NEAT. The NEAT's design included the assessment of four key English skills: listening, reading, speaking, and writing. The test was adapted for in three versions for different test populations: Level 1 for university students and adults and Level 2 and 3 for high school students. Level 1 was designed to measure business English skills to replace the Test of English for International Communication (TOEIC) designed by Educational Testing Service (ETS) in the United States, while both Level 2 and 3 were designed for university admissions to replace the English subject in the College Scholastic Ability Test (CSAT) in Korea (Korea Institute for Curriculum and Evaluation [KICE], 2011). Level 2 measured the English skills required in academic contexts, while Level 3 measured the English skills concerning everyday life situations (KICE, 2011). Universities had the option to use either Level 2 or Level 3 for university admissions: departments that required academic English skills tended to use the Level 2 scores, while departments that required more practical English skills usually used Level 3 scores (Kim et al., 2013).

The NEAT was initiated with two political purposes: to improve English education systems and to curb private spending on English education in Korea. As ways to disseminate the test, the NEAT was presented as the more effective substitute for the existing CSAT that only assessed the receptive reading and listening skills (Lee and Lee, 2016). However, the media covered the negative issues and problems, such as private education expenditure, raters, and scoring credibility (Shin and Cho, 2018), and it led to politicians' apprehensiveness about the NEAT. The substitution plan in the context of the CSAT system was not decided until 2013, and the state-administered NEAT was finally suspended by the subsequent government in 2014. Levels 2 and 3 were abolished in 2014, along with Level 1 in 2015, due to a lack of awareness and practicality. The development and use of the NEAT ceased after only seven years (2008–15).

The rise and demise of the NEAT demonstrates the influence of these sociopolitical factors. However, until this point, there has been little analysis of the sociopolitical factors associated with the introduction and termination of the full administration of the test (Lee and Lee, 2016; Shin, 2019; Shin and Cho, 2018). The purpose of this chapter is to understand the sociopolitical factors surrounding the rise and demise of the NEAT as well as the social impact of the NEAT on the Korean society and its education. Specifically, we discuss the sociopolitical factors surrounding the NEAT controversy as they relate to

Levels 2 and 3 because these two levels were supposed to be used for high-stakes decisions (i.e., university admissions).

Method

To explore the sociopolitical factors around the NEAT, a variety of sources were collected: (1) press releases by the Korean government, (2) research reports and forum documents issued by the Korean Institute for Curriculum and Evaluation (KICE), (3) the related media reportage, and (4) an interview with the team manager of the English education policy department in the Ministry of Education. Documents collected from these various sources helped us gain insights into the relevant research problem (Merriam, 1988). The press releases, research reports and forum documents, and the interview helped us identify the Korean government's intentions and perspectives toward the NEAT.

The KICE is a government-affiliated institute and conducts "a wide-range of research on curriculum and evaluation in elementary and secondary schools" (KICE, 2018, August 21, para 1). It played a main role in developing the NEAT. Therefore, research reports and forum documents from the institute were analyzed. NEAT-related news articles were gathered from two major newspapers in Korea, *Chosun Ilbo* and *JoongAng Ilbo*, which are the Korea's first and second daily newspapers by circulation (MediaX, 2018, February 2) and also are considered conservative. We wanted to examine the conservative newspapers' reaction to the testing policy when the conservative president made radical changes in English education and English language testing systems.

The news articles from *Chosun Ilbo* published between January 1, 2008, and January 31, 2014, were collected to provide clear examples for the perspectives of various stakeholders such as the government, teachers, professors, students, and parents. This time period was selected because it spanned the period from when the NEAT was initiated and terminated. To identify the pattern of the media's perspectives to the NEAT, two journal articles (Shin, 2012) were used because these studies were the first to look at the media's perspectives on the NEAT in Korea. Newspapers used in Shin (2012) was *JoongAng Ilbo*, which is the Korea's second top daily newspapers by circulation (MediaX, 2018, February 2). In Shin's (2012) studies, the scope of data collection of news articles from *JoongAng Ilbo* was restricted to the content appearing between December 21, 2007, and August 31, 2012. The year, 2007, was when excessive

Table 8.1 Overview of Data Collection

Time Published	Data Collected	Sources
January 2008–September 2013	Twenty press releases from the Ministry of Education	http://www.moe.go.kr
January 2006–December 2013	Three research reports and two forum documents from KICE and Ministry of Education	http://www.kice.re.kr http://www.moe.go.kr
January 1, 2008–January 31, 2014	Ninety-five newspaper articles from *Chosun Ilbo*	Newspaper archive
December 21, 2003–August 31, 2012	Twenty newspaper articles from *JoongAng Ilbo*	Newspaper archive
August 29, 2011	An interview with a team manager (Suk-Hwan Oh) in the Ministry of Education Science and Technology	Munhwa Broadcasting Corporation (MBC)

Table 8.2 Themes and Categories

Theme 1: A Push for a Domestic English Test
  Improving communication skills
  Private education
  TOEFL crisis

Theme 2: A Potential Trigger of Private Education
  Quality of test preparation in public schools
  Low difficulty in the NEAT

Theme 3: A Lack of Viability/Feasibility
  Raters
  Insufficient equipment and facilities for internet-based testing (IBT)

Theme 4: Heightened Consequences
  Unintended consequences
  Negative consequences

demand for the TOEFL iBT caused the TOEFL crisis in Korea. Then the urgent need for a standardized and externally developed test of English proficiency was widely discussed not only to gain credibility in the global market but also to demonstrate competitiveness compared to locally developed tests in Korea (Shin, 2012). Table 8.1 illustrates our data collection process.

This study adopted a document analysis procedure, which is an iterative process for researchers to skim, read, and interpret the document data (Bowen, 2009). This analysis involved two types of analysis: content analysis and thematic analysis. Content analysis includes organizing information into categories, and thematic analysis involves uncovering themes from the categories (Bowen, 2009). Codes were inductively generated from the data, followed by organizing the initial codes into categories and generating themes from the categories. The categories and themes identified in this study are illustrated in Table 8.2.

Our findings are reported by themes, and we provide relevant quotations and events to support the themes.

Findings

Kyung-ae Jin (2012), a director of the NEAT division at the KICE, provided the rationale for developing the NEAT. Lyle F. Bachman (2013), an eminent scholar in language testing, also endorsed the development of the NEAT, because measuring four skills, he thought, would result in positive washback on classroom teaching and learning in Korea—a similar situation that aimed to bring about positive washback through the Hong Kong Certification of Education in English (HKCEE) three decades ago (Cheng, 2005). However, testing is interrelated with sociopolitical factors (Cheng, 2014; Shohamy, 1998, 2001, 2007; Spolsky, 2000) and may result in unintended consequences. In this chapter, we describe the sociopolitical factors around the NEAT according to the following themes: a push for a domestic English test; a potential trigger of private education; a lack of viability/feasibility; and heightened consequences. Figure 8.1 illustrates how

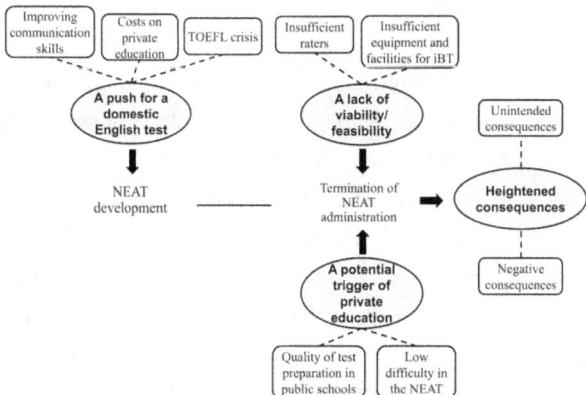

Figure 8.1 Themes and categories interrelated with the NEAT.
Note: Squircle = category; patterned oval = theme; black straight arrow = an indicator of casual relationship.

themes and categories are interrelated to the development and termination of the full administration of the NEAT and its consequences.

It should be noted that we could not find any discourses about the content of the NEAT. As of 2014, there were some pilot studies for the NEAT, but the test was not fully administered and it was subsequently terminated. Notably, the content of the NEAT was not a big concern to politicians and other stakeholders.

A Push for a Domestic English Test

In Korea, private education is a hotly contested social issue. Kang (2008, January 2) estimates the cost of private English education to be 10 trillion Won (i.e., US$885 million), but it is believed that Koreans' English proficiency levels still lag behind that of English language learners from Singapore and Hong Kong. Furthermore, the gap of access to educational resources in English between those who are economically advantaged and disadvantaged is getting bigger. The government stated that this social inequity can be resolved by enhancing English education in public schools. One of the ways the government sought to address this problem was to introduce a new English test, the NEAT. Suk-Hwan Oh, the team manager in the Ministry of Education Science and Technology, stated in the interview that "the government decided in 2008 to support changes to English education at school by developing the National English Ability Test" (Munhwa Broadcasting Corporation, 2011). He also mentioned that teachers at schools hardly taught English communication. He thought the CAST resulted in a negative washback effect, but by adopting the NEAT, there would be a positive washback effect to help students both improve their English communication skills and prepare for the test in schools. In line with the central government's plan for introducing the NEAT, local governments also planned to administer English programs to help students prepare for the test (S. H. Choi, 2008, August 26).

Indeed, the urge to develop a domestic English test in Korea was further stimulated by Koreans' lack of English communication skills since the existing CSAT did not measure speaking and writing skills. This shortcoming is also illustrated by media coverage that reported on Korean test takers' markedly low-ranking performance in international English tests, such as International English Language Testing System (IELTS) and TOEFL. Y. Oh (2008, June 5) in *Chosun Ilbo* stated that Korean test takers' scores on IELTS ranked nineteenth out of twenty countries, even though costs of English private education were a staggering 15 trillion Won (i.e., US$1.33 billion) per year in Korea. The article further stated that "Koreans' English communication skills are not . . . good enough because they have focused on grammar and reading comprehension." This is substantiated in a research report published by Jin (2006) who attributed Koreans' lack of confidence in English communication to the CSAT's negative washback. It was pointed out that the Korean government could address these issues by developing a domestic English test that would measure all four core English skills.

Another motivation to introduce the NEAT was frequent web server outages and the high demand for the TOEFL iBT in Korea, which was described as the "TOEFL Crisis" in 2007 (Shin, 2012). TOEFL scores became a necessity for Koreans who wished to study in universities in the United States and who applied for secondary school and university admissions in Korea. As mentioned earlier, the TOEFL crisis broke out due to insufficient test slots for Korean TOEFL takers. In addition to this insufficient supply of test-taking slots, the web server was down, preventing Koreans from registering the test. Some Koreans resorted to traveling to other countries to take the test (Lee, 2007, May 14). According to Shin's (2012, 2019) analysis, *JoongAng Ilbo*, like the other Korean newspapers, called for the development of a trustworthy domestic test to replace TOEFL. A new test was thus needed.

These factors resulted in the development of the NEAT. In a press release on December 19, 2008, the Korean government explicitly stated the purposes of the NEAT: to improve English communication skills, reduce dependence on international English tests such as TOEIC and TOEFL, and use the NEAT scores for university admissions, hiring, and overseas study.

A Potential Trigger of Private Education

Originally, the Presidential Committee announced that the English subject in the CAST would be replaced by the NEAT in 2013. Do-yoen Kim, the minister of education, science and technology, stated in an interview with *Chosun Ilbo* that "because 40% of costs on private education were spent for English education, it is the key to success how English education can be provided in public education" (Ahn, 2008a). He conceived a scoring system in the NEAT that reflected "pass" or "fail" on the report cards so that students would not compete with each other to get a higher score in the NEAT, which in turn would significantly reduce costs on private education. Unlike the government's purpose of the NEAT (i.e., reducing costs on private education), there had been much concern that the

NEAT would promote private education spending. Because of questionable teacher qualifications to effectively teach speaking, parents sent their children to private education for NEAT preparation.

JoongAng Ilbo strongly asserted that the government-developed English test be implemented after 2008, but the outlet often included articles that discussed the increased burden on the test preparation education, while implicitly advocating its continued use. According to Shin's (2012, 2019) analysis, as most of the authorities consulted in these articles were the representatives of private education, the media featured the following phrases and headlines in 2008: "excited in the market of private education," "private education industry is getting bigger," "*hakwons*[2] expecting benefit and smiling," "can public school teachers handle it?" "hakwons affirm that the number of enrolled students will increase," "stock values of test prep companies increase," "private education increasing," and "double burden" (Shin, 2012, 2019). In *Chosun Ilbo*, S. Oh (2008, June 30) reported that hakwons administered English to primary students in grades 1 or 2 with native English-speaking teachers and sought to provide educational facilities for English education such as libraries and English zones (i.e., places for English conversation with native English speakers). *Chosun Ilbo* (2011a, June 14) reported that there were not many English teachers in public schools who can teach communicative English in public schools, and due to this, private education will proliferate if the CSAT would be replaced by the NEAT. Furthermore, *Chosun Ilbo* (2011b, June 14) surveyed 545 Korean people to see their perceptions of administration of the NEAT and reported that 73 percent (398 votes) opposed the administration while 27 percent (147 votes) supported it. To deal with private education and for the government's policy to be disseminated properly without unintended consequences such as promoting private education, the Ministry of Education, Science and Technology announced that government officials would crack down hakwons' exaggerated advertisements that would likely influence parents to be concerned about English teaching and promote private education.

Another potential trigger of private education that resulted in the termination of the NEAT administration was concerns about the NEAT's low item difficulty as score inflation may arise due to the low item difficulty of the NEAT. Yoo showed that (2011a, May 27), for example, Level 2 of the NEAT had one thousand less vocabulary items and the percentage of correct responses in the NEAT would be increased 5 to 10 percent points above those in the English portion of the CSAT (Ministry of Education, Science and Technology, 2011). In this case, Korean universities may be concerned about selecting qualified candidates using NEAT scores for university admissions and, consequently, may administer and use additional processes or criteria. Citing teachers' testimonies, Yoo (2011a, May 27) reported that "other types of private education would be proliferated to fill the gap in difficulties between the NEAT and the CAST," presumably in the areas of essay writing, examinations in schools, academic awards in foreign language, mathematics, and science contests for university admissions.

A Lack of Viability/Feasibility

The other factor that delayed the replacement of the CAST was insufficient equipment for internet-based testing (IBT) and raters. Not long after the Presidential Committee announced the introduction of the NEAT, the government delayed the plan to replace the CSAT with the NEAT because of concerns regarding viability and feasibility of administering the NEAT. *JoongAng Ilbo* often discussed the technological challenges of English proficiency testing (Shin, 2012, 2019). It forecasted that it would be extremely difficult to implement sufficient equipment such as recorders and computers, and that unexpected technical issues would occur if hundreds of thousands of students were tested on the same day. It assumed that it was impossible to "objectively" rate test results. Even within the government, some officials doubted the possibility to administer the NEAT (Ahn, 2008b, November 17). Kim also reported,

> The number of test-takers who can take the NEAT on the same day is estimated to be 50,000. However, students in grade 12 number over 550,000 and the number of test-takers would be over one million if high school students in grade 10 and 11 would take the test on that day. Therefore, the KICE should have a number of servers which can accommodate this number of students. In addition, there is a need to provide high-end computers to prevent potential hacking, as well as headsets and soundproofing devices to prevent cheating. It took ETS ten years to develop TOEFL iBT and build facilities for internet-based testing. However, it is doubtful about whether the Korean government can handle just for four years. As for the speaking test, fair marking is crucial. For marking in the TOEFL iBT, there are at least three to six raters to mark responses of one test-taker. One official at the KICE says we will have 25,000 to 30,000 raters who meet qualifying conditions and pass the calibration test and they will be trained and refers to scoring manuals. (2008, April 29)

With these concerns, the KICE held a public forum for discussing the directions of the NEAT and English curriculum in 2011. At the forum, further plans were presented for training English teachers as item writers and raters and for building iBT systems and test locations (Jin and Kim, 2011). The KICE was planning to train six hundred English teachers as item writers through online and offline training during summer and winter vacations, with the target of having one hundred certified raters in 2009, five hundred in 2010, and one thousand in each of the following years until 2014. For scoring procedures, the KICE planned to assign four raters each for speaking and writing tests pertaining to one test taker's responses. For IBT testing venues, five hundred test locations in 2011, six hundred in 2012, and six hundred in 2013 nationwide were planned for allocation. The popularity of the NEAT was increasing in Korea in tandem with the number of universities that used the NEAT scores for admissions. However, system errors occurred when 1,116 students took the NEAT on June 2, 2013. Of that group, fifty-eight students reported that they could not see the responses that they entered and instead, an irrelevant screen suddenly popped up. Cho (2013, June 11) reported that the government was on the cusp of terminating the plan to replace the CAST with the NEAT due to lack of reliability of the NEAT. At that time, thirty-six universities and colleges were using the NEAT scores for rolling-based university admissions. The earlier concerns regarding the viability and feasibility of administering the NEAT were thus realized in actual testing.

Heightened Consequences

One of the critical purposes of the administration of the NEAT was to curb private education as shown in the interview with Do-yoen Kim, the minister of education, science and technology (Ahn, 2008a, April 28). However, parents' concerns about whether test preparation for the NEAT could be provided in public education resulted in a continued boom of private education. Ahn (2009, February 28) reported that costs of English private education increased 11.8 percent points in 2009 from 68,000 to 76,000 Won (US$60 to US$67.29) per family. This increase was the highest among school subjects such as Korean essay writing, Korean, and mathematics. In the news article, one parent sent her grade 4 child to an English hakwon and said, "If English listening and speaking are assessed in English examinations, it is necessary to go to an English hakwon to get a high score." In the previous year (i.e., in 2008), the government announced that five thousand teachers who specialized in English communication teaching were supposed to be allocated to schools across Korea, and the government would train the teachers intensively. However, parents did not trust the government's promise that "public schools will take care of students' English skills," and this distrust resulted in a private education boom, contrary to the primary purpose of the NEAT.

Indeed, the turnover rate at two English hakwons had increased from 43.6 billion to 78.6 billion Won (from US$38 million to US$69 million) and from 62.8 billion to 83 billion Won (from US$55 million to US$73 million), respectively (Ahn, 2009, February 28). Parents also sent their children to English-speaking countries to prepare for the NEAT. For example, one parent sent her eleven-year-old son to Canada to help him prepare for the NEAT because there would be a higher possibility for him to pass the NEAT when he entered grade 12 (Yoo, 2011b, October 4). "Moms are concerned about whether their kids would be behind the class unless they learn English since they are young," declared the parent (Yoo, 2011b, October 4). The parents' concerns also led to requests for the replacement of the English teacher who was in his fifties with a young female English teacher because parents generally perceive that females are better at teaching languages than males. This happened in a private high school near Seoul when the older male teacher was assigned to teach English for three classrooms out of ten (Oh and Jung, 2008, June 21).

Oh and Jung (2008, June 21) reported the pressures English teachers encountered from teaching English speaking and writing in the classroom. One teacher stated that English teachers who are old are worried about whether they should change their subjects of teaching. Some English teachers actually applied for teaching different subjects. "It is the first time for English teachers to apply for changing their teaching subject," said one supervisor at the Seoul Education Office (Oh and Jung, 2008, June 21). This pressure also led to highly competitive and intense English teacher training run by the government. Regarding these unexpected consequences, Myunghee Lee, a professor at Kongju University noted that "because education is dealt with based on perspectives of teachers and education officials rather than students and their parents, educational reformation comes to nothing" (Ahn, 2008b, November 17).

In addition to these unintended consequences, the introduction of the NEAT also led to confusion and distrust among parents and the consumption of a significant amount of the national budget (approximately US$34 million in test design and administration). In a newspaper report (Kim and Kim, 2013, May 13), Byungman Ahn, the minister of education, announced in 2010 that "the NEAT would be used for rolling-based university admissions in the academic year of 2013. Whether the NEAT would replace the CSAT will be decided in 2012. If the decision is made, the NEAT will replace the CAST in the academic year of 2016." However, the government did not decide by 2012 and delayed the decision, saying, "it would be better for the next administration to decide." In another report (Kim, 2014, January 16), Namsu Seo, the new minister of education in the following administration, said that "it would be likely that student workload and dependence on private education would be increased if the CAST is now replaced with the NEAT. It is not desirable to replace it until schools are ready to prepare for the NEAT." One parent, however, said, "I have heard the importance of the NEAT for university admissions since my kid was a primary student. So I sent him to English hakwon when he was a middle school student to prepare for the test, but the news is absolutely preposterous to me." Furthermore, students, their parents, and teachers responded that the government lied again; criticisms were ubiquitous among Korean people (Kim and Kim, 2013, May 13). In sum, the introduction of the NEAT became a problem instead of the solution that it was meant to be.

Discussions and Conclusions

Government-driven testing in Korea has a long history, dating back to the Chosun Dynasty (1392–1987) when standardized testing was used to hire government officials (I.-C. Choi, 2008). A successful undertaking of the test entitled, *Kwage Sihem*,[3] was mandatory for those who wished to be hired as a government official, and the chance to take the test was given to all males except serfs (I.-C. Choi, 2008). Ever since, the Korean government has made societal changes through introducing tests and has maintained its vise-like grip on its authoritative power. Recently, the government considered English language ability as a top priority and yet again used its power to instill societal changes with the emerging global society. The NEAT was introduced by the Korean government to reduce the costs of private education and to improve Koreans' English language proficiency by providing English education in public schools. The NEAT is a prime example that testing is initiated to achieve political ends (Fulcher, 2009; McNamara, 2005; Shohamy, 1998, 2001, 2007; Spolsky, 2000). The NEAT's purpose of curbing private education was designed to give economically disadvantaged students the opportunity to learn. This goal, however, has been a controversial issue in Korea in light of Kunnan's (2018) definition of fairness because students who have more access to private education had higher chances to be admitted in universities. As illustrated in this chapter, the themes (a push for a domestic English test, a potential trigger of private education, and a heightened consequence) derived from the data clearly show that the Korean government and Korean people emphasize equitability in testing, that is, equal access to assessment, equal opportunity to prepare for the assessment, and equal access to educational resources and opportunities to learn (Bachman and Palmer, 2010; Cheng, 2014).

Although the abovementioned equitability concerns fundamentally led to the development of the NEAT, the concerns also led to its demise due to a lack of confidence in the efficacy of public education in preparing students for the NEAT and its variability and feasibility, leading to a proliferation of private education. Right after the Korean government announced the introduction of the NEAT, unintended consequences emerged: advertisements for NEAT preparation from private institutes appeared in newspapers (Ahn, 2009, February 28), and stories outlining how parents were requesting teaching staff changes (Oh and Jung, 2008, June 21) and sending their children to English-speaking countries for NEAT preparation (Yoo, 2011b, October 4) began to appear. Furthermore, as the government delayed the replacement of the CSAT with the NEAT, students and their parents experienced confusion and concern. These factors accumulated and resulted in the termination of the full administration of the NEAT, consuming a significant amount of national budget.

In short, policy makers' intentions and public opinions have affected the rise and demise of the NEAT. This case has implications for test validity and test validation. Since Messick's (1989) seminal work on the validity (specifically including value implications into validity), stakeholders' beliefs about testing have been paid little attention as the inclusion of value implications into validity may place a big burden on validity researchers (O'Loughlin, 2011) because value implications are too complex to be investigated. Despite this methodological difficulty, value implications need to be investigated as they shape stakeholders' interpretations and uses of test scores (Im and McNamara, 2017). In addition, researchers may need to use policy analysis, cultural awareness, and critical discourse analysis to understand value implications in a given context.

Another factor that brought about the termination of the full administration of the NEAT was the issue of the practicality of testing. Bachman and Palmer (1996) proposed six qualities of *test usefulness* corresponding to test validity: construct validity, reliability, authenticity, interactiveness, practicality, and impact, each of which needs to be weighed when designing a test. Practicality is one of the important qualities in designing what type of and how much resources such as human resources (e.g., item writers, raters, and technical support), material resources (e.g., computers and test spots), and time (e.g., development time) are required for the stages of the design, operationalization, and administration. The lack of raters and insufficient equipment and facilities for the NEAT triggered the termination of the full administration of the NEAT after a server error occurred. This serious technical mishap led to invalid test scores and potentially erroneous decision making.

In the investigation of sociopolitical factors surrounding the NEAT, it is evident that testing has been intertwined with sociopolitical factors in testing contexts where stakeholders' values affect the initiation and termination of testing. These factors need to be investigated beyond traditional scientific inquiry. In closing, we want to emphasize that the case of NEAT is representative of how language testing has universally been initiated to achieve political purposes (Fulcher, 2009; McNamara and Roever, 2006; Shohamy, 2001). Future research should thus include policy studies that provide methodological frameworks to investigate sociopolitical factors in testing.

Notes

1 As of 2007, ETS did not allocate sufficient test slots for Korean test takers of TOEFL after switching from computer-based to the internet-based test format because of security concerns and preventing cheating. Most TOEFL takers then experienced registration failure.
2 Hakwon refers to private institutes in Korean. In hakwons, students from primary to high schools are taught the same subjects that are taught in public schools. It may look like an add-on curriculum, but the majority of students take additional classes after school.
3 The test was the national civil service examination under the Chosun Dynasty of Korea.

References

Ahn, S. B. (April 28, 2008a). *Kyoywukpi 40%ka yenge⋯Kongkyoywuk anulo hupswuhayya*. [40% of on the budget in education are allocated to English learning: English should be taught in public education]. *Chosun Ilbo*, p. A33.

Ahn, S. B. (November 17, 2008b). *Kyoywukkongyak 1nyento antway cwulcwuli hucipwuci* [Campaign pledges about education broken within a year]. *Chosun Ilbo*, p. A8.

Ahn, S. B. (February 28, 2009). *Hye kkoinun MBcengpu yengekyoywuk: Tutki wuycu silyongyenge cengchayk 1nyen, sakyoywuk pwuchwukye "tilleyma"* [English education in the Myung-Bak Lee's administration gets complicated: The educational policy that focuses on English listening education is in dilemma as it promotes private English education]. *Chosun Ilbo*, p. A6.

Bachman, L. F. (2013). NEAT to have a positive impact on language learning. *The Korea Times*. Retrieved August 1, 2018 from http://www.koreatimes.co.kr

Bachman, L. F. and Palmer, A. S. (1996). *Language Testing in Practice: Designing and Developing Useful Language Tests*. Oxford: Oxford University Press.

Bachman, L. F. and Palmer, A. S. (2010). *Language Assessment in Practice: Developing Language Assessments and Justifying Their use in the Real World*. Oxford: Oxford University Press.

Bowen, G. A. (2009). Document analysis as a qualitative research method. *Qualitative Research Journal, 9*(2), 27–40. doi: 10.3316/QRJ0902027

Cheng, L. (2005). *Changing Language Teaching Through Language Testing: A Washback Study*. Cambridge: Cambridge University Press.

Cheng, L. (2014). Consequences, impact, and washback. In A. J. Kunnan (Ed.), *The Companion to Language Assessment* (pp. 1130–46). Chichester: John Wiley & Sons. doi:10.1002/9781118411360.wbcla071

Cho, C. H. (June 11, 2013). *Kokyosayngyong NEAT siem censanolywu···Tayippanyeng nonlan* [Technical errors found in NEAT for high-school students: Raising doubts for its use in university admissions]. *Yonhap News*. Retrieved August 1, 2018 from http://www.yonhapnews.co.kr

Choi, I.-C. (2008). The impact of EFL testing on EFL education in Korea. *Language Testing, 25*(1), 39–62. doi: 10.1177/0265532207083744

Choi, S. H. (August 26, 2008). *Taykwuey cenyongkyosil 200kay* [200 classrooms for English education in Daegu]. *Chosun Ilbo*, p. A14.

Chosun Ilbo. (June 14, 2011a). *Swunungtaycheyhantamyen sakyoywuk simhaycilket* [If the NEAT replaced the CAST, private education will boom]. *Chosun Ilbo*, p. A33.

Chosun Ilbo. (June 14, 2011b). *Kwukkayengenunglyekphyengkasihem toip pantay 73%* [73% of the participants in a survey object to the introduction of the NEAT]. *Chosun Ilbo*, p. A33.

Fulcher, G. (2009). Test use and political philosophy. *Annual Review of Applied Linguistics, 29*, 3–20.

Im, G.-H. and McNamara, T. (2017). Legitimate or illegitimate uses of test scores in contexts unrelated to test purposes. *English Teaching, 72*(2), 71–99. doi: 10.15858/engtea.72.2.201706.71

Jin, Y. (2006). On the improvement of test validity and test washback: The CET washback study. *Foreign Language World, 6*, 65–73.

Jin, K.-A. (2012). Will new English test facilitate communication in the classroom? *The Korea Herald*. Retrieved August 1, 2018 from http://www.koreaherald.com

Jin, K.-A. and Kim, H. (2011). Kwukkayengenunglyekphyengkasihem kaypalpangan [Plan for developing the NEAT]. In Korea Institute for Curriculum and Evaluation, *Kwukkayengenunglyekphyengkasihem mit kyoywukkwaceng kayceng panghyang kongkay tholonhwoy* [Public forum for the National English Ability Test and direction for revision of English curriculum] (pp. 3–41). Seoul: Korea Institute for Curriculum and Evaluation.

Kang, K. H. (January 2, 2008). Yenge, nalaka chaykimcye! [English education: The nation's responsibility]. *Chosun Ilbo*, p. A31.

Kim, N.-I. (April 29, 2008). *Nancey manun "yengenunglyekphyengkasihem"* [The NEAT that has intractable problems]. *Chosun Ilbo*, p. A10.

Kim, S. H., Kim, Y.-M., Lee, B. C., Park, J.-S., Hwang, P.-A. and Kim, K. H. (2013). *Swucwunpyel swunung yenge yengyek sihem kaysen yenkwu* [A study on the reform of the foreign language domain of CSAT] (Research report CAT 2013-30). Seoul: Korea Institute for Curriculum and Evaluation.

Kim, Y. (January 16, 2014). "Kokyosayng hankwukhyeng thophul" phyeyci⋯Kyoywukcangkwan pakkwuymyen malto pakkwuye [Termination of the Korean version of the TOEFL for high-school students: Every time the minister of education changes, the educational policies change]. *Chosun Ilbo*, p. A14.

Kim, Y. and Kim, H. (May 13, 2013). "Hankwukhyeng thophul" swunung yenge taycheyhantateni⋯400ek nallil phan [Plan to replace the CAST with the NEAT: Losing $34 million USD]. *Chosun Ilbo*, p. A12.

Korea Institute for Curriculum and Evaluation. (2011). *Kwukkayengenunglyekphyengkasihem mit kyoywukkwaceng kayceng panghyang kongkay tholonhwoy* [Public forum for the National English Ability Test and direction for the revision of the English curriculum] (ORM 2011-18). Seoul: Korea Institute for Curriculum and Evaluation.

Korea Institute for Curriculum and Evaluation. (August 21, 2018). *President's Message*. Retrieved from http://www.kice.re.kr/sub/info.do?m=0101&s=english

Kunnan, A. J. (2018). *Evaluating Language Assessments*. New York, NY: Routledge.

Lee, H. and Lee, K. (2016). An analysis of the failure(s) of South Korea's National English Ability Test. *Asia-Pacific Education Researcher*, 25(5/6), 827–34. doi: 10.1007/s40299-016-0301-6

Lee, S.-H. (May 14, 2007). High demand causes "Toefl crisis" in South Korea. *The New York Times*. Retrieved August 1, 2018 from www.nytimes.com

McNamara, T. (2005). 21st Century shibboleth: Language tests, identity and intergroup conflict. *Language Policy*, 4(4), 351–70.

McNamara, T. and Roever, C. (2006). *Language Testing: The Social Dimension*. London: Blackwell Publishing.

MediaX. (February 2, 2018). *Cwuyo ilkanci palhayngpwuswuwa maychwulayk pikyo* [Comparison of daily circulation and turnover among Korean newspapers]. *MediaX*. Retrieved August 21, 2018 from http://www.mediax.kr/?p=744&ckattempt=1

Merriam, S. B. (1988). *Case Study Research in Education: A Qualitative Approach*. San Francisco, CA: Jossey-Bass.

Messick, S. (1989). Validity. In R. L. Linn (Ed.), *Educational Measurement* (3rd ed.) (pp. 13–103). New York, NY: American Council on Education & Macmillan.

Ministry of Education, Science and Technology. (2011). *Hakpwumo cengchayk selmyeong calyo- Kwukkayengenunglyekphyengkasihem annay* [Policy description for school parents: Information on the NEAT]. Seoul: Ministry of Education, Science and Technology.

Munhwa Broadcasting Corporation. (2011). *Isywu24: Silyongyenge cwungsim "NEAT" toip, mwunceyepna?* [Introduction of the NEAT for improving practical English: Any issues?]. Available from http://imnews.imbc.com//replay/2011/nw2400/2916458_18770.html

Oh, S. (June 30, 2008). Wuenemin swuephwakday-Yengetosekwan sinsel tungulo kyengceyng [Expanding English classes run by native English speakers: Competing to build new facilities for English education]. *Chosun Ilbo*, p. D2.

Oh, Y. (June 5, 2008). Mitchen tulenan hankwukin yengesillyek…20kaykwuk cwung 19wuy [Koreans' English ability rankings came out: Ranked 19th out of 20 countries]. *Chosun Ilbo*, p. A9.

Oh, Y. and Jung, H. J. (June 21, 2008). Yengeey ttenun kyosatul [English teachers afraid of English]. *Chosun Ilbo*, p. A9.

O'Loughlin, K. (2011). The interpretation and use of proficiency test scores in university selection: How valid and ethical are they? *Language Assessment Quarterly*, 8(2), 146–60. doi: 10.1080/15434303.2011.564698

Shin, D. (2012). TOEFL daylaney kwanhan sinmunkisabwunsek: Pipanjekdamlonbwunsekul kibanulo [Analyzing newspaper articles on TOEFL Crisis through critical discourse analysis]. *Foreign Languages Education*, 19(1), 187–210.

Shin, D. (2019). Analyzing media discourse on the development of the National English Ability Test (NEAT) in South Korea. *Language Testing in Asia*, 9. doi: 10.1186/s40468-019-0081-z

Shin, D. and Cho, E. (2018). How was a government-led test of English suspended? Examining discursive conflicts in the media. Manuscript submitted for publication.

Shin, D. and Im, G.-H. (2011). Cengchayktokwulo sayongtwoynun enesihem: Kwuknay yengesihem cwungsimulo [Language tests as language policy tools: English tests in Korean contexts]. *English Teaching*, 66(4), 281–305. doi: 10.15858/engtea.66.4.201112.281

Shohamy, E. (1998). Critical language testing and beyond. *Studies in Educational Evaluation*, 24(4), 331–45.

Shohamy, E. (2001). *The Power of Tests: A Critical Perspective on the Uses of Language Tests*. London: Pearson.

Shohamy, E. (2007). Language tests as language policy tools. *Assessment in Education*, 14(1), 117–30.

Spolsky, B. (2000). Language testing in the modern language journal. *The Modern Language Journal*, 84, 536–52.

Yoo, S. J. (May 27, 2011a). Swunung taychey ywulyek "hankwukhyeng thophul" ko3ttay twu pen ponta [High possibility for the CAST to be replaced with the NEAT: Students in grade 12 take the NEAT twice a year]. *Chosun Ilbo*, p. A12.

Yoo, S. J. (October 4, 2011b). Coki ywuhak palam tasi solsol: Ipsi silyongyenge wuycwulo pakkwuymye 4nyenmaney cungkasey [Revival of sending young Korean students overseas: Showing a rate of increase four years after focusing on practical English for university admissions]. *Chosun Ilbo*, p. A14.

The Disconnect between English Tests and English Proficiency: Two South Korean Jobseekers' Perceptions and Performances

Miso Kim and Mari Haneda

Introduction

"Measurement drives performance" (YBMNET, n.d.) is the claim made on the website of the Test of English for International Communication (TOEIC). The TOEIC and TOEIC Speaking tests, developed by the Educational Testing Service (ETS) and administered in South Korea by a local language education institute called YBM, are used by large Korean corporations for initial screening for employment (YBMNET, 2018a). Consequently, these tests have become rites of passage for entry-level jobseekers looking for domestic employment such that some take them multiple times in order to receive scores high enough to pass the screening process.

Does measurement really drive performance? Previous research has identified the disconnect between test content and the features of workplace communication through the analysis of surveys, media reports, and test items (e.g., Choi, 2008; Nicholson, 2015; Park, 2011). However, left unexamined are jobseekers' perceptions of the disconnect and their different performances under the test and non-test formats. An investigation of both of these aspects may yield meaningful evidence to corroborate the previous studies on the disconnect. We address this gap in research by reporting the findings of a qualitative case study of two Korean jobseekers, focusing on (1) the case-study participants' perceptions of the tests and real-life communication and the way in which these affected their English learning experiences and (2) their different oral performances on two tasks—one simulating a TOEIC Speaking item and the other simulating interactive communication. In what follows, we review previous research on the aforementioned disconnect and present the design of the current study, followed by findings and discussion.

The Disconnect between the Tests and Workplace Communication

TOEIC is a typical paper-and-pencil English proficiency test composed of 100 multiple-choice questions assessing reading and listening. It "measures the everyday English skills of people working in an international environment" (ETS, 2015, p. 2). TOEIC Speaking is a computer-delivered test that consists of eleven questions "designed to measure a person's ability to communicate in spoken English in the context of daily life and the global workplace" (ETS, 2016, p. 2). Although ETS provides TOEIC Writing, it is not commonly used in the Korean job market and thus is excluded from this study.

Even though the TOEIC purports to measure English competence, there is controversy regarding the validity of this claim (Choi, 2008; Nicholson, 2015; Park, 2011). A quantitative study by Powers and Powers (2014) found that the TOEIC test can predict performance on real-life tasks. However, Nicholson (2015) challenged the validity of TOEIC, arguing that it lacks clear underlying theoretical constructs and ways of measuring productive skills.

In addition to the controversy over its validity, its implementation in the local Korean context is often considered problematic. Private test preparation schools, called *hakwons*, provide a number of test-taking tips and strategies to help test takers achieve high scores without developing actual communicative competence (Booth, 2012, 2018; Jang, 2015; Kim, Choi, and Kim, 2018). In order to combat this particular weakness of the test, major Korean corporations and their subsidiaries, including Samsung, Hyundai, SK, and LG, require TOEIC Speaking test scores in addition to TOEIC (YBMNET, 2018a, 2018b). However, the problem of teaching test-taking strategies at the expense of proficiency persists (Jang, 2015; Kim, Choi, and Kim, 2018).

Park (2011) argued that the transition from TOEIC to TOEIC Speaking is linked to the decreased discriminatory power of TOEIC scores. As jobseekers invested in TOEIC, the mean score of TOEIC increased to the point that having a high score became the norm for every jobseeker. Because a TOEIC score alone cannot distinguish competent jobseekers from others, corporations recalibrated the preferred mode of assessment from TOEIC to TOEIC Speaking or other speaking tests. For example, the participants in Jang's (2015) study who could afford to study English abroad sought to distinguish themselves by practicing oral communication skills in English language schools and during internships in Canada. Those who remain in Korea, however, struggle to attain the desired scores, often attending private classes, taking practice tests, purchasing test preparation books, and attending lectures online to keep up with the higher bar for TOEIC scores. They also boost their résumés by presenting TOEIC Speaking scores (Booth, 2012, 2018).

In contrast to the limited formats of TOEIC and TOEIC Speaking, all forms of workplace communication, including discussions of work-related manners, teleconferencing, and presentations (Kassim and Ali, 2010), are highly interactive and cannot be measured on paper and/or by computers. Managers and employers stress the ability to communicate with professionalism. Moreover, personal qualities such as leadership, sociability, and flexibility are seen as key to successful interactions, whereas TOEIC scores function only as a symbol of the importance of English to employees (Kubota, 2013). As Firth (2009) points out, communication is achieved not just through verbal language but also through paralinguistic features, including voice, stress, intonation, and pacing. Research on workplace communication has also shown that English spoken at work is highly interactive, pragmatic, context-dependent, multimodal, and hybrid. For example, employees actively employ multimodal artifacts, such as graphs, objects, and spreadsheets (Kleifgen, 2013), and the spatial organization of such artifacts affects communication as well (Caronia and Cooren, 2014). Also important are communicative strategies, including comprehension checks and repetition (Canagarajah, 2017). Finally, real-life utterances are often partial, simplified, and incomplete, and it is the norm to use different codes simultaneously (Canagarajah, 2013; Higgins, 2009; Otsuji and Pennycook, 2010).

Previous research has problematized the disconnect between the test contents and real-life workplace communication by analyzing test items (e.g., Nicholson, 2015), survey results (Choi, 2008), media reports (e.g., Park, 2011), and ethnographic interviews (e.g., Booth, 2012, 2018; Jang, 2015). While meaningful, these studies either approach the disconnect from a broad discursive perspective and leave the jobseekers' perspective unaddressed or rely primarily on interview data that do not reflect the jobseekers' actual performances in English. The studies have problematized the TOEIC website's slogan, "measurement drives performance" (YBMNET, n.d.); however, jobseekers' perceptions and oral performances have not been investigated. Therefore, this study investigates jobseekers' perceptions of the disconnect, the impact of their perceptions on their learning experience, and their oral performances in the test format and non-test interactive format. By doing so, the study yields empirical evidence to bolster the argument of the previous studies. Therefore, we address the following two research questions: (1) How did two jobseekers' perceptions of the tests and English proficiency influence their English learning experiences? (2) How did two tasks, simulating a TOEIC Speaking item and actual interactive communication, respectively, elicit oral performances in English?

The Study: Investigating Korean Jobseekers' Perceptions and Performances

The data for this study were taken from a larger study conducted in a four-week course led by the first author, Miso Kim, in the Seoul metropolitan area. At the time, Kim, a native of South Korea, was a doctoral student in applied linguistics in the United States. The course aimed to help jobseekers improve business-related English-speaking skills and their oral performance on the TOEIC Speaking test. Participants were recruited through online advertisements posted on university websites and job information websites. Out of the eighteen participants who signed up, eleven participants satisfied all of the following recruitment criteria: (1) juniors, seniors, or recent graduates from four-year colleges in Korea; (2) entry-level jobseekers who planned to apply for full-time white-collar jobs in domestic corporations; and (3) individuals who were interested in practicing TOEIC Speaking tasks and developing English skills for business communication. All eleven were in their mid to late twenties, but they were heterogenous in terms of their disciplinary training, desired position, level of English proficiency, previous exposure to English, and test scores.

Kim, a Korean–English bilingual, acted as a teacher-researcher. She used Korean as a medium of instruction for the majority of time but occasionally used English when providing examples. The class met twice a week, once in a whole-group session and once in a pair session, for two hours per meeting. Each week of the course focused on a single topic. In pair sessions, a set of two participants who had been grouped according to similar job interests and majors worked with Kim. She used two types of tasks in teaching, one simulating TOEIC Speaking and the other approximating interactive communication, providing detailed feedback on the participants' task performances. For the purpose of her research, she also conducted semi-structured interviews in pair sessions and video-recorded the participants' task performances.

Participants

For this study, we focused on two students and their oral task performances on the topic "proposing a solution" (Week 3) because this topic elicited longer and more interactive responses than other topics, thus allowing for a more in-depth analysis. Two participants, Sunwoo and Pyoung (both pseudonyms), were selected because they had experience taking standardized tests, and their job-seeking efforts were more serious than the other, younger pairs. Sunwoo was a senior studying electrical engineering who had scored 850 on the TOEIC.[1] Pyoung had graduated from college with a degree in physics six months before the study and had reached TOEIC Speaking Level 5.[2]

The Test-Simulated and Interactive Tasks

The tasks selected for analysis addressed the topic "proposing a solution." Table 9.1 shows how the tasks were organized within the whole-class and pair sessions during the third week of classes. There were two types of tasks: (1) simulated TOEIC Speaking tasks, which required participants to propose a solution according to the test requirements of a monologue format and time limit; and (2) interactive tasks, which required participants to interact without conforming to the test format. The participants used English to propose and negotiate solutions to problematic situations interactively with one another, drawing on both verbal and multimodal resources. Their performances in the monologue test format and the interactive non-test format were then compared. In this chapter, we analyze the participants' video-recorded performances on both types of tasks during the Week 3 pair session.

During the Week 3 pair session, Sunwoo and Pyoung first reviewed the recorded responses from the whole-group session and worked on the two types of tasks. The first task was a simulation of a question on TOEIC Speaking that required a sixty-second response (monologue), and the second task was a natural interaction between Sunwoo and Pyoung. Before beginning the first task, the participants listened to the following directions: "In this part of the test, you will be presented with a problem and asked to propose a solution. You will have 30 seconds to prepare. Then you will have 60 seconds to speak. . . . In your response, be sure to show that you recognize the problem, and propose a way of dealing with the problem" (ETS, 2016, p. 14). They then listened to a fifty-second conversation about the problem: fifty people had signed up for a real-estate seminar but only thirty computers were available in the room. A laptop

Table 9.1 Test-Simulated and Interactive Tasks during Week 3 (Topic: Proposing a Solution)

Tasks\Sessions	Simulated Tasks of TOEIC Speaking (Test-Simulated Tasks)	Interactive Tasks
Whole-class session	• Learn how to respond to the task according to the test requirements • Record responses to the test-simulated tasks	• Propose solutions to general business problems with other participants
Pair session	• Receive individualized feedback on the responses recorded in the whole-group sessions • Practice more test-simulated tasks with guided help	• Propose solutions in situations of interest and receive individualized feedback

screen placed in front of the participants displayed the time remaining for preparation and response. The second task, which had no time limit, modeled natural interaction between the two participants in negotiating a solution to a problematic situation. Sunwoo took the role of a student who had received a low grade, and Pyoung played the role of the professor. They then negotiated a solution acceptable to both parties.

Data Sources and Analysis

We used transcripts of semi-structured interviews conducted with the two focal participants in order to address the first research question on the influence of their perceptions on their English learning experiences. These interviews were conducted individually in Korean, focusing on the participants' backgrounds; previous English learning experiences; and their perceptions of TOEIC, TOEIC Speaking, and their English proficiency. The interviews were transcribed in Korean and translated into English for analysis. Drawing on Saldaña's (2009) coding process, we first iteratively labeled the transcripts with descriptive codes. Then we selected the codes relevant to the first research question and recategorized the codes into two larger themes: (1) the participants' perceptions of TOEIC, TOEIC Speaking, and their English proficiency; and (2) their English learning experiences. Using this recategorization, we analyzed the relationship between the codes grouped under each larger theme. For instance, a part of Sunwoo's transcript showed that his perception of his accent motivated him to study abroad and work hard to reduce it. The code "bad accent" was categorized under the "Sunwoo's perception of English proficiency" theme, and the other code, "study-abroad," was assigned to the "Sunwoo's learning experience" theme. The relationship between the two codes was then labeled as "motivating." In this way, we explored links between the participants' perceptions and experiences. Sunwoo's data map is presented in Appendix A.

To address the second research question, which considers the participants' differential oral performances on the tasks simulating a TOEIC Speaking item and real-life interaction, we transcribed their video-recorded performances on both types of tasks. When transcribing the performances, we included both verbal and multimodal features, including words, pauses, intonation, stress, volume, speed, gestures, eye gaze, and use of objects. The participants' performances on the test-simulated task were analyzed with a publicly available rubric and scoring guide provided by ETS (2016), as the full score description and rater training resources were not accessible. The participants' performances on the interactive task were assessed based on Kubota's (2013) conceptualization of the ability to communicate in transcultural workplace settings, which requires both linguistic skills and strategic competence to achieve a shared goal. Finally, we juxtaposed the analytical results of the test-simulated task performance with those of the interactive task performance to investigate the differences between them.

The Jobseekers' Perceptions and Performances

The Influence of the Jobseekers' Perceptions of Learning Experiences

Drawing on the interview data, we first describe Sunwoo's and Pyoung's perceptions of the TOEIC, TOEIC Speaking, and their English proficiency. Then we present their accounts of how their perceptions influenced their experiences learning English.

Sunwoo. Sunwoo considered the TOEIC and TOEIC Speaking to be merely requirements for the job market, requirements that were unrelated to his actual English competence, as connoted in his utterance, "TOEIC is just TOEIC." He scored 850 out of 990 on the first test and believed that his test-taking skills would also prove effective during the second test. However, his familiarity with the multiple-choice TOEIC test did not transfer to the computer-based TOEIC Speaking test, which requires a test taker to record their response (monologue). Sunwoo perceived that the TOEIC Speaking test was distinctly different from authentic communication, noting, "If it's a natural conversation, I don't feel like this at all. I feel much more comfortable. There's a big difference between taking the test and speaking with others." It led him to be anxious whenever he had to speak using the test format: "I'm not used to this, so my brain goes blank; I hesitate a lot, and I panic, and then I can't think of anything."

While Sunwoo believed the tests were job requirements, he defined "real" English competence as the ability to speak English fluently without a Korean accent. This perception was shaped by what he perceived as a critical event during his trip to Europe. At a Christmas party in a hostel in the UK, he was utterly shocked by his complete inability to communicate in English. Before the trip, he was confident about his English. He had received a good score on the TOEIC, and he had practiced speaking English by watching many American sitcoms. Nonetheless, at the party, he not only had difficulty expressing himself but realized that his English was not comprehensible to others because of his Korean accent. He described this experience, saying, "Everyone was laughing and chatting merrily, but I couldn't join in. I felt, ah, I really need to practice English. Really." This experience taught him that the ability to communicate is the hallmark of English proficiency, and that he had failed to develop it despite his studying for tests and watching sitcoms.

Just as Sunwoo differentiated among the TOEIC, the TOEIC Speaking, and English proficiency, he prepared for each of them with a different strategy. He gave the TOEIC the least attention, as he thought he could easily "brush up on [his] TOEIC skills" to earn a better score. "TOEIC skills" meant his familiarity with "answering multiple-choice questions on reading and listening comprehension." However, his perception of the TOEIC Speaking was that it had an "artificial" format that required him to complete timed tasks by using correct grammar and American pronunciation. It led him to practice how to perform to the TOEIC Speaking test format. For instance, he tried to avoid using non-American accents when practicing test-simulated tasks because he imagined that ETS would give high scores to those individuals who used American pronunciation.

To develop authentic English competence, Sunwoo focused exclusively on oral skills during his study abroad program because of his perceived need to improve oral proficiency and to eliminate his accent. For example, when he attended an English language school in the Philippines, he focused on oral skills only, conversing in English with his teacher for eight hours a day. He recorded these conversations and constantly asked his teacher for corrections. After four months of working on basic oral skills in the Philippines, he moved to the UK to attend English language schools for six more months. He soon became dissatisfied with his classes because his British teachers did not explicitly address pronunciation and accent reduction: "They [English-language schools in the UK] didn't care about pronunciation at all. French people spoke with a French accent, Chinese people with a Chinese accent. . . . It [the quality of UK language schools] is poor."

Pyoung. Pyoung believed that TOEIC tests did not gauge actual communicative skills in English. He viewed tests as anxiety-provoking rather than natural. He explained that he can interact in English but is too afraid to take the TOEIC test, saying, "When I talk in English, foreigners wait for me and understand me. But the TOEIC test is different. I feel my performance on the test won't reflect the work I've put into preparing for it, and I'll be devastated." Pyoung was well aware of the importance of the TOEIC in securing a desirable position at a large corporation. However, due to his high level of test anxiety, he had not taken it yet. Pyoung blamed himself for acting like a "fool" who was too nervous to take this basic step to prepare himself for the job market. He had the same problem with the TOEIC Speaking test. In Excerpt 1, Pyoung describes his perception of the test as having a "specific format" that requires good grammar and vocabulary. This provoked his anxiety about producing correct answers. For him, the test was different from real-life communication in which grammar mistakes are allowed.

Excerpt 1

But on the test [i.e., TOEIC Speaking], I need to get a good score. I get nervous, and the test requires a specific format, right? I have to pay attention to grammar and vocabulary. But when I hang out with a foreign friend [and make a mistake]—for example, "conversation" is a noun but I use it as a verb—he understands anyway. But on the test, that's a problem. . . . If someone asks me to speak English, I can do that. It's a little difficult, though. But during the test, I get super anxious about things like grammar and verbs.

In contrast to his ideas about the tests, Pyoung perceived oral proficiency as a practical competence for negotiating meaning with interlocutors to accomplish real-life tasks. In Excerpt 1, Pyoung gives the example of using *conversation* as a verb with a foreign friend; this minor error does not obscure his meaning. His pragmatic orientation was also evident when he described his experience working a part-time job at a mobile phone store near Myeongdong, a popular tourist attraction for foreigners. He had interacted with a number of foreign customers and had had to discuss complicated details about carriers and contracts despite his self-described limited proficiency. When asked how he had managed it, he explained, "When I interact in English, the people know that I'm not from an English-speaking country and I'm not good at English, so they speak slowly and use easy words. So it's not a problem for me, and I can speak with confidence." The features of these interactions, including mutual cooperation and accommodation, shaped Pyoung's perception of authentic communication in English.

Pyoung's perception of the TOEIC and TOEIC Speaking tests as requirements, combined with his high level of test anxiety, led him to postpone taking these tests as long as possible; he then rushed to take them at the last minute. He saw no reason to invest in extended test preparation and was fearful of testing situations. When he could no longer avoid the tests, he crammed for both tests by memorizing sample answers. This was based on a friend's advice to "memorize the books and sample answers" and "don't dare give your own response in the TOEIC Speaking test." Following this advice, Pyoung rushed to take the test and achieved Level 5 (the mean score of Korean jobseekers). Having minimally prepared for the tests, making no conscious effort to develop oral English proficiency, he expressed satisfaction with his pragmatic competence in negotiating meaning with foreigners, saying, "I can negotiate meaning with foreigners. I am not good at it, but we can communicate." His experience working at the mobile phone store gave him confidence that he could function with limited grammar and fluency.

Performances on Two Different Types of Tasks

In this section, we examine Sunwoo's and Pyoung's transcribed performances on a test-simulated task and an interactive task in the Week 3 pair session. Transcript conventions are provided in Appendix B. The performances on the test-simulated task were evaluated using the rubric and scoring guide for the TOEIC Speaking test provided in the ETS examinee handbook (2016). According to the rubric and guide, the test taker must (1) demonstrate a clear understanding of the problem; (2) provide a relevant and detailed solution; and (3) show good control of both simple and complex grammatical structures, use precise vocabulary choices, and exhibit an intelligible and well-paced flow when speaking. The performance on the interactive task was assessed by determining how proficiently the speakers could accomplish a shared goal by drawing on both linguistic and strategic competence. It was based on the ability to communicate, as defined by Kubota's (2013) study on communication in the transcultural workplace.

The Test-Simulated Task

Transcript 1. Sunwoo's performance on the test-simulated task

1   **Sunwoo**: Hi this is Sunwoo speaking↓. Well, we have a problem about . . . the (1.1) ahh. . .
2   vacancies of this seminar↑, and (1.4) I think we should ah change the place to (.) ah present our
3   ah presentation↑, (1.9) and, uh because ah >we just have only< <thirty> ah seats for using
4   computers↑. So after that↑ we post, we'll post the notice >on the website< and if someone has
5   laptop, or personal, ah, mobile, like ah (1.5) ((drawing a box with a right hand)) iPad, ah (1.2) if
6   they bring that kind of (.) items uh we will give them (.) discount. ((laughter)). °If you have any
7   . . . ((laughter))

The transcript above shows that Sunwoo attempted to fulfill the requirements of the task but made some mistakes. He attempted to summarize the problem and suggested two solutions: moving to a different room and giving discounts to attendees who could bring mobile devices. His summary of the problem in lines 1–2 is unclear because he used an imprecise word, "vacancies," in line 2. His first solution (lines 2–4) was intelligible to Kim, but it was awkward due to his repetition of "present" in the phrase, "present our ah presentation," in lines 2–3, as well as the 1.9-second pause in line 3 and the use of six gap fillers, "ah" or "uh," in lines 3–4. The second solution (lines 4–7) was clearly delivered except his self-initiated repair, "we post, we'll post," in line 4 and two pauses in line 5. He tried to come up with the phrase, "a mobile device," in line 5 but substituted "iPad." Sunwoo gave up on completing his response in lines 6–7 because the laptop showed his time was up.

Transcript 2. Pyoung's performance on the test-simulated task

1   **Pyoung**: >Hello this is Pyoung speaking.< I heard your problem about ah: (1.7) <lack of
2   seat?>. (2.8) Uh how about the (4.0) how about (.) make a <u>two</u> class for the seminar (.) If a (3.1)
3   ah with a: (1.7) some internet broadca, broadcast service like >a AfreecaTV< then you can 아
4   시간 왜케 걸리냐 [Ah why does it take this much time] ((covers face with hands)) ((smiles)) then
5   you can (2.0) ah: have a seminar ah two you can have seminar↑ <another place> (4.2)
6   °아 씨[damn]° Thank you ((laughter))

Pyoung's response required considerable effort for Kim to comprehend. The problem indicated in the listening script was that there were not enough computers to accommodate fifty people in the seminar room, but Pyoung's use of the phrase, "lack of seat," in lines 2–3 did not sufficiently summarize the problem. In lines 2–6, Pyoung attempted to suggest using an internet broadcasting service, such as AfreecaTV (a YouTube-like live broadcasting website in Korea), to livestream the seminar to other locations. The meaning was not successfully conveyed because of the long pauses in lines 2 and 5; a failed self-initiated correction in line 5; code-switching to Korean in lines 3, 4, and 6; and an incomplete ending in line 6.

The Interactive Task

Transcript 3. Sunwoo's and Pyoung's performances on the interactive task.
*S: Sunwoo, P: Pyoung, K: Kim (the instructor)

1 S: Can I come in?
2 P: No
3   ((All laugh))
4 P: Just a moment. ((drinks juice)) Okay come in.
5 S: Ah hi, <I'm,> my name is Sunwoo Jang. I'm your student↑ (.) and >I think there is problem
6   with my< ah grade because I think (.) I I did my test (.) well↑ (.) but my grade is C+↑.
7   I cannot accept this grade. Can I see my test sheet.
8 P: >Here you are<. You doing very well and in tech exam but I don't know your face and your
9   name that is mean, that's mean is ah (.) you doesn't attend my class anytime. So (.) you just
10   attend exam and not, not coming in my class↑, so I can't give a good grade for you.
11 S: No. There's no evidence for ((laughter)) prove that. Because I always attend your class
12   but you didn't call my I no, my name. And (1.5) if I didn't, ah, ahh, ((waves hands)) if
13   don't attend your class, uh I cannot receive this kind of ah score. So this score prove that I
14   attend your class and I studied hard (1.3) >that's why I complain about< the C+ grade.
15 P: Okay, um (2.0) , you always ah very (8.1)
16 K: 본분? [your duty?]
17 P: ((laugh)) Okay um I °I heard your word° well but haaa (3.4) correctly, I don't like you so,

18		because uh, ((clears throat)) 뭐라고 하지[what to say] (2.9), you always uh (.) sleep in my
19		class or sit just corner not look at me or °the° whiteboard (1.6) ((looks at and points to a
20		whiteboard behind him)) and you you using you always using phone in my class. If you say
21		(1.7) uh studying hard, high grade is a result, result, of result ah studying hard, there's not (.)
22		I will say no. I say, I say that is not true because (2.1) uhh (10.1) ((scratches nose)).
23		((Kim interrupts to give the turn to Sunwoo))
24	S:	Actually I did not sleep in your class and (1.8) uh your (1.9) your saying is str<u>ange</u> because
25		ah (.) if someone always attend your class↑ and always sits, seated in the first row↑ but his
26		uh score is really low↓, if his score is really low, then you, you, will you, will you give hi::m
27		(.) an A grade? Um I think this not make sense because ah the test is the, one of
28		the criterian? (.) to estimate the student (.) and I get I get a really high score so you have to
29		give me a A grade, not C+.
30	P:	Okay um I suggest (1.6) one (2.5) 뭐 하나 제안하겠다고 하면 [I want to suggest one thing]
31		((looks at Kim and puts his index finger up))
32	K:	Let me suggest one thing.
33	P:	Let me suggest one thing. I will ask some something about our major. It is a very (3.8) base::
34		one. If you explain about Maxwell law↑ to me very exactly so I will change your grade.
35	S:	Max what?
36	P:	Maxwell
37	K:	Maxwell's law
38	S:	Maxwell's law (2.0) Okay see you next time.
39		((all laugh))
40	P:	See you

Sunwoo tried to negotiate a solution using the following moves: He described the problem in lines 5–7, explained the reason for his complaint in lines 11–14, presented arguments against Pyoung's position in lines 24–29, and finally gave up when Pyoung offered his solution in line 38. Sunwoo demonstrated reasonable use of linguistic skills to make these moves, aside from some minor lapses that did not significantly affect meaning (e.g., grammatical errors such as "no evidence for prove that" in line 11, "this score prove that" in line 13, "your saying is strange" in line 24, and self-initiated repairs in line 12). In general, Sunwoo showed strategic competence in supporting these moves, including negotiating his grade based on his test scores (lines 13–14), repeating part of an earlier utterance so that he had more time to construct a sentence (line 26), and pinpointing the contradiction in Pyoung's earlier utterance (lines 25–28). However, occasionally Sunwoo seemed too direct or arrogant, such as when he said, "I cannot accept this grade" (line 7) and "so you have to give me a A grade, not C+" (lines 28–29). This degree of directness might be attributed to the familiarity between Sunwoo and Pyoung since they had been participating in the pair session together for three weeks.

Pyoung attempted to address Sunwoo's concern by explaining the reasons for Sunwoo's poor grade in lines 8–10 and lines 17–22 and by proposing a solution in lines 30–31 and 33–34. His linguistic skills limited his ability to fully construct his intended meaning, as indicated by numerous grammatical errors (e.g., "you doing very well and in tech exam" in line 8, "you doesn't attend my class anytime" in line 9, and "not coming in my class" in line 10), limited vocabulary and expression (e.g., "I heard your word" in line 17, "correctly" in line 17, and "base" in line 33), long pauses (lines 15, 17, 22, and 33), failed self-correction (line 22), and code-switching to Korean (lines 18 and 30). Pyoung used strategic competence to compensate for his limited linguistic skills, such as by letting go of minor errors without attempting to correct them in almost all of his utterances, using gestures to point to the real whiteboard behind him (lines 19–20), and explicitly calling for external help by looking at the instructor and gesturing "one" to indicate "one suggestion" (lines 30–31). Like Sunwoo, Pyoung was too direct ("I don't like you" in line 17) and did not hedge, likely due to their familiarity.

A comparison of their performances on the test-simulated and interactive tasks revealed two points. First, measuring linguistic skills alone did not fully account for the participants' task performance. Their performances on the test-simulated task showed that their linguistic skills were not sufficient for them to meet all of the test requirements, especially in Pyoung's case. These limitations, however, did not cause a communication breakdown during the interactive task. Sunwoo waited for Pyoung's long pauses and ignored Pyoung's minor errors using the let-it-pass strategy (Firth, 1996); Sunwoo also paid attention to the reasons Pyoung gave for his low grade. Similarly, Pyoung ignored Sunwoo's minor mistakes and compensated for his own limited linguistic skills by using gestures and drawing on external help. In this sense, an assessment of language ability alone cannot account for the interactive aspects or strategic competence that enhanced their ability to communicate.

Second, the monologue, audio-based, and timed response requirements severely limited participants' performances. During the test-simulated task, the two participants were not allowed to communicate with interlocutors to negotiate meaning. The responsibility of expression was placed solely on the test takers, but real-life communication is always a two-way street (Kubota, 2001). In addition, an audio-based test format did not account for the participants' use of multimodal resources, such as Sunwoo's gesture for "a mobile device" in line 5 in Excerpt 1, which he used to clarify meaning. The time limit also meant that neither participant was able to complete his response on the test-simulated task. The test did not reflect the features of natural interaction, even though the purpose of the TOEIC Speaking test is to measure communicative ability in the workplace (ETS, 2016).

Discussion and Conclusion

The first research question concerns how the jobseekers' perceptions of the tests and proficiency influence their learning experience. Our interview analysis shows that Sunwoo and Pyoung perceived the TOEIC and TOEIC Speaking tests to be mere job requirements, disconnected from their English proficiency. Accordingly, they prepared for the tests by working to develop their test-wiseness (Booth, 2018), including their test-taking skills and their level of familiarity with the test format, mainly by cramming and memorizing. With respect to English proficiency, because Sunwoo considered fluent, accent-free English the ultimate goal, he strove to develop fluency and eliminate his accent. In contrast, Pyoung saw English as a means to achieve a communicative goal through interaction with his interlocutors; as a result, he was satisfied with his current level of ability.

The second research question addresses how the test-simulated task and the interactive task elicited the participants' oral performances in English. Recall that the TOEIC Speaking test assesses their oral linguistic skills using only a timed monologue. This test format requires participants to produce monologic responses in the given time; the rubric and scoring guide are used to evaluate the responses based primarily on linguistic accuracy. The limited test format and evaluation criteria do not take into account jobseekers' real-life competence, which includes nonverbal communicative behaviors, collaboration with interlocutors, and meaning negotiation. Indeed, the TOEIC Speaking test may prompt prescripted and memorized responses among highly anxious test takers. Test takers seem attuned to this highly artificial dynamic, as Pyoung reported that his friend had said, "Don't dare give your own response in the TOEIC Speaking test."

The results raise three questions regarding the politics and ideologies of English language testing. First, whose definition of workplace communication is used to create the tests? While ETS claims to measure workplace communication skills, it does not explicitly provide the theoretical constructs (Nicholson, 2015) undergirding its tests. If ETS's constructs do not include the interactive, multimodal, pragmatic, context-dependent, and hybrid aspects of communication, the tests will provide only a partial measurement of a test taker's skills. Second, who decides to use the tests for gatekeeping purposes? More than 1,100 corporations in Korea adopt the tests for recruitment purposes (YBMNET, 2018a) because the scores are an expedient way to estimate candidates' English competence and determine their eligibility for job positions (YBM Korea TOEIC Committee, 2015). This reliance on scores implies that the scores are objective and credible. Third, given that ETS and corporations set the standards, whose responsibility is it to meet them? The jobseekers take responsibility to achieve as high of scores as possible, even though they may perceive a discrepancy between the tests and real-life communication. It has become normalized practice to use the tests in the corporate recruitment procedure given the tests' claim to assess workplace communication skills and their widespread corporate adoption. However, this seemingly commonsensical ideology is built on an unclear definition of communicative competence.

As noted at the beginning of this chapter, the slogan that appears on the TOEIC website is "Measurement drives performance" (YBMNET, n.d.). However, the findings of this study suggest that test takers perceive the measurement as having little connection to their actual performances. The limited formats of the tests may not fully capture the test takers' workplace communication skills. This poses a challenge to the commonly accepted ideology that the tests are legitimate means of recruiting candidates with competent business communication skills. To borrow the language used on the TOEIC website, to drive competent performance, it is essential for the measurement to reflect important features of workplace communication.

Notes

1. The maximum score of the test is 990.
2. The test has eight proficiency levels. Level 5 indicates that the test taker has "limited success at expressing an opinion or responding to a complicated request" (ETS, 2016, p. 25).

References

Booth, D. K. (2012). *Exploring the Washback of the TOEIC in South Korea: A Sociocultural Perspective on Student Test Activity* (Unpublished doctoral dissertation). The University of Auckland, Auckland, New Zealand.

Booth, D. K. (2018). *The Sociocultural Activity of High Stakes Standardised Language Testing*. Cham, Switzerland: Springer.

Canagarajah, S. (2013). *Translingual Practice: Global Englishes and Cosmopolitan Relations*. New York: Routledge.

Canagarajah, S. (2017). *Translingual Practices and Neoliberal Policies: Attitudes and Strategies of African Skilled Migrants in Anglophone Workplaces*. New York: Springer.

Caronia, L. and Cooren, F. (2014). Decentering our analytical position: The dialogicity of things. *Discourse and Communication, 8*(1), 41–61.

Choi, I. (2008). The impact of EFL testing on EFL education in Korea. *Language Testing, 25*(1), 39–62.

ETS. (2015). Examinee handbook: Listening & reading. Retrieved from https://www.ets.org/Media/Tests/TOEIC/pdf/TOEIC_LR_examinee_handbook.pdf

ETS. (2016). Examinee handbook: Speaking & writing. Retrieved from https://www.ets.org/Media/Tests/TOEIC/pdf/TOEIC_Speaking_and_Writing_Examinee_Handbook.pdf

Firth, A. (1996). The discursive accomplishment of normality: On "lingua franca" English and conversation analysis. *Journal of Pragmatics, 26*(2), 237–59.

Firth, A. (2009). Doing not being a foreign language learner: English as a lingua franca in the workplace and (some) implications for SLA. *IRAL—International Review of Applied Linguistics in Language Teaching, 47*(1), 127–56.

Higgins, C. (2009). *English as a Local Language: Post-Colonial Identities and Multilingual Practices*. Bristol: Multilingual Matters.

Jang, I. C. (2015). Language learning as a struggle for distinction in today's corporate recruitment culture: An ethnographic study of English study abroad practices among South Korean undergraduates. *L2 Journal, 7*(3), 57–77.

Kassim, H. and Ali, F. (2010). English communicative events and skills needed at the workplace: Feedback from the industry. *English for Specific Purposes, 29*(3), 168–82.

Kim, M., Choi, D.-I., and Kim, T.-Y. (2018). A political economic analysis of commodified English in South Korean neoliberal labor markets. *Language Sciences*, *70*, 82–91.

Kleifgen, J. A. (2013). *Communicative Practices at Work: Multimodality and Learning in a High-Tech Firm*. Bristol: Multilingual Matters.

Kubota, R. (2001). Teaching world Englishes to native speakers of English in the USA. *World Englishes*, *20*(1), 47–64.

Kubota, R. (2013). "Language is only a tool": Japanese expatriates working in China and implications for language teaching. *Multilingual Education*, *3*(4), 1–20. https://doi.org/10.1186/2191-5059-3-4

Markee, N. (2015). *The Handbook of Classroom Discourse and Interaction*. Oxford: Wiley-Blackwell.

Nicholson, S. J. (2015). Evaluating the TOEIC® in South Korea: Practicality, reliability and validity. *International Journal of Education*, *7*(1), 221–33.

Otsuji, E. and Pennycook, A. (2010). Metrolingualism: Fixity, fluidity and language in flux. *International Journal of Multilingualism*, *7*(3), 240–54.

Park, J. S.-Y. (2011). The promise of English: Linguistic capital and the neoliberal worker in the South Korean job market. *International Journal of Bilingual Education and Bilingualism*, *14*(4), 443–55.

Powers, D. E. and Powers, A. (2014). The incremental contribution of TOEIC® listening, reading, speaking, and writing tests to predicting performance on real-life English language tasks. *Language Testing*, *32*(2), 151–67.

Saldaña, J. (2009). *The Coding Manual for Qualitative Researchers*. Thousand Oaks, CA: SAGE.

YBM Korea TOEIC Committee. (2015). TOEIC newsletter. Retrieved from http://upsisa.ybmsisa.com/si/exam_ybmsisa_com/newsletter/pdffile/89.pdf

YBMNET. (2018a). Gieop chayong si yeongeo hwalyong hyeonhwang boonseok [The analysis of how English scores are used in corporation recruitment]. Retrieved from http://exam.ybmnet.co.kr/news/media_view.asp?id=685&page=1

YBMNET. (2018b). Hwalyonghyeonhwang [The current state of how it's used]. Retrieved from http://exam.ybmnet.co.kr/toeic/status/recruit_company.asp

YBMNET. (n.d.). YBM eohaksiheom TOEIC [YBM language test TOEIC]. Retrieved from http://exam.ybmnet.co.kr/toeic/

Appendix A. Sunwoo's Data Map

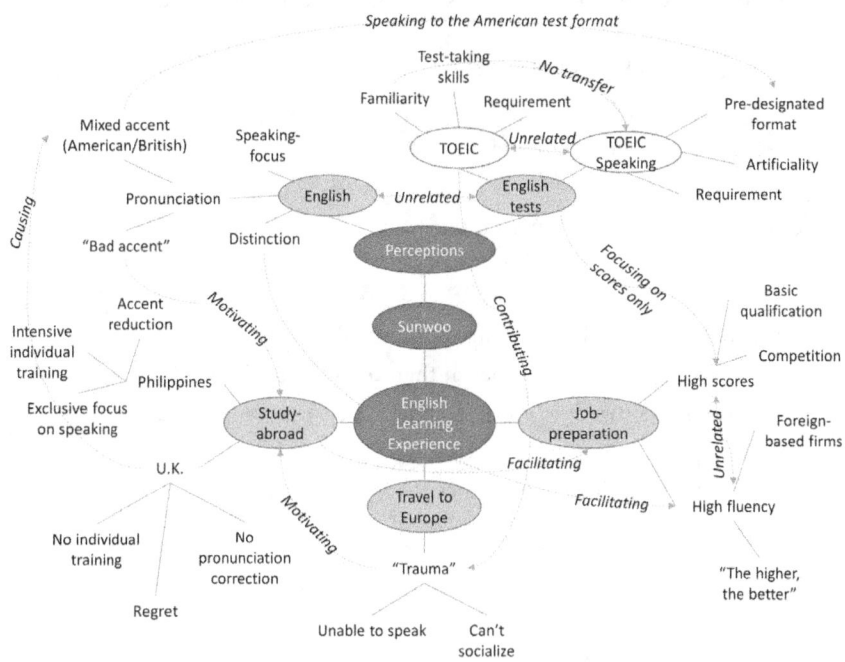

Appendix B. Transcription Conventions

It is a modified version of Markee's (2015) transcription conventions.

(0.3) a 0.3-second pause
? rising intonation
base:: lengthening of sound or syllable
<u>va</u>cancies marked stress
seminar↑ rising shifts in intonation

↓

°the° quieter speech than the surrounding talk
>....< indicates speeded up speech than the surrounding talk
<...> indicates slowed down speech than the surrounding talk
(( )) description of nonverbal actions
[ ] translation of a Korean utterance

10

Sanctioning the IELTS for Enrolling in ELT: A Critical Perspective from Oman

Ali S. M. Al-Issa

English and ELT Today

English today is a global phenomenon. It stands head and shoulders above all its linguistic counterparts leading to their marginalization and subordination. Its spread and importance as a global lingua franca are not accidental. It is a commodity that was promoted by the British colonial legacy and supported today by the American empire as a part of the wider Anglo-American linguistic and cultural imperialism and neoliberal project. This project has cultural, economic, and political interests in the developing world (Phillipson, 1992, 2008), especially in the "corporate globalization" era (Templer, 2004), which can be described as "renewed imperialism" (Hamel, 2006). At the heart of such a project lies a class of context-specific powerful individuals and influential social and political agencies with sanctioning power that undervalue internal dynamics, while reinforcing and marketing external interests and creating the dependence of the dominated peripheries on the dominant center (Phillipson, 1992, 2008). Such a phenomenon has turned the former into passive and submissive receivers of goods and values, which in turn has led to choice restriction and minimization, the legitimization of English cultural hegemony, and the unequal division of material and nonmaterial power and resources (Tsui and Tollefson, 2007).

One of the powerful forces driving linguistic imperialism at the present time is the widely promoted and rapidly expanding practice of English Language Teaching (ELT), which is value-laden and provides native English-speaking countries with a new form of growing and expanding international trade. When narrowing the focus down, we see the British designed and disseminated International English Language Testing System (IELTS) representing a fundamental component and aspect of this huge business worldwide. The IELTS today widely controls the definition of the English language knowledge, despite the test being described as "tricky," "deceptive," "top-down," "biased," "manipulative," "oppressive," and "discriminatory" (Al-Issa, 2018). It is an internationally recognized test that provides a benchmark for making comparisons. The IELTS is currently managed by the British Council, IELTS Australia, and the University of Cambridge ESOL Examinations, through more than 1,100 locations in 140 countries. It is administered for the purposes of immigration to an English-speaking country or acceptance into university by international students where English is used as the first language. The IELTS is further used by multinational corporations to assess the English ability of their workers or to get a job in some cases.

Khan (2009) argued against a culturally biased ready high-stakes standardized exam like the IELTS. She considered it invalid for various local contexts. Instead, she called for central education agencies in the so-called Third World to free themselves from what Phillipson (1992) described as "postcolonial education" and "educational imperialism" and develop local norms of proficiency that test ELT candidates' information about the curriculum and their ability to interact in English with speakers of other varieties in English as an international language.

Templer (2004) thus described the IELTS as a "testing cartel" and an integral part of the ELT industry and commercialization and a powerful tool for socialization, social manipulation, control, class stratification, and reproduction. Templer, who examined the ideological influence pertaining to levels and standards and resulting from the cultural bias of the IELTS from a materials and program design perspective, identified two factors that contributed to washback effects. Templer argued in favor of using and adapting other low-cost tests.

The IELTS is hence a form of benchmark used to define and control the English language proficiency and knowledge for a specific category of non-native English language speakers. It is accepted and promoted worldwide due to the cultural and economic support it has been receiving from the West and the developing world, which in turn perpetuates cultural dependency on the West. The next section will shed light on how the IELTS was introduced as a language proficiency benchmark for Omani NNESTs.

Contextual Background

Several language assessment scholars (Fleckenstein, Leucht, Anand Pant, and Köller, 2016; Richards, 2017 and Tajeddin and Adeh, 2016) have emphasized the central role of English language proficiency for non-native English-speaking teachers (NNESTs). These researchers also highlighted its implications for such teachers' confidence and performance inside and outside the ELT classroom and for students' language learning.

Relatedly, a large number of students who graduate every year from high school in Oman have failed to reach the required competence in English, which has been partly attributed to the teachers' linguistic inadequacy (Al-Issa, 2005; Moates, 2006). Such failure has had negative implications for Oman's nationalization and modernization plans since English is important for science and technology acquisition, pursuing higher education, finding a white-collar job, conducting business, and engaging in interlingual communication (Al-Issa, 2015). Therefore, the Omani Ministry of Education and in response to a recommendation by Jane Moates (2006), a British ELT consultant hired to produce a curriculum framework for grades 11 and 12 and to advise on the new course materials development, decided to recognize the academic IELTS as an officially valid benchmark to assess the ELT Sultan Qaboos University (SQU) graduates' English language proficiency. SQU was established in 1986 and is the only state-owned university in Oman. Interestingly, Moates recommended that SQU sanction the IELTS as a language proficiency requirement indicator prior to joining the ELT program. However, SQU ignored this recommendation since SQU is being evaluated by the Oman Academic Accreditation Authority against national standards. The ministry therefore approved an overall Band 6 as a minimum requirement to be eligible for applying for an ELT job at its schools in order to (1) help facilitate the implementation of the linguistically demanding Communicative Language Teaching (CLT)-oriented Basic Education System (BES) innovation and (2) prepare linguistically adequate students fit to join the ever-increasing challenging job market. It is noteworthy that candidates who score Band 6 in the IELTS generally have an effective command of the language despite some inaccuracies, inappropriacies, and misunderstandings. They can use and understand fairly complex language, particularly in familiar situations, however.

Importantly, the choice of the IELTS as an English language proficiency indicator has generated substantial debate in the Omani ELT education community due to different technical issues related to the test. It is noteworthy that the sultanate has been culturally dependent on the West—as represented in North America, Britain, and Australia (NABA)—to formulate its policies and help it implement them (Al-Issa, 2006). In fact, and like all other aspects of ELT, assessment, too, has been ideologically driven and oriented in Oman (Al-Issa, 2005).

Furthermore, the quality of the College of Education ELT program came under the microscope, as its validity was questioned, given that SQU has been pursuing accreditation and international recognition through the National Council for Accreditation of Teacher Education (NCATE) and the American Council on the Teaching of Foreign Languages (ACTFL) for its different programs over the past two decades to improve its world ranking. Hence, SQU has invested generously in this regard.

The next section will thus review literature about the concept of language proficiency and what it means to be proficient in English language and whether an instrument like the IELTS could define such concept when applied to English teachers.

Problematizing English Language Teachers' Proficiency

Proficiency is a contentious construct that has divided scholars worldwide (Canh and Renandya, 2017; Richards, 2017; Tsang, 2017). These authors problematized the concept of proficiency and pedagogy. They asserted that language proficiency and teaching ability were two different things, and that the relationship between them was indirect and complex and not straightforward. Canh, Renandya, and Tsang, who found that those who scored Band 7 or Band 8 or achieved a high level on internationally received language proficiency certificates such as the Common European Framework of Reference for Languages (CEFR) were more confident in language use and provided a good language model to their students and could motivate and engage them better. By contrast, they found that teachers who were considered less linguistically proficient performed better. The authors suggested that teachers' functional competence or discourse skills comprised of classroom English proficiency and general English language proficiency, with the former including knowledge of and about the language. They stressed that the two types of proficiency are interrelated in a complex way and need to be addressed using a balanced approach. They further held that measuring language proficiency required for teaching English through English or as generally applied to contexts in which teaching a foreign language is conducted through a foreign language is a challenge. This is especially the case if the aim is to use the test for professional training benchmarking purposes defining and identifying "best practices" (Richards, 2017). Richards (2017) was critical of the fact that certain developing countries used imported tests and benchmarks to measure teachers' general level of language proficiency and correlated it with those teachers' teaching competence, which he deemed to be unrealistic.

Freeman et al. (2015) thus discussed a reconceptualization of English language teacher proficiency to prepare and teach English lessons in English in public-sector schools. The aim was to support national policy and help students develop a useable knowledge of the target language. Freeman et al. proposed a "bounded form" of English for Specific Purposes and called it "English-for-Teaching." The construct advocated that teachers developed a sense of authority and expertise as a result of their knowledge of the "local" tasks and responsibilities of their teaching situations and the social and interactional contexts of their classrooms while using English as a global language.

In addition, Freeman et al. (2015) stated that their English-for-Teaching construct highlighted the essential English language skills teachers would need to be able to "prepare and enact the lesson in a standardized (usually national) curriculum in English in a way that is recognizable and understandable to other speakers of the language" (p. 132). The authors were critical of the connection established between improving teachers' English language proficiency on the one hand and improved instructional quality and student learning on the other hand. They saw such a concept as promoting and marketing the pervasive native-speakerism ideology to ELT.

Critical of the lack of the loosely defined demands of language use in the classrooms by Western agencies like the CEFR and ACTFL, Freeman et al. (2015) maintained that their proposed construct had important implications for designing teacher education programs with the capacity to address teachers' language development in terms of "tangible" and "classroom-based outcomes" (p. 137), thus enhancing program face validity and allowing for better use of teachers' time and energy. In sum, it has become evident that English language proficiency is a complex and subjective construct that needs to be measured subjectively. The next section will review literature about the IELTS's validity to see to why this test cannot be used as an English language proficiency benchmark.

The IELTS' Validity

Griffiths (2003) stated that neither the "expensive and time consuming" (p. 38) TOEFL nor the IELTS "is universally accepted as a valid measurement of proficiency" (p. 37). Hinton (2009) further acknowledged the comprehensiveness of the IELTS as a test with high face validity or the degree to which a test appears effective in terms of its stated aims. Nonetheless, Faust (2012) held that "face validity is not really a scientifically based criterion but an impressionistic one" (p. 65).

On the subject of the suitability of the IELTS for enrollment in ELT, Al-Malki (2014) questioned the IELTS's construct validity or the degree to which a test measures what it claims, or purports, to be measuring. She collected ninety-four graduate freshmen Omani English teachers' IELTS, grade point average (GPA), and teaching competencies. The author found a moderate significant relationship between the IELTS and the participants' GPA. However, the relationship between the IELTS and teaching competencies was weak. Al-Malki recommended that the Omani Ministry of Education reconsider its overall Band 6 requirements on the IELTS for appointing the College of Applied Sciences graduates as full-time English teachers. She also recommended that the ministry allow those who scored below Band 6 on the IELTS to teach since they had been learning at the college for five years to become teachers.

A different dimension of the IELTS's cultural bias was found in Freimuth's (2013) study. She found that the cultural bias perceived by the twenty-four Emirati university students IELTS Task One takers had some validity problems, given the sociocultural and educational background of the students, which is largely similar to the Omani students'. She hence concluded that the IELTS was invalid for some candidates with different needs.

Furthermore, Freimuth (2016) found a different perspective of the IELTS's cultural bias. The author found sixty reading passages she had investigated referred to 139 places or regions around the world with only five references pertaining to the Middle East and none to the UAE, which slowed students down and significantly impacted on their reading scores. Freimuth recommended avoiding using the IELTS as a one-size-fits-all instrument for determining language proficiency on a mass scale.

Hinton (2009) further viewed the IELTS as having a negative washback effect at the micro level due to the large number of discrete-point item types, which lack communicative authenticity and allow for too much guessing. As a consequence, this negatively impacted on teaching and learning. Interestingly, Dooey and Oliver (2002) found no link between the IELTS scores and academic performance. By contrast, other researchers (Arcuino, 2013; Avdi, 2011) found generally positive (although sometimes weak or inconsistent) correlations between the IELTS entry levels and GPAs. Arcuino (2013), for example, suggested that external and cultural factors played a part in student's academic success when the relationship between the IELTS score and final GPA is weak and that a high score in this international test was not a true reflection of one's academic success.

In short, one can argue that the IELTS cannot be used as an English language proficiency benchmark, due to its lack of predictive validity,[1] construct validity,[2] and concurrent validity.[3] This leads to the conclusion that the acceptance of the IELTS as a language proficiency benchmark is hence ideologically motivated and entails a hidden agenda.

Defining Ideologies

The aforementioned discussion argued that choice of the IELTS as a language proficiency benchmark is imbued with ideology. Therefore, this section attempts to see what Western-based ideologies are embedded in the IELTS and how they determine its choice as a language proficiency benchmark.

Meritocratic Ideology

Meritocracy is a British-originated social ideology and system and a principle of distribution of rewards by "merit," which results from fierce competition. It creates and promotes hierarchy, discrimination, and inequality and cultivates the talented. It further creates social divisions among ELT student teachers (STs) as potential future teachers on the basis of their scores on a highly "selective tradition" (Williams, 1989) and "interested knowledge" (Pennycook, 1989) like the IELTS to safeguard the ELT policy from incompetent teachers.

Colonialist/Culturalist Ideology

The British-originated and American-cultivated colonialist/culturalist ideology is a form of ideology that gives supremacy to one powerful class and culture over another weak one. Power is tied to knowledge and the cultural capital and space occupied by the internationally recognized IELTS. The IELTS stresses communicative knowledge of the four skills and the target language culture through a process of acculturation, while delegitimizes, subordinates, marginalizes, and oppresses all other forms of local and context-specific knowledge held by the ELT STs at SQU. The dominated class or "proletarian culture" (Gramsci, 1971) is the SQU ELT STs, who try to revolt against the "bourgeoisies" (the Ministry of Education in this case) by contesting meritocratic ideology and colonialist/culturalist ideology that (1) are manipulative, biased, discriminatory, oppressive, and power-abusive and (2) favor one type of culture and knowledge over another, thereby leading to the creation of social hierarchy and stratification.

The Economic/Rationalist/Neoliberalist Ideology

The Australian-originated economic/rationalist/neoliberalist ideology is a social philosophy and a value-laden political ideology. It rejects monopoly while promotes individualist, competitive, and libertarian values. Meantime, it conflicts with values of equality and cooperation (Stokes, 2014).

In today's knowledge-based economy, the members of this ideology thrive to liberate themselves from the power exercised over them by the dominant group, which attempts to promote knowledge specifically produced to promote its cultural values and traditions, as it is the case with the IELTS, which hinders Omani SQU STs' enrollment in ELT. Members of the periphery are self-motivated to introduce change to improve the quality of the selection criteria. SQU ELT STs try to create space for themselves through arguing, questioning, negotiating, and contesting their place on the knowledge and power hierarchy, which creates tension at the micro- and macro-structure levels and struggle over power and cultural space. They provide scientific reasoning to try and sound rational and to explicitly and implicitly justify their epistemological merit. Moreover, they view all members of their group as equally knowledgeable and meriting involvement in formulating policies leading to introducing positive change to the system in an untraditional manner. Members of this ideology are manipulative too "but as a form of opposition or dissent, or ad hoc, on the basis of personal characteristics" (van Dijk, 2006, p. 362).

Hence, there is an evident conflict among the ideologies that govern the use of the IELTS as a language proficiency benchmark. This conflict is embedded in discourse and necessitates analysis from a critical perspective.

Method

The Omani ELT system is imbued with ideologies and mind control, which have contributed to the emergence and persistence of a lack of democratic education (Al-Issa, 2015). Nonetheless, there is an evident lack of studies that focus on Critical Discourse Analysis (CDA) to reveal the ideologies embedded in the multiple discursive layers to provide a "fresh" perspective on the construction of the Omani ELT system (Al-Issa, 2015). Therefore, guided by van Dijk's (2006) social cognitive theory, my aim in this CDA study is to analyze, understand, and expose inequality and injustice generating from bias, manipulation, and power abuse as exercised by the Ministry of Education and related to sanctioning the IELTS as a prerequisite for enrollment into ELT in Oman and leading to victimizing STs. STs within this study are being deceived and discriminated against. They are unaware of the consequences of such biased decision due to a lack of specific and relevant knowledge resulting from the cultural space they occupy. This provides an important platform for understanding the ideologies that inform the views of the six STs about the role of the IELTS as the only English language proficiency selection criterion for becoming an English language teacher in the Sultanate of Oman and any alternative language proficiency selection criteria used for the same purpose.

Participants

The major source of data in this study came from six STs at the College of Education at SQU. They were selected out of a total of fifty-eight (twenty-one males and thirty-seven females) graduating ELT majors, who took the academic version of the IELTS. I had two higher achievers (above Band 6 on the IELTS), two lower achievers (below Band 6), and two who matched the Ministry of Education criterion (Band 6).

Data Collection

I conducted semi-structured personal interviews with the participants. I interviewed each one of them separately after getting their consent. I used the six questions appearing below as my main questions.

1. Why did you take the exam in the first place? How important to you is taking the IELTS exam?
2. How important is it to you to know your language proficiency level?
3. Do you think that setting an IELTS score as a precondition for working as an English teacher is a fair requirement? Why/why not? Can you suggest alternative means of assessing graduates' language proficiency?
4. In your opinion, is the score you obtained a true representation of your language proficiency? Why/why not?

5. What aspects of the test may have affected your score?
6. In your opinion, how may this score in the IELTS exam affect you in the future either positively or negatively?

To improve the quality, reliability, and validity of the interview questions, I sent them along with the study aims to an expert jury with expertise about using the IELTS and the policies underlying its imposition in the Third World. The jury gave its feedback about some of the items.

Another equally important and substantial source of data was the pertinent literature on the various ELT selection criteria. I used it to help enhance the construct validity of the study and make theoretical contributions to the teachers' selection process in the Omani ELT system.

Data Analysis

Guided by Greckhamer and Cilesiz's (2014) approach to discourse analysis, I tabulated "the discourse analysis process to represent the process of analysis and interpretation by providing anchors connecting data units, specific points of reasoning (i.e. concepts), and building blocks" (p. 431). In the first column, I included segments of the raw data. The next column included textual units from the pertinent literature. I used the data from the first and second columns to describe the concepts and highlight their main features in the third column. The last column included the name of the code the previous three columns logically led to (see Tables 10.1 and 10.2).

Table 10.1 Tabulating the Discourse Analysis Process of the IELTS as a Selection Criterion

Data Unit in Context	Data Unit	Concept	Building Block
"Maybe when I apply for a teaching job, that's what will define our language proficiency because they will only take some people and some people will be left behind" (Informant 6).	Canh and Renandya (2017) and Tsang (2017) found no relationship between good and effective teaching and achieving a high score in the IELTS.	Participant believed the IELTS could predict her language proficiency. She hence accepted its role as a fair tool for granting her an ELT full-time position.	Meritocratic ideology and colonialist/culturalist ideology.

Table 10.2 Tabulating the Discourse Analysis Process of the Alternative Selection Criteria

Data Unit in Context	Data Unit	Concept	Building Block
"Actually, the best way in my opinion is to visit us in schools. Observation I think is the best way. So, you can know the teacher, you can see the teacher in the classroom. This is the most important point here. Because we are teachers, you can see us in the place where we work in. It's all about practice! About delivering!" (Informant 3).	Address teachers' language development in terms of "tangible" and "classroom-based outcomes" (Freeman et al., 2015, p. 137).	Participant suggested classroom-based performance observation as a selection criterion due to the IELTS's lack of construct validity.	Economic/ rationalist/ neoliberal ideology.

Results

The IELTS Predictive Validity

The previous section discussed the ideologies governing the validity of the IELTS. This section of the study reports results pertinent to the ideologies governing the predictive validity, construct validity, and concurrent validity of the IELTS. Participant 1 mentioned the high face validity of the IELTS in Oman and how its uses define talent, control economic rewards, and produce social hierarchy, division, and stratification. He spoke about correlating language proficiency with teaching competence and the use of Band 6 as a cut-off score for finding a teaching job beyond the Ministry of Education, where financial and academic rewards are better.

> Looking for a job and maybe to continue my higher education. So, some of the universities ask for the IELTS in order to accept you and they need a certain band in the IELTS. Some of the local institutions look for the IELTS exam such as the Air Force and the Army. They want the candidate teacher to have a minimum of Band 6 in the IELTS exam.

Participant 6 problematized language proficiency as a construct. She tried to define it in order to predict her level. However, she was uncertain about how to define it due to its complexity and subjectivity.

> Somehow, I know my strength and weakness in language proficiency. Somehow we can say, for example, being able to read and write and communicate in English. I don't know my proficiency level exactly but I know my strengths and weakness.

Participant 6 then correlated language proficiency with teaching competence and saw the former as a prerequisite for the latter. She believed the IELTS could objectively define her language proficiency as an English teacher and linked this belief to the selection criterion practice adopted by the Ministry of Education. She said, "Maybe when I apply for a teaching job, the IELTS will define our language proficiency because they will only take some people and some people will be left behind."

Similarly, sanctioning the IELTS made Participant 5 believe that it could predict his English language proficiency. He believed it could give him self-confidence as a language user through identifying his areas of weaknesses and work toward improving them.

> I think taking the IELTS is very important. I want to see my efficiency to which degree I have reached and another question I have in my mind that do I want more to improve my language or is it o.k. now, or what I can do for the future to improve? Even I graduated with a good competence of language, I feel I need to improve, because English language doesn't end at a certain point.

Participant 4 also believed that the IELTS could predict his general and classroom English language proficiency and help him identify his language weaknesses. He too correlated language proficiency with teaching competence and accepted the IELTS as a benchmark for his classroom English proficiency. He believed that a high score in the IELTS would make him a more self-confident, motivated, and efficient teacher.

> I wanted the IELTS to see my score, my level in English. I took it mainly for career reasons. It's very important because I want to see my level. For instance, if I am an English teacher, I have to be professional in my career so that when I go to the field, I face many students. It's embarrassing somehow to find a student who is better than you. So, it is preferable to develop yourself, to improve your skills, and in the IELTS you will meet these levels.

Similarly, Participant 3 believed the IELTS could predict her language proficiency. She too correlated her teaching competence with her language proficiency. Nonetheless, she did not think Band 6 as a cut-off score was a justifiable benchmark for becoming a competent English teacher.

It means that I have to improve my language. So, how can I be a teacher in the future and teach my students and my level will be 6 on the IELTS. Also, how will the students benefit from me in the future? So, I want to give them the right format of the English language.

Nevertheless, Participant 3 did not think the IELTS was sufficient for predicting her language proficiency. She proposed employment interviews to validate the IELTS's weak predictive validity. She wanted her classroom English language proficiency to be tested too to demonstrate to the Ministry of Education that there was another aspect of her language proficiency that would be equally important for teaching.

They can also make interviews with students asking them about what they have taken so far in the English Language Department. For example, in the English Curriculum, the Curriculum Systems, about our methods of teaching, in the English Language Department we talk about literature. How we can apply all these things in our teaching. How you can group students together. How you can teach them specific skills.

Participant 3 then linked classroom English language proficiency in general and pedagogical competence to argue how English could be used to teach in a local context. She suggested classroom-based performance observation as a selection criterion to argue against the weak predictive validity of the IELTS. She also suggested being appointed as a full-time teacher first and then being observed in action to judge one's all-round performance.

Actually, the best way in my opinion is to visit us in schools. Observation I think is the best way. So, you can know the teacher, you can see the teacher in the classroom. This is the most important point here. Because we are teachers! You can see us in the work place! It's all about practice! About delivering!

The IELTS Construct Validity

Participant 3 looked at the IELTS's cultural sensitivity and bias. She used her SQU ELT program as a benchmark to critically highlight certain irrelevant aspects tested by the IELTS. She tried to highlight the lack of alignment between the IELTS and instruction at her program.

The writing part, we have different parts, which is describing a diagram. So, we don't know how to describe a graph. It's my first time to see a graph and how to describe it. We don't have the skill of describing the graph. So, I had difficulty in that part.

She then continued addressing the culturally insensitivity and bias of the IELTS to further highlight the lack of alignment between the IELTS and her program. She talked about the speaking test and highlighted her needs as a language teacher as well as the type of English she needed to teach in her local context.

> They asked me about a company in your village, and in our village we don't have a company. So, I told her about a company in Muscat. I found it very difficult because I can't find a company and what's going in these companies. Talk about companies is not about my experience, because I encounter them and read about them for interest, not to focus on them or how to apply them in my teaching or in the future as well.

Unlike the previous participant, Participant 4 was critical about the reading test. He spoke about discrete points in the reading passages, which allowed for guessing and led him to obtain a low score.

> I can promise that with the reading passages, I didn't read the passages at all. Just doing by guessing and I got 5.5. If you are asking me about the headlines of the passages, I'll tell you I don't know and I actually don't know anything about them.

Participant 2 underscored the lack of suitability of the IELTS for different needs and the lack of justice and equality emerging from this practice. She critiqued the speed factor of the IELTS and how it slowed down other students and impacted their scores.

> I don't think it is fair because frankly the IELTS is a speed test and you are challenged very much by the time. Maybe there are learners who are slow but they can produce accurate results even when they are working slowly. Fast is not always correlated with accurate.

Similarly, Participant 6 criticized the IELTS for being a speed test and its failure to meet STs' individual difference. She tried to correlate the IELTS with her SQU ELT program to highlight the former's weak construct validity. She argued against its failure to accurately reflect the language proficiency of STs.

> I don't think it is fair because it is a speed test. It doesn't capture the students' ability even though they are active. Because the test has a tight time limit, they will not respond according to their real level. For some students, for example, their GPA is somehow high, but their ability in English is not that much. Maybe they are good in one skill but not in others.

The next three participants criticized the IELTS for lacking cultural sensitivity. They used certain nonlinguistic external factors to argue against the IELTS's construct validity. Participant 4 talked specifically about feeling hungry and how such factor affected his performance.

> I was sick on the exam day and I was hungry when I got into the speaking, the interview. I was shaking! The first word in my mind I want to say to the interviewee "maybe I'll fall down" because I was very hungry and I was shaking. I didn't eat anything. So, I'm just struggling with the speaking.

Participant 5 considered a different dimension of nonlinguistic external factors, which was a lack of preparation. He argued against the IELTS's cultural insensitivity and complained about time pressure and how it could affect individual differences.

> We were at a workshop at the night before the exam and until 12 o'clock. Moreover, I didn't prepare for the exam. Moreover, the time! Being under pressure! I also found it a bit difficult because personally sometimes I require more time to work, to understand. I need more time! When I read or listen to something, my character is analytic person.

Participant 6 also spoke about certain biased and culturally insensitive nonlinguistic external factors to highlight their effect on her performance. She explained her unfamiliarity with certain rules and guidelines pertinent to taking the IELTS, which were different from those implemented at school or SQU and led to a cultural drift.

> I was under stress because it was the first time to go and wait for an hour before our name is called in order to go to each room. This created some stress and anxiety. When we went to the room we were calm somehow but the instructions were somehow tough. You don't do this and somehow even they say "don't use your pencil!" "Use this pencil!" It created extra pressure.

Participant 6 then separated language proficiency from teaching competence to highlight the IELTS's failure to test STs' pedagogical competence. She argued for adopting a different locally designed and standardized test to validate the IELTS.

> The employer may give them another exam which might not impact the language skills. But I think if one doesn't have the IELTS certificate and you don't employ them is not acceptable. A professor from the university here told us "why do they give you the IELTS in order to employ you? You are graduates from SQU! You should be employed as soon as possible!"

Similarly, Participant 4 tried to create more space for his pedagogical competence. He, too, separated language proficiency from teaching competence to highlight the IELTS's failure to test STs' pedagogy competence. He accepted the predictive validity of the IELTS as a language measurement benchmark. However, he quoted his friends' opinion to argue for the ability of the SQU ELT program to test language proficiency and teaching competence.

> We have been discussing this with my mates. I asked them, "We are graduating from SQU and we have a bachelor certificate." So, they don't care if you got the certificate. But we are focusing on the IELTS. It's important, really important to take the IELTS, but not as much as taking a bachelor degree.

Different reasoning was provided by the different participants in this section using manipulative language to resist dominance, control, and marginalization; contest their space on the power hierarchy; highlight the controversy behind the sanctioning of the IELTS as a selection criterion; and introduce change.

The IELTS Concurrent Validity

Participant 1 correlated the IELTS with his personal knowledge. He tried to compare between his score in the IELTS and his personal knowledge to highlight the inaccuracies of the former.

> Sometimes it's tricky in the IELTS exam. For example, I scored the lowest grade in writing, while I was expecting to get a higher grade. Because I know myself and from my writing courses that I'm good at writing, because my speaking is not that good especially in terms of accuracy and fluency, but surprisingly in the IELTS exam I got the highest grade in speaking and the lowest grade in writing.

Unlike Participant 1, Participant 2 tried to measure the IELTS against her knowledgeable acquaintances to highlight the IELTS's inaccuracies. She questioned the measurement scale and the relationship between the different aspects of performance and the overall judgment of her proficiency.

> I am not fully satisfied with my 7.5 because those who know me said you could have gotten more than that and I had the same view. I am satisfied with it! It is satisfactory, but I could have gotten more.

Similarly, Participant 3 questioned the measurement scale. She tried to compare her writing and listening scores in the IELTS with those in the SQU ELT course by highlighting the inaccuracies of the former. Nevertheless, she believed that the IELTS reflected her language proficiency more accurately than her SQU ELT program.

> Actually to be honest with you I'm not happy with 6 and my writing skill and listening skill as well, because my marks at the Department of English. I got

at least 8 out of 10 in the writing skill, because all my exams are writing, just writing. So, how will it come 5.5 in the IELTS? Actually, I decided to do my IELTS again, because I want to see if it will be just 6 or above.

To corroborate her argument and to emphasize the IELTS's poor concurrent validity, Participant 3 singled out her friends as significant knowledgeable individuals as cases in point. She underscored the IELTS's subjectivity and problematized the accuracy of the speaking assessment, suggesting instead that the scale development be rethought.

I will tell you something about the speaking part. Me and my friend, we had the same topic, and with different examiners. So, most of the students who got that particular teacher got 7 in speaking. Actually, the majority of us who got a different teacher, they got 6.5. The examiners are from the Language Center. We know them! I communicated with my friends and asked them about what they talked about in speaking, what your topic was about, and what you said about it. So, we discussed our topics and I discovered finally that some of them got 7, while others got 6, although we have the same level, we share the same ideas, we have the same level of speaking as well, but the strangest thing that the teacher gave them 7. How? Why?

Participant 3 continued to cite more examples. This time she correlated the IELTS with the GPA and highlighted the weak relationship between them. She believed that her GPA was a more objective measurement since it was based on measuring her overall academic success.

My GPA is higher than my friends' and my friends got more in the IELTS. So, how can they compare between our grades? For example, my GPA is higher than my friend's, but she got 6.5 in the IELTS and I got 6. So, how can they compare between us? Who will be the teacher in the future?

Participant 1 problematized assessing teachers' language proficiency and found it to be challenging for setting a benchmark and defining and identifying best practices. He accepted the hegemony of the IELTS as a language proficiency benchmark. However, he was critical of its choice as the only dominant benchmark and linked it to a lack of justice. He wanted his classroom English proficiency to be tested as well and suggested adopting interviews to validate the IELTS and solve this problem.

It's very difficult to have a criterion for accepting candidates, but the IELTS could be one option and interviews could be another option. If we combine the two it will be more fair, because mainly this is what most of the institutions now are doing. They are asking for the IELTS as a starting point for your application to get accepted, but for you to get accepted you have to go through many interviews.

Discussion

This study used CDA to investigate the ideologies of six SQU ELT STs about the sanctioning of the IELTS as a selection criterion for enrollment in ELT in the Sultanate of Oman. The participants spoke about the IELTS's predictive validity, construct validity, and concurrent validity. Almost all participants accepted the hegemony of the IELTS as a language proficiency benchmark due to its sanctioning by the Ministry of Education. The results suggested that the adoption of the IELTS caused substantial harm to the participants' thinking and behavior due to different validity problems. For example, Participants 3, 4, 5, and 6 believed that language proficiency could be measured objectively and that achieving the IELTS would make them competent teachers. This is counter to the results reported by Canh and Renandya (2017), Richards (2017), and Tsang (2017). Constructs like language proficiency and pedagogical competence are complex, different, and very difficult to measure. However, the Ministry of Education abused its power. It used the face validity of the IELTS to control the minds of SQU ELT STs and make them believe that the IELTS could predict their language proficiency and be a benchmark for pedagogical competence. This can have negative implications for the BES CLT-based policy implementation. It also has negative implications for teacher selection, as it promotes discrimination and inequality, cultivates the wrong talent, and distributes economic rewards unjustly.

Moreover, results suggested that the construct validity of the IELTS played an important role in perpetuating the colonialist/culturalist ideology and meritocratic ideology in the context under investigation. It additionally showed the gulf between the IELTS and assessment in the Omani ELT education system. Certain participants like 4, 5, and 6 raised important issues pertinent to "locus of control" (Shannon, 2008). They had low locus of control due to the weak correlation between the construct validity of the IELTS and that of the tests used in the Omani school and higher education system. The nature of the IELTS's test-taking strategies introduced a new kind of challenge that some of the STs were not familiar with and preferred to surrender to.

Students in the ideologically imbued Omani ELT education system lack voice and empowerment. Decisions are made on their behalf. The rigidly centralized, top-down, teacher-fronted, textbook-based, and exam-oriented system at school and higher education oppresses students' needs and interests and spoon-feeds them with selective traditions and interested knowledge (Al-Bulushi, Al-Issa, and Al-Zadjali, 2018). This, according to Al-Bulushi et al., has had negative implications for their communicative language proficiency. The aforementioned participants were confronted by failure and frustration and hence decided to surrender in a competitively demanding situation like taking the IELTS.

Furthermore, other participants looked at the weak correlation between the IELTS and the Omani ELT education from a different perspective. Participant 2, Participant 3, Participant 4, and Participant 6 talked about problems with their language learning strategies. In a system almost entirely dominated by the textbook, students in the Omani ELT system find themselves with no choice but to memorize the textbook content, speak the textbook, and write the textbook. This is contrary to the language and knowledge promoted by the IELTS, which is beyond textbooks and which poses cognitive and social challenges to students (Al-Issa, Al-Bulushi, and Al-Zadjali, 2016). In fact, the IELTS broadly measures whether candidates are ready to study or train in the medium of English. It covers the four language skills, which are equally weighted. Focus in the IELTS is more on demonstrating high-order thinking skills and strategies in listening, reading, speaking, writing, and vocabulary using a wide range of materials and task and text types and forms. This kind of performance measurement should help "achieve a more accurate understanding of language proficiency in relation to real-world target domains" (Biber, Gray, and Staples, 2014, p. 4).

My results further suggested that the Ministry of Education was culturally dependent over the West for formulating its policies. As a local agency, it used its power in an abusive way to delegitimize, subordinate, marginalize, and oppress different locally designed valid and reliable measurement tools in favor of an imported, invalid, and culturally inappropriate instrument like the IELTS. In that respect, my findings align with those of Cranston (2012) who questioned the administrators' current hiring practices and the extent to which they lead to recruiting strong and capable teachers. He held that teacher hiring should be more thoughtful and include more deliberative criteria that indicate teacher effectiveness. Participants 1 and 3 thus suggested personal interviews, which coincidentally were also ranked highest in Cranston's study by twenty-eight school superintendents in helping them decide on whether to offer individuals a teaching job. In fact, "structured" employment interviews were found to have a high level of construct validity (Macan, 2009). Furthermore, Participant 3 recommended conducting classroom observations, and Participant 6 suggested administering a test that would test STs' professional knowledge as alternative selection criteria. This echoed the English-for-Teaching construct proposed by Freeman et al. (2015). Moreover, Participants 3, 4, and 6 spoke about the predictive and construct validity of their SQU ELT program, and they questioned the Ministry of Education's decision to marginalize and inhibit such a program, while giving ultimate legitimacy and supremacy to the IELTS.

Such suggestions could help usher in justice and equality in the Omani ELT system due to their predictive and construct validity. Nonetheless, research suggested that the SQU ELT program largely failed to prepare linguistically proficient graduates due to problems pertinent to content knowledge and teaching methods (Al-Bulushi, Al-Issa, and Al-Zadjali, 2018).

Conclusion

This CDA study proved to be a classic case of policy-practice disparity due to power relation issues. A powerful ideologically driven agency like the Ministry of Education fell prey to postcolonial education and educational imperialism. It submitted to the West and supported an aspect of the Anglo-American linguistic and cultural imperialism neoliberal project in the corporate globalization era. The discussion suggested that the ministry needs to rethink its selection criteria to allow for more justice and equality leading to more efficient and successful policy implementation. One of the key reasons for the Omani Spring in 2011 in which the people revolted against the government was power abuse. Hence, there is an urgent need for the Ministry of Education and another powerful agency like SQU, which was found responsible for STs' unsatisfactory language proficiency level, to engage in a constructive dialogue to reach solutions that can help establish quality and public accountability in the Omani ELT system and better serve nationalization and modernization.

Notes

1. In the context of preemployment testing, predictive validity refers to how likely it is for test scores to predict future job performance.
2. The degree to which a test measures what it claims, or purports, to be measuring.
3. A type of evidence that can be gathered to defend the use of a test for predicting other outcomes.

References

Al-Bulushi, A., Al-Issa, A., and Al-Zadjali, R. (2018). Qualitative perspectives on the English language content knowledge and methods on communicative language proficiency: Implications for succeeding in the IELTS. *Khazar Journal of Humanities & Social Sciences, 21*(3), 67–89.

Al-Issa, A. (2005). An ideological discussion of the impact of the NNESTs' English language knowledge on Omani ESL policy implementation. *Asia EFL Journal On-line, 7*(3). Retrieved from http://www. asian-efljournal.com/September_05_asmai.php

Al-Issa, A. (2006). The cultural and economic politics of ELT in the Sultanate of Oman. *Asia EFL Journal On-line, 8*(1). Available from http://www. asian-efl-journal.com/September_06_asmai.php

Al-Issa, A. (2015). Making a case for new directions in English language teaching research at an Omani university: A critical qualitative content analysis report. *The Qualitative Report, 20*(5), 560–95. Retrieved from http://nsuworks.nova.edu/cgi/viewcontent.cgi?article=2131&context=tqr

Al-Issa, A. (2018). A critical perspective on "best practice" in ELT: Implications for policy and practice. Paper presented in 18th International English Language Teaching Conference, The Language Centre, Sultan Qaboos University, Muscat, Sultanate of Oman.

Al-Issa, A., Al-Bulushi, A., and Al-Zadjali, R. (2016). Arab English language candidates climbing the IELTS mountain: A Qualitatively driven hermeneutic phenomenology study. *The Qualitative Report, 21*(5), 848–63. Retrieved from http://nsuworks.nova.edu/cgi/viewcontent.cgi?article=2367&context=tqr

Al-Malki, M. (2014). Testing the predictive validity of the IELTS Test on Omani English candidates' professional competencies. *International Journal of Applied Linguistics and English Literature, 3*(5), 166–72.

Arcuino, C. (2013). *The Relationship between the Test of English as a Foreign Language(TOEFL), the International English Language Testing System (IELTS) Scores and Academic Success of International Master's Students*. Unpublished doctoral dissertation, Colorado State University, Fort Collins, Colorado, USA.

Avdi, E. (2011). IELTS as a predictors of academic achievement in a master's program. *EA Journal, 26*(2), 42–49.

Biber D., Gray, B., and Staples, S. (2014). Predicting patterns of grammatical complexity across language exam task types and proficiency levels. *Applied Linguistics, 36*(1), 1–31.

Canh, L. V. and Renandya, W. A. (2017). Teachers' English proficiency and classroom language use: A conversation analysis study. *RELC Journal, 48*(1), 67–81.

Cranston, J. (2012). Evaluating prospects: The criteria used to hire new teachers. *Alberta Journal of Educational Research, 58*(3), 350–67. Retrieved from http://ajer.journalhosting.ucalgary.ca/index.php/ajer/article/view/1053/893

Dooey, P. and Oliver, R. (2002). An investigation into the predictive validity of the IELTS test. *Prospect, 17,* 36–54. Retrieved from https://www.ielts.org/~/media/researchreports/ielts_rr_volume12_report5.asx

Faust, D. (2012). *Coping with Psychiatric and Psychological Testimony* (6th ed.). Oxford: Oxford University Press.

Fleckenstein, J., Leucht, M., Anand Pant, H., and Köller, O. (2016). Proficient beyond borders: Assessing non-native speakers in a native speakers' framework. *Large Scale Assessment in Education, 4,* 19. Retrieved from https://link.springer.com/article/10.1186/s40536-016-0034-2. DOI 10.1186/s40536-016-0034-2

Freeman, D., Katz, A., Gomez, P., and Burns, A. (2015). English-for-teaching: Rethinking teacher proficiency in the classroom. *ELT Journal, 69*(2), 129–39.

Freimuth, H. (2013). A persistent source of disquiet: An investigation of the cultural capital on the IELTS exam. *International Journal of Education, 1*(1), 9–26.

Freimuth, H. (2016). An examination of cultural bias in IELTS Task 1 non-process writing prompts: A UAE perspective. *Learning and Teaching in Higher Education: A Gulf Perspective, 13*(1), 1–16.

Gramsci, (1971). *Selections from the Prison Notebooks,* translated and edited by Q. Hoare and G. N. Smith. New York: International Publishers.

Greckhamer, G. and Cilesiz, S. (2014). Rigor, transparency, evidence, and representation in discourse analysis: Challenges and recommendation. *International Journal of Qualitative Methods, 13,* 422–43.

Griffiths, C. (2003). *Language Learning Strategy use and Proficiency.* Unpublished doctoral dissertation, University of Auckland, Auckland, New Zealand.

Hamel, R. (2006). The development of language empires. In U. Ammon, N. Dittmar, K. Mattheier, and P. Trudgill (Eds.), *Sociolinguistics—Soziolinguistik: An International Handbook of the Science of Language and Society. Ein internationales Handbuch zur Wissenschaft von Sprache und Gesellschaft.* (2nd ed.) (vol III, 2240–58). Berlin, New York: Walter de Gruyter.

Hinton, T. (2009). Retrieved from http://www.birmingham.ac.uk/Documents/college artslaw/cels/essays/testing/THintonTesting.pdf

Khan, S. (2009). Imperialism of international tests. In F. Sharifian (Ed.), *English as an International Language: Perspectives and Pedagogical Issues.* Bristol: Multilingual Matters.

Macan, T. (2009). The employment interview: A review of current studies and directions for future research. *Human Resource Management Review, 19,* 203–18.

Moates, J. (2006). *Final Report.* Sultanate of Oman: Ministry of Education.

Pennycook, A. (1989). The concept of method, interested knowledge, and the politics of language teaching. *TESOL Quarterly, 23*(4), 589–615.

Phillipson, R. (1992). *Linguistic Imperialism.* Oxford: Oxford University Press.

Phillipson, R. (2008). The linguistic imperialism of neoliberal empire. *Critical Inquiry in Language Studies, 5*(1), 1–43.

Richards, J. (2017). Teaching English through English: Proficiency, pedagogy and performance. *RELC Journal, 48*(1), 1–24. Retrieved from http://www.professorjackrichards.com/wp-content/uploads/Teaching-English through-English.pdf. DOI: 10.1177/0033688217690059https://org/10.1

Shannon, S. (2008). Using metacognitive strategies and learning styles to create self directed learners. *Institute for Learning Styles Journal 1*, 14–28. Retrieved from http://citeseerx.ist.psu.edu/viewdoc/download? doi:10.1.1.576.3658&rep=rep1&typepdf

Stokes, G. (2014). The rise and fall of economic rationalism. In J. Uhr and R. Walter (Eds.), *Studies in Australian Political Rhetoric* (pp. 195–220). The Australian National University, Canberra, Australia: Australian National University Press.

Tajeddin, Z. and Adeh, A. (2016). Native and nonnative English teachers' perceptions of their professional identity: Convergent and divergent. *Iranian Journal of Language Teaching Research, 4*(3), 37–54.

Templer, B. (2004). High-stakes testing at high fees: Notes and queries on the international English proficiency assessment market. *Journal of Critical Educational Policy Studies*, 2(1), 189–226. Retrieved from http://www.jceps.com/wpcontent/uploads/PDFs/02 1-07.pdf

Tsang, A. (2017). EFL/ESL teachers' general language proficiency and learners' engagement. *RELC Journal, 48*(1), 99–113.

Tsui, A. and Tollefson, J. (2007). Language policy and the construction of national cultural identity. In A. Tsui and W. Tollefson (Eds.), *Language Policy, Culture, and Identity in Asian Contexts* (pp. 1–21). Mahwah, NJ: Lawrence Erlbaum.

Van Dijk, T. A. (2006). Discourse and manipulation. *Discourse and Society*, *17*(2), 359–83.

Williams, R. (1989). Hegemony and the selective tradition. In S. de Castell, A. Luke, and C. Luke (Eds.), *Language, Authority and Criticism* (pp. 56–60). London: Falmer Press.

11

Neoliberal Placemaking and Ideological Constructions of Standardized Tests in Nepal's Linguistic Landscape

Prem Phyak

Introduction

Standardized tests have been used as popular tools to assess students' second language and academic proficiency. Studies have shown that there is an increasing trend, particularly in developing countries, to make high-stakes tests mandatory for students in their educational programs (Moore, Stroupe, and Mahony, 2009). Although these tests are primarily used for assessing students' linguistic abilities, critical scholars have unraveled the sociopolitical dimensions of these tests (Shohamy, 2014). At the center of critical language testing studies remains the question of how standardized tests reproduce sociopolitical inequalities among students from diverse linguistic and cultural backgrounds (Au, 2010). Furthermore, scholars have consistently argued that the use of standardized tests to assess students' abilities reproduces social privilege and power of upper-class people while marginalizing the identity and knowledge of minority children. For other scholars, standardized tests function as a controlling mechanism for student and teacher agency (Menken, 2008; Shohamy, 2007). Menken (2008), for example, claims that standardized tests have "damaging effects" on minority youth and contribute to their drop-out and low graduation rates.

In the context of Nepal, standardized tests are used mostly for testing English language proficiency of the students who wish to study abroad. Such tests are not adopted in the mainstream formal education system; they are administered by private educational consultancies. Annually, several thousands of students leave the country to pursue their higher education abroad, mostly in the United States, Australia, UK, and other European countries. As English language test scores are mandatory for enrollment in the universities in English-speaking countries, Nepali students who aspire to go abroad for studies invest a significant amount of time and money for test preparation. They take test preparation classes run by private institutes, popularly known as "educational consultancies." Following neoliberal state policy, such institutes are established and operated by private investors, with a very loose form of state regulation, primarily for business purposes. Within the broader package of providing educational consultancy services, these private institutes use standardized tests as a major component of their business. In this chapter, I will discuss how standardized tests have been portrayed, by educational consultancies, in public spaces of Kathmandu the capital city of Nepal. More specifically, I analyze the construction and reproduction of ideologies in the use of standardized tests as a placemaking tool of educational consultancies. I also consider standardized tests as an important placemaking tool in Nepal's urban linguistic landscape. In this consideration, I discuss how standardized tests are used as a tool to support broader neoliberal ideology of language commodification and native-speakerism. Specifically, I analyze how educational consultancies use standardized tests to construct and reproduce ideologies that support neoliberal imaginations such as flying abroad for higher education and ensuring better job opportunities. This chapter contributes to an ongoing critical discussion on the use of standardized tests by focusing on their ideological meanings in a developing country where young people aspire to study abroad for migration and better life opportunities.

Standardized Tests, Study Abroad, and Educational Consultancies

The use of standardized tests is becoming increasingly popular across the globe. Smith's (2014) study showed that high-stakes tests have been used as a tool to assess quality of education in relation to global standards. His study further revealed that high-stakes tests are used for making teachers accountable for students' achievement and accreditation purpose. However, Smith (2014) claimed that mandating standardized testing has resulted in reduced instructional time, nonteaching of curriculum content that is not focused on testing, and increased use of test preparation materials. Two decades ago, Shohamy (1998) warned us that high-stakes tests serve the interests of specific groups, mostly the elite and privileged, while marginalizing minority and multilingual learners. In theorizing her critical language testing perspective, she argued that standardized tests should be considered as "political subjects in a political context" and as tools that are "deeply embedded in cultural, educational and political areas where different ideological and social forms struggle for dominance" (p. 332).

Shohamy (1998, p. 332) further asserted that in order to fully understand sociopolitical dimensions of language tests, it is important to ask what "vision of society" language tests construct and what "vision of society tests subserve." From this perspective, language tests should not be considered only as the tool to assess language proficiency; rather, they should be understood as a tool that constructs and reproduces particular social imaginaries and ideologies. Critical perspectives pay attention to the impacts of standardized tests on the lives of test takers. Lomax et al. (1995), for example, analyzed the impacts of mandated standardized testing on minority students. Their study revealed that standardized tests do not necessarily assess minority students' ability nor do they motivate them to learn further. Kearns' (2011) analysis further showed that standardized tests contribute to low level of learning motivation of minority youth and marginalize them by positioning their identity as low-achieving students.

Although a critical language testing perspective has drawn our attention toward the impact of standardized tests on test takers, what is still missing from the literature is how such tests are used as a tool in placemaking that supports a neoliberal market ideology. Hamid et al. (2018) viewed standardized tests as "linguistic gatekeeping" tools for the students who wish to study abroad. Based on multiple students' case studies who have taken IELTS tests to study in Australia, they claimed that there is gap between the purpose of IELTS tests and the aims of test takers. In other words, the students who take such standardized English language tests consider these tests as part of their bigger dream to emigrate to foreign countries where they have better opportunities for settlement upon completing their education. Thus, for Hamid et al. (2018), standardized tests are used as a means to support a neoliberal ideology of migration and profit-making business. As the students from developing countries such as Nepal increasingly choose to fly to English-speaking countries for their higher education, standardized tests are assigned more value and importance and are thus used as a commodity in the placemaking processes by educational consultancies.

In the case of Nepal, however, standardized tests are not used to assess students' academic and language proficiency in the mainstream education system. Except for very few schools that run Cambridge University's A level programs, English language competencies are assessed through regular local classroom and national examinations. However, the market of test preparation centers is growing in urban spaces. Reports have shown that about 2,500 education consultancies have sprouted across the country (Aryal, 2017). These consultancies are affiliated with three major organizations—Educational Consultancies Association of Nepal (ECAN), Free Educational Consultancies Organization of Nepal (FECON), and International Education Representatives' Initiative of Nepal (IERIN). In this chapter, I focus on how such private educational consultancies use standardized tests in public space and what underlying ideologies they construct in the broader public sphere. In what follows, I discuss the presence of standardized tests in the cityspace of Kathmandu.

Standardized Tests and Neoliberal Placemaking in Kathmandu

Critical language testing scholars have interpreted the role of standardized tests from multiple perspectives. Building on Foucault's "governmentality," Graham and Neu (2004) analyzed how standardized tests cannot simply be used as a tool to assess students' educational achievement. They claim that "although standardized testing may serve its stated rationale of measuring student performance, it functions as a mode of government control and a method of constructing governable subjects" (p. 1). From this perspective, standardized tests are considered as a mechanism to control students from learning as per their needs. Graham and Neu (2004) further argue that standardized tests promote "pedagogical narrowness" and are unable to "measure the essence of learning" (p. 2). Recent studies have further considered standardized testing as a major component of neoliberal education market. Taking such testing as a "linguistic gatekeeping" tool for international migration, Hamid, Hoang, and Kirkpatrick (2018) argue that standardized tests support "market fundamentalism" and promote profit-making motive of the companies that develop and administer standardized tests. Although these studies have critically assessed the ideologies that standardized tests support, their role in the placemaking process has been ignored in the existing literature. What ideologies standardized tests construct and reproduce through their display in public space has not yet been studied. In light of this gap, I focus on ideological meanings of standardized tests as they are displayed in the public space of Kathmandu.

In the context of Nepal, although there is lack of exact data, various sources, including the Ministry of Education, show that more than sixty thousand students annually receive a "no objection letter" to apply for student visa (The Himalayan Times, 2018). Studies have further shown that these students consider countries such as the United States, Australia, the UK, New Zealand,

and Canada as major destinations for study abroad (The Himalayan Times, 2018). As requirements for admission, these students have to take standardized tests and other counseling services, including visa processing, from "brokers" who are famously known as "educational consultancies" (Thieme, 2017). Registered as educational counseling and test preparation centers, such educational consultancies engage in professionalized educational brokering to cater to the needs of young middle-class Nepalis who aspire to study abroad. This professional services include setting up offices, with sophisticated infrastructure, and recruitment of professional counselors, receptionists, and teachers for test preparation classes.

Education consultancies occupy an important space in the placemaking process of Kathmandu cityspace. In their signboards, of different sizes and colors, they use various strategies to attract public to their places. This kind of placemaking process has been interpreted from a number of perspectives. Lew (2017) considers it as a set of "planned and intentional global theming" processes involving multiple actors such as the government and other authorities. In Kathmandu, streets such as Putali Sadak, New Baneshwor, Bag Bazzar, and Lagankhel have been popular target places for educational consultancies that run test preparation classes and visa counseling services. These consultancies use multiple advertising strategies such as "visa guaranteed," "no consultancy fee," "test preparation classes by experienced teachers," and "best IELTs/TOEFL/GRE preparation centers in the city" to lure their prospective clients. Dolker Gurung (2015) reports that thousands of young Nepalis who have just finished their tertiary education (known as +2) join these educational consultancies "that promise student visas to Australia, New Zealand, Canada or Europe" (p. 1). The signboards of such consultancies advertise their standardized test preparation classes that "mostly feature Caucasian faces" (p. 1). What is most intriguing is that many such consultancies are "fly-by-night outfits" that charge heavy fees by promising students and parents visas for foreign countries. Parents believe that sending their children abroad as students is "the easiest way to obtain a visa to North America, Europe or Australia" (Dolker Gurung, 2015, p. 1). As study abroad is seen as an "exclusive privilege" for parents, the number of Nepali students taking standardized tests is growing every year. While very few students have a long-term plan to return home after the completion of their higher education abroad, most students find jobs and eventually become permanent residents of the host country (Dolker Gurung, 2015, p. 2). Educational consultancies thus capture these aspirations and advertise their own places, through various semiotic resources in public display, as an ideal place where students are provided with the best counseling services and test preparation classes to ensure their flight to foreign countries.

An analysis of such placemaking processes provides critical insights into understanding how global ideologies and agendas, particularly, neoliberalism, play a critical role in unraveling the meaning of a particular place. As a global political-economic ideology, neoliberalism has impacted on the modes of thinking, doing, and creating of individuals, communities, and governments all over the world. Through the flows of people, money, and ideas, neoliberalism has contributed to restructure and reconfigure places that support specific ideologies such as commodification of place (Harvey, 2005). As places are restructured according to free-market forces, placemaking processes involve multiple semiotic resources that add economic value to a specific place. Thus, on the major streets of Kathmandu, standardized tests have been used as a key resource for creating a neoliberal place where students, who aspire to go abroad for higher education, come to buy their services, including standardized test preparation classes, from educational consultancies.

The study of language display in public places, linguistic landscape, provides a critical framework to analyze ideologies constructed and reproduced by the use of standardized tests in public places. Shohamy and Gorter (2009) consider linguistic landscape as "language in the environment, words and images displayed and exposed in public spaces" (p. 1). While expanding the scenery of linguistic landscape, Blackwood, Lanza, and Woldemariam (2016) have paid a close attention to political and economic perspectives on identity construction in public display of languages. At the center of their analysis lies how analysis of linguistic landscape helps to understand the creation of identity, both local

Figure 11.1 Signboard of one educational consultancy.

and global, and analyze how such creations impact on people's imaginations about a particular place. Studies have also focused on how languages used in public places contributes to making sense of a particular place (Thurlow and Jowarski, 2014). Building on these and other studies that focus on linguistic landscape as a placemaking process, this paper focuses specifically on the theory of placemaking to analyze how standardized tests are used in building neoliberal cityspace of Kathmandu. While analyzing standardized tests as part of linguistic landscape in the broader placemaking process, this chapter focuses on how standardized tests construct multiple ideologies, imaginaries, and identities of place.

The Study

This study is based on my ongoing ethnographic research on multilingualism and linguistic landscape of urban spaces in Nepal. I have used observation, field notes, and photography as major methods of data collection for the study. For this paper, I have analyzed one hundred images, collected by myself, from four major streets of Kathmandu, Bag Bazzar, Putali Sadak, Lagankhel, and New Baneshwor. Between February 2017 and October 2018, I have collected some six hundred images related to educational consultancies by using Cannon Rebel T3i camera and iPhone 5c. These images include signboards, testimonials, leaflets, and other promotional materials developed by educational consultancies. The photos have included multiple information such as visa processes, counseling services, and English, Japanese, and Korean language classes. For this paper, I have selected only those images that include standardized tests.

For the analytical purpose, I first grouped these images according to their common themes. English language ideology, commodification of tests, native-speakerism, and identity construction are major themes that emerged from the reading of the images. After grouping them, I analyzed the images by using a multimodal approach (Bezemer and Jewitt, 2010; Kress, 2009). In this approach, language is considered as part of broader semiotic system and analyzed in relation to other signs such as images, colors, and overall environment. In the process of analyzing the images, I focused on language, signs, and other related semiotic resources that are used to promote standardized tests in public places. The major research questions I have addressed in this paper include the following: (a) what ideologies are constructed and supported by the use of standardized tests in public space? (b) What imaginaries are created by the use of standardized tests? In the remainder of this chapter, I analyze the ideologies and imaginaries that are constructed and reproduced through the use of standardized tests in places created by educational consultancies. I begin the discussion with native-speakerism and English language ideology associated with the standardized tests.

Native-Speakerism and English Language Ideology

One major component of the educational consultancies is standardized test preparation classes. As mentioned above, the number of educational consultancies that provide test preparation classes is increasing in Kathmandu. Registered as institutes for providing educational counseling services for study abroad, the educational consultancies use a number of strategies to attract students to their place and take test preparation classes. The educational consultancies deploy multiple semiotic resources such as multiple colors, size of letters, and statements to make their advertisement more attractive. Using pieces of flex boards and zincs, the signboards of the educational consultancies construct and reproduce multiple language ideologies related to English. As seen in Figure 11.2, *Big Bang Education* consultancy runs IELTS preparation classes. The signboard is posted on the third floor of a building in New Baneshor of Kathmandu. In order to attract students, they advertise the institute as a place where "native speaking foreign teachers" teach IELTS classes. The language used in this signboard reproduces the dominant "native speaker ideology" (Davies,

Figure 11.2 Bing Bang.

1991; Holliday, 2006), which assumes that native-speaker teachers are better than the local teachers. The native-speaker ideology is deeply rooted in English colonial history. Considering it as "the colonialist myth," Holliday (2006) claims that native speaker ideology is "implicit in the native-speakerist 'moral mission' to bring a 'superior' culture of teaching and learning to students and colleagues who are perceived not to be able to succeed on their own terms" (p. 385).

The native-speaker ideology, as seen in the signboard, reproduces a neoliberal imaginary of international migration and "international opportunity" by learning English. In other words, the test preparation institutes remain as an ideological place to reproduce the ideology of English as the language of international job opportunity. As seen in Figure 11.3, another test preparation institute highlights the number of universities from different countries as a strategy to attract students to their place. In creating the hierarchy of the list of the countries, the owner of the institute puts Anglophonic countries—the United States, the UK, Canada, Australia, and New Zealand—at the top. Alongside this, the consultancy labels its own identity as a "world-class" test preparation center where the classes of standardized tests such as IELTS, TOEFL, GRE, GMAT, and SAT are offered. This kind of strategy captures the future dream of young Nepali youth who wish to study in Anglophonic countries not only for better education but also for better job market and lifestyle.

Standardized tests contribute to the placemaking process of Kathmandu city in multiple scales. While most standardized test preparation centers are located in well-furnished high-rise buildings, some test preparation classes are run in cheap private buildings. As seen in Figure 11.4, electric poles and public walls

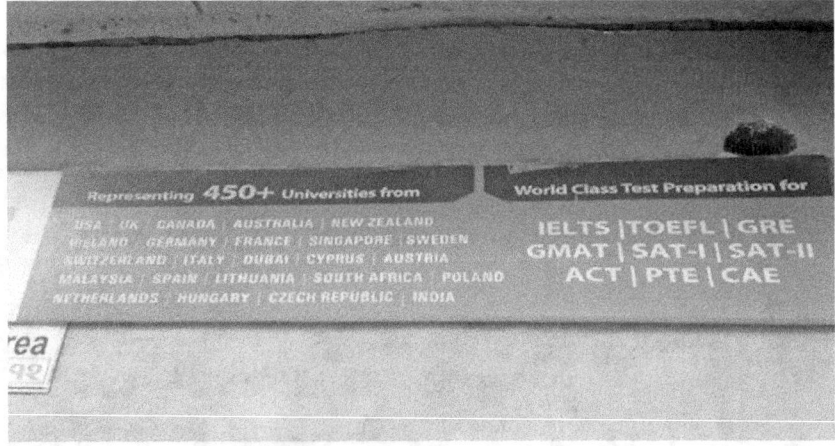

Figure 11.3 "World class" test preparation.

Figure 11.4 Advertisement of IELTS/TOEFL/SAT on an electric pole.

are covered with the advertisements of standardized tests such as IELTS and TOEFL. Such advertisements use attractive slogans to highlight the features of their places. Figure 11.4 shows that the test preparation institute guarantees the "success rate up to 9 out of 9 in IELTS." The advertisements of standard tests consistently portray English as a commodity. In Figure 11.4, the test preparation center uses the Nepali language to attract students who are not much proficient in English. By doing this, the institute hopes to spread the message to a wider audience. Such cheap advertisements are mostly pasted at bus stops and narrow streets where people walk on foot. The center promises that they provide "career counseling" for the students who do not have any English language proficiency.

Imagining Job Placement and Standardized Tests

Internationalization of job market is a major dimension of global neoliberal market of education. In Kathmandu, the educational consultancies use "job placement" in foreign countries as a major trope in the making of a particular place. In one of the major commercial places of New Baneshwor, "Beyond Boundary" institute has been established for providing test preparation classes and study abroad counseling. The institute (see Figure 11.5) asks "job placement assurance after study?" and appeals to students to make "informed decisions!" In other words, the institute appears to guarantee that the students who take their test preparation classes will get jobs after their study abroad.

Using a big, highly sophisticated and colorful flex board in front of the building, this institute displays their "consistent performance record" in different standardized tests. Their consistent score shows 7.5, 8, and 8.5 in TELTS and 110, 112, and 118 in TOEFL. Similarly, the institute includes 334,

Figure 11.5 Job placement.

Figure 11.6 We are not magicians.

326, and 320 as consistent GRE scores obtained by the students who have taken their test preparation classes. More strikingly, the institute claims that they are "NOT MAGICIANS" but "SIMPLY EXPERTS." This self-labeling strategy implies that the test preparation classes are conducted by "experts" in the field of standardized tests. More importantly, this particular institute constructs, through language, their place as the place where "experts" can help its clients obtain a high standardized test score.

Significantly, all test preparation centers use English dominantly in their signboards. For these centers, sloganization becomes a key strategy to promote themselves as the best place for test preparation classes. As seen in Figure 11.7, the institutes label themselves as a "right preparation" place for gaining the "key to success." Such institutes use creative slogans to justify their relevance.

Figure 11.7 Right preparation.

Figure 11.7, for example, shows that the students should join test preparation centers "because when you prepare, you make things happen." Pasted on the wall of the building, the signboard advertises that this test preparation center can help students achieve better scores in IELTS, TOEFL, GRE, GMAT, and SAT tests. Like other test preparation institutes, this institute also uses "English language course" as an integral part of their place.

"Mission USA": Building Imagined Future, Standardized Test, and Study Abroad

Educational consultancies often highlight the names of English-speaking countries such as the United States, the UK, and Australia as a strategy to attract the attention of students. As seen in Figure 11.8, educational consultancies use the name of the English-speaking countries as a commodity. By doing this, they construct an imagined future among the students that by joining IELTS classes in the consultancies they will ensure their entry to the United States. Although the list of the countries includes India, Cyprus, and Europe, the educational consultancies focus on the developed countries such as the United States.

While commodifying their own place, the educational consultancies also offer free test preparation classes. Some institutes offer "free IELTS" (Figure 11.9) for the students who would come to their place for study abroad counseling services. Located at one of the buildings of Bag Bazaar, Umbrella Education Foundation uses a multimodal signboard that features images of young Nepalis with happy faces and the Statue of Liberty placed on the top. A "streamlined visa process" and a "full scholarship" to study in New Zealand, the United States, Australia, the

Figure 11.8 Mission USA.

Figure 11.9 Free IELTS.

UK, and Canada are also offered to the students. In building an imagined future, the institute claims that they also help students "live, work & study" in Australian colleges and universities of their "choice." As scholars (e.g., Harvey, 2005) note, an element of "choice" constructs individuals as neoliberal subjects. In this context, the prospective student clients are conceived as individuals who have some level of choice in deciding which tertiary institutions they would like to attend.

Standardized tests, in particular, have been portrayed as a means to find the right "choice" when it comes to selecting universities and colleges abroad. Such a portrayal of standardized tests lures the Nepali youth into thinking that by attending test preparation classes they can obtain better scores and subsequently move abroad where their life and career opportunities would be better. Figure 11.10 shows that students should "prepare better" to "aim higher." In other words, students' aspirations would be fulfilled by joining test preparation centers, as claimed by the educational consultancies.

Making their signboards multimodal, the test preparation institutes use a Caucasian female image. Such an image further sustains the imagined future of the students who seek to study abroad in search of better life opportunities. As Figure 11.10 indicates, test preparation institutes consider standardized tests as a

Figure 11.10 Prepare better.

Figure 11.11 Study abroad.

tool to construct a desirable future by "opening doors" and "creating opportunities" for studying and settling overseas. More interestingly, standardized tests are presented as an integral part of the study abroad program that the educational consultancies offer. As seen in Figure 11.11, IELTS preparation classes are also offered to students who wish to study in Japan, Germany, Finland, Norway, and Denmark. The education consultancies such as "Epicenter" educational consultancy maintain that they can help "make your dream come true." This implies that educational consultancies use standardized tests to construct themselves as a place where students' dreams to study will be fulfilled.

Mobilizing Testimonies and Neoliberal Subjects through Standardized Tests

Educational consultancies not only use images of individuals but also use their testimonies in their signboards. One of the most popular consultancies, Alfa Beta, which has its branch offices throughout the country claims to be "celebrating 26 years of academic excellence" (in 2017) in providing study abroad services and test preparation classes. Located in a prime place in Kathmandu, Alfa Beta has posted signboards of various sizes and in various places, ranging from its entrance to walls of the building. They identify countries such as the UK, the United States, Australia, Japan, Thailand, Ireland, and China as destinations for their study abroad program and include IELTS, PTE, SAT, and TOEFL as part of their test preparation services. Educational consultancies thus mobilize their students as neoliberal subjects in their multimodal and colorful signboards. They use images and testimonies of their high-achieving students to justify their existence as one of the most appropriate places for fulfilling students' dreams. For example, Alfa Beta invokes the discourse of high-achieving students (Figure 11.12) as follows:

> In my conviction, one can be successful only if there is proper guidance, counselling, and knowledge. Today I feel so happy that I enrolled in Alfa Beta for IELTS classes which provided me needful resources and helped me achieve 8 out of 9 in IELTS Exam.

The testimony of another student, who had obtained 1,420 in the SAT, describes Alfa Beta as a place with "supportive and friendly teachers" that helped students experience the institute as a "quite amazing" place. All students show their gratitude to the educational consultancy for helping them achieve high test scores. More importantly, the students, through their testimony, construct the education

Figure 11.12 Testimonies and test scores.

consultancy as a place where they were able to achieve what they had never thought of achieving prior to signing up for their test preparation classes. For example, one of the high-achieving students who had taken test preparation classes at Alfa Beta claimed, "Before I joined Alfa Beta, I never considered the possibility of securing 90 out of 90 in PTE-A. But Alfa Beta offered hands on learning with one to one interaction which helped me a lot to achieve such a score."

While constructing the identity of their students as appreciative neoliberal subjects, the educational consultancies also use the testimonies of the students who have taken their test preparation classes and gone abroad to study. Such testimonies further construct the educational consultancies as a place where students are able to fulfill their dream to go abroad, after securing a good test score. For example, the testimony (Figure 11.13) of one of the students who was pursuing her higher education in Australia expressed her feelings as follows:

I am happy that I selected Alfa Beta. They not only helped me get admitted into one of the best universities in Australia but also guided me throughout the application process. Even now they are in constant touch with me and help me whenever there is a need. Their dedication to perfection and quality service is very impressive.

Another student, who is also pursuing her higher studies in Australia, had a similar feeling. As seen in Figure 11.13, she was grateful to the educational consultancy,

Thank you so much Alfa Beta for assisting me to achieve what I had dreamt of. I experienced great quality guidance and counseling and every member of Alfa Beta works hard for the bright future of each student. I am happy that I chose Alfa Beta for the guidance.

Thus, the linguistic landscape of education consultancies constantly constructs the identity of young Nepalis as neoliberal subjects by presenting them as individuals who have achieved their study abroad dreams by taking test preparations classes offered by them. The students' testimonies support a neoliberal ideology of

Figure 11.13 Testimonies and study abroad.

choice to attract more students for the profit of educational consultancies. As test reparation classes are run by private educational institutes, such institutes claim to be the best choice for their students to fulfill their neoliberal dreams.

Free Test Preparation Classes, English and Neoliberal Dream

Standardized tests become major components of a neoliberal placemaking process in Kathmandu. While considering these tests as part of their placemaking strategy, educational consultancies use standardized tests to promote a neoliberal free-market ideology. "Englishers" (Figure 11.14), one of the educational consultancies in Kathmandu, which provides counseling services for study abroad in Europe,

Figure 11.14 Englishers.

Figure 11.15 Connect Globe.

Korea, Japan, the United States, and Australia offers "Free IELTS" preparation classes. The name of the educational consultancies itself shows that they are the place where students become proficient English speakers. On their signboard, they use the image of a girl with a smiley face to make it more attractive.

As mentioned above, standardized tests are presented as an important aspect of the study abroad program. 'Connect Globe', one of the educational consultancies, displays the United States, Canada, Australia, New Zealand, Portugal, Poland, Cyprus, Spain, and European countries as destinations for their study abroad program. This institute invites students to "enroll for IELTS, TOEFL and SAT." The standardized tests are further taken as a core part of English language commodification through a neoliberal placemaking process.

One of the educational consultancies, as reflected in Figure 11.16, which claims that they provide counseling services for study abroad programs in Australia, the UK, the United States, Ireland, New Zealand, Denmark, and Poland, also offers IELTS and TOEFL preparatory classes. On a signboard, posted on the ground wall of the building, their English language classes and IELTS and TOEFL are highlighted. The institute claims that they provide English classes (written as *Angrejee* in Nepali) for 2,000 Nepali rupees. In highlighting the role of English in the placemaking process, the institute states "I speak English" at the top and "English language for all" at the bottom.

Standardized tests also become commodity of private banks, which are complicit in promoting neoliberally oriented education. As seen in Figure 11.17, one of the private banks, Kumari Bank, offers online services to register for

Figure 11.16 English language for all.

Figure 11.17 Online services.

TOEFL, IELTS, SAT, ACT, GRE, GMAT, GED, and PTE test dates. The bank also helps students to pay fees for SEVIS, WES, and college application.

Discussion and Conclusion

The analysis of the use of standardized tests in the placemaking process of Kathmandu provides some unique insights into understanding the sociopolitical ideologies embedded in the display of standardized tests. As discussed in this chapter, standardized tests should not be understood simply as a tool for assessing students' English language proficiency; rather, they should be considered as a major resource of neoliberal placemaking to support the profit-making agenda of private educational consultancies. As Hamid et al. (2018) argue, standardized tests are major gatekeepers of higher education and transnational migration. Such tests are mostly used for maximizing the profit of educational consultancies. The evidence from this study consistently shows that it is important to consider standardized tests as part of a broader neoliberal market of education. On the one hand, such tests are presented as a major commodity in the market of private education consultancies. The commodification of standardized tests, as used by the educational consultancies, is less concerned with assessing the students' language proficiency than with supporting the global profit-making agenda of local education consultancies. In this process, standardized tests construct and support three major ideologies—English language commodification, neoliberal free market, and transnational migration.

As discussed in this chapter, standardized tests embody the ideology of English language commodification. Although most educational consultancies do not have English native-speaker teachers, these consultancies often support a native-speaker ideology in their advertisements that generally promote standardized tests. Education consultancies provide free English language classes for the students who join their test preparation sessions. The presence of standardized tests in the linguistic landscape of educational consultancies sustains the widely held ideology of English as a language of global career opportunities (Park, 2011; Price, 2014). This implies that educational consultancies use standardized tests to promote their study abroad programs and circulate a neoliberal imaginary of finding jobs, among the aspirers, in a competitive educational marketplace.

Returning to Shohamy's (1998, p. 332) argument, standardized tests should be understood as an ideological tool that defines the identity of test takers as "political subjects within a political context." In the placemaking of educational consultancies, standardized tests are used as a major semiotic resource to construct the identity of test takers as "neoliberal subjects" (Flores, 2013) who have dreams to migrate and find jobs in developed countries. Furthermore, these tests should be taken as part of the strategy of the educational consultancies to promote themselves as a place that would facilitate students' dream to fly abroad and study in Anglo-American and European colleges of their "choice." In this sense, standardized tests play a critical role in enabling the neoliberal placemaking process of private educational consultancies. As education around the globe is deeply influenced by neoliberal ideologies, standardized tests are deployed to restructure educational spheres as a place where students' aspirations to achieve a high test score for study abroad is achieved.

While considering standardized tests as an ideological tool, it is also important to question the agendas that tests serve (Shohamy, 1998). Previous studies have focused on the impact of standardized tests on test takers' lives on the basis of the test scores they have obtained. These studies have claimed that standardized tests serve the interests of students from the dominant group and culture. However, this interpretation is not sufficient to understand the sociopolitical dimension of standardized tests. As Hamid et al. (2018) have argued, standardized tests are major components of transnational migration. Standardized tests, mostly English language tests, should be viewed as a driving force to construct the dream of transnational mobility for the students from low-income countries like Nepal. As evidenced in this study, standardized tests are entangled with the study abroad program agenda of educational consultancies. This entanglement is not accidental; it is purposeful and ideologically charged. The standardized tests in the placemaking process thus contribute to constructing neoliberal imaginaries that support transnational migration and dreams for better job opportunities.

Two major insights can be drawn from this study with regard to language policy. First, it is important for government to have an explicit policy regarding the use of language for private educational consultancies. The government should have a regulating mechanism for these consultancies so that standardized tests are not (mis)used in placemaking processes that support the profit-making agenda of a neoliberal educational market. Second, it is necessary for the government to monitor whether the educational consultancies fulfill what they have claimed, that is, to help students secure high scores in standardized tests. As demonstrated, educational consultancies mostly use standardized tests as a tool to promote their business of sending students to foreign countries. Although such consultancies are established with the approval of the government, they are free to use attractive language to advertise their neoliberal place. So the display of standardized tests by educational consultancies becomes a de facto policy that targets the public.

References

Aryal, B. P. (2017). *Consultancies into Human Trafficking, Money Laundering.* Retrieved from https://myrepublica.nagariknetwork.com/news/consultancies-into-human-trafficking-money-laundering-govt

Au, W. (2010). *Unequal by Design: High-Stakes Testing and the Standardization of Inequality.* New York: Routledge.

Bezemer, J. and Jewitt, C. (2010). Multimodal analysis: Key issues. In L. Litosseliti (Ed.), *Research Methods in Linguistics* (pp. 180–97). London: Continuum.

Blackwood, R., Lanza, E., and Woldemariam, H. (Eds.) (2016). *Negotiating and Contesting Identities in Linguistic Landscapes.* London: Bloomsbury Publishing.

Davies, A. (1991). *The Native Speaker in Applied Linguistics.* Edinburgh: Edinburgh University Press.

Dolker Gurung, T. (2015). *Losing Our Young.* Retrieved from http://archive.nepalitimes.com/regular columns/Between-the-lines/More-Nepali-students-settle-overseas

Flores, N. (2013). The unexamined relationship between neoliberalism and plurilingualism: A cautionary tale. *TESOL Quarterly, 47*(3), 500–20.

Graham, C. and Neu, D. (2004). Standardized testing and the construction of governable persons. *Journal of Curriculum Studies, 36*(3), 295–319.

Hamid, M. O., Hoang, N. T. H., and Kirkpatrick, A. (2018). Language tests, linguistic gatekeeping and global mobility. *Current Issues in Language Planning, 20*(3), 226–44.

Harvey, D. (2005). *A Brief History of Neoliberalism.* Oxford: Oxford University Press.

Holliday, A. (2006). Native-speakerism. *ELT Journal*, *60*(4), 385–87.

Kearns, L. L. (2011). High-stakes standardized testing & marginalized youth: An examination of the impact on those who fail. *Canadian Journal of Education*, *34*(2), 112–30.

Kress, G. (2009). *Multimodality: A Social Semiotic Approach to Contemporary Communication*. London: Routledge.

Lew, A. A. (2017). Tourism planning and place making: Place-making or placemaking? *Tourism Geographies*, *19*(3), 448–66.

Lomax, R. G., West, M. M., Harmon, M. C., Viator, K. A., and Madaus, G. F. (1995). The impact of mandated standardized testing on minority students. *Journal of Negro Education*, *64*(2), 171–85.

Menken, K. (2008). High-Stakes Tests as de facto language education policies. In *Encyclopedia of Language and Education* (pp. 2529–41). Boston, MA: Springer.

Moore, S., Stroupe, R., and Mahony, P. (2009). Perceptions of IELTS in Cambodia: A case study of test impact in a small developing country. In J. Osborne (Ed.), *IELTS Research Reports* (pp. 1–109). Australia: IDP-IELTS Australia and British Council.

Park, J. S. Y. (2011). The promise of English: Linguistic capital and the neoliberal worker in the South Korean job market. *International Journal of Bilingual Education and Bilingualism*, *14*(4), 443–55.

Price, G. (2014). English for all? Neoliberalism, globalization, and language policy in Taiwan. *Language in Society*, *43*(5), 567–89.

Shohamy, E. (1998). Critical language testing and beyond. *Studies in Educational Evaluation*, *24*(4), 331–45.

Shohamy, E. (2007). Language tests as language policy tools. *Assessment in Education*, *14*(1), 117–30.

Shohamy, E. (2014). The weight of English in global perspective: The role of English in Israel. *Review of Research in Education*, *38*(1), 273–89.

Shohamy, E. and Gorter, D. (Eds.) (2009). *Linguistic Landscape: Expanding the Scenery*. New York: Routledge.

Smith, W. C. (2014). *The Global Expansion of the Testing Culture: National Testing Policies and the Reconstruction of Education*. An unpublished doctoral dissertation. The Pennsylvania State University.

The Himalayan Times. (2018). *More Students Opting for Studies Abroad*. Retrieved from https://thehimalayantimes.com/kathmandu/more-students-opting-for-studies-abroad

Thieme, S. (2017). Educational consultants in Nepal: Professionalization of services for students who want to study abroad. *Mobilities*, *12*(2), 243–58.

Afterword

Constant Leung

It has been a real treat to be given the opportunity to read this collection of papers and to mull over them in terms of the issues and challenges they raise for future developments in English language assessment and testing. The team of contributing authors provides a panoramic view of the state of play in different world locations. The issues they address are wide-ranging—validity and utility claims made on behalf of testing, policymaking, bureaucratic and administrative support, influence of public media, public opinion, teacher assessment literacy, teacher professionalism, etc. Although the chapters cover a diverse range of language assessment contexts—English as a school language (also generally taken to be *the* language for public communication in wider society), as an additional language (for members of minoritized communities in English-speaking countries), as a foreign language (for learners of English in societies where English is not used for public communication)—several challenging issues have emerged as common cross-chapter themes; these include inappropriate and/or inadequate policy, operational and/or implementational problems, a lack of test validity, the need for teacher professionalism and support, unfair and unjust use of testing, and so on. I will focus on two issues—standards and teacher professionalism—in this discussion, as I believe they are at the heart of the problems and challenges alluded to by the authors in this volume. In this discussion, *assessment* is used as a general term to refer to any attempt to establish what a person knows and can do, and *testing* refers to the use of standardized assessment instruments such as a formal examination or a test such as TOEFL.

Perhaps the single most important justification for public support for language assessment and testing is related to the idea of (setting of and maintaining) *standards*. And yet standards seem to be difficult to operationalize or problematic in one way or another, as noted by the discussions in this collection. Standards in assessment have come to be understood in a number of different ways, including desirable or ideal qualities to be acquired or aspired to (e.g., Standard English is meant to be the model for English language learners), benchmarks for making judgments about the performance and/or abilities of individuals (e.g., sixty marks or above = Pass), and criteria for comparison (e.g., Grade A is higher than Grade B). On the whole, standards are regarded as safeguards against unchecked low quality and poor performance. Yet many of the authors in this collection take issue with the choice and/or implementation of standards within their context. So, why does the idea of "standards" seem to be problematic? Perhaps it is worth a moment to consider why standards have become a necessary part of the sort of assessment that many of us have grown accustomed to through schooling education.

Standards in language testing do not represent some sort of naturally occurring phenomena; they are very much an artifact created by a particular approach to testing and public policy. Indeed, one can say that standards in most large-scale academic and professional tests are the products of a norming and benchmarking process within psychometrically oriented test/examination design. The bedrock of psychometric testing is a commitment to the idea that we can set up standards against which individuals' knowledge and abilities can be measured; this is in essence a key meaning of standardized testing (in addition to control of test administration and test conditions). Standards are explicit articulations of the constructs underlying tests, and they are used to judge test takers' performances. Constructs are building blocks for test development; they are specified and determined by experts and professionals (often comprising testing specialists, senior education administrators, subject specialists, and sanctioned by policy makers). A well-established definition of construct in language assessment is the following: "The nature of the knowledge and ability we want to measure, by defining it abstractly" (adapted from Bachman and Palmer, 1996, p. 89). This view is expanded further as the following:

> We can consider a construct to be the specific definition of an ability that provides the basis of a given assessment or assessment task and for interpreting scores derived from this task. The construct definition for a particular assessment situation becomes the basis for the kinds of interpretations we can make from assessment performance. (Bachman and Palmer, 2010, p. 43)

To elaborate, a prespecified level of ability in or amount of knowledge of, say, the use of tenses in English grammar forms the basis of assessment tasks. Individuals' ability to perform the tasks can be judged in terms of the prespecified ability and/or knowledge (construct), which are expressed by the desired *standards* (which can be arrayed along a continuum of grades or levels). So the construct/s underlying any particular test do not generally represent any preexisting standards (for a further discussion on standard setting, see Kenyon and Römhild, 2014; Manias and McNamara, 2015). Within the psychometric testing tradition, standards emerge from the norming process within the test development itself; there is an element of circular reasoning in this approach. (For a fuller discussion on this point, see Jenkins and Leung, 2019.) Given the near-global predominance of psychometric approaches to testing in general and English language testing in particular in the past one hundred years, it is no accident that there is widespread acceptance that testing can tell us who have achieved certain standards and who have not.

Perhaps it is not very difficult to see the inherently design-derived consequences of the operationalization of constructs and standards if we consider the shifting foci in English language assessment over time. Up until the 1970s, English language proficiency had been largely interpreted and assessed in terms of grammar knowledge. With the advent of the concept of communicative competence from the 1970s onward, English language proficiency was reconceptualized as an ability to communicate with others in spoken and written modes taking into account not just grammatical knowledge but also social and pragmatic conventions of use in context (see Bachman and Palmer, 1990; Leung, 2011; Leung and Lewkowicz, 2006). Thus, the "constructs" and "standards" in English language testing have changed with the shifting intellectual paradigms over time. Any cursory glance at the individual tests from the different time periods would attest to the shifts in focus and orientation over the past forty years. (For historical overviews, see Davies, 2007; Weir and O'Sullivan, 2017. For a related discussion on the ways in which views of validity of testing have changed over time, see Newton and Shaw, 2014.)

Many of the standards-related issues discussed in this collection (and elsewhere) can be understood as a problem inherent in the conceptualization of construct itself. A construct has to be prespecified in test development and, once specified and operationalized, the test concerned should only be used to assess the construct that underpins it. In language assessment and testing, prespecification in effect delimits the range of language forms, uses, and proficiencies being regarded as allowable; this in effect is tantamount to imposing a monochromic palette on a variegated communication scape. This reduced representation of a complex reality makes sense when a purposefully designed test is used to tap into a highly specific ability in a circumscribed context.

In everyday life, individuals use their language/s in a variety of ways to achieve communication for their purposes. Indeed, the concept of communicative competence is built on the insight that the manners and forms of language with which people make and take meaning are context- and purpose-related within particular sociocultural environments (Halliday, 1973; Hymes, 1964, 1974; Leung, 2005; Widdowson, 1975). Thus, the fabric and form of language tend to change as part of the wider shifts in social practice and technological development over time. The myriad ways in which people use language for communicative purposes in particular circumstances can be observed and described. The work in genre studies has tapped into this aspect of language use in different domains such as business and higher education (e.g., Bhatia, 1993; Hyland, 2004; Paltridge, Starfield, and Tardy, 2016).

However, genres in any specific domain cannot be prescripted and prescribed as fixed linguistic recipes for all time. The descriptive adequacy of any pattern of language use should be checked from time to time, as communicative practices can shift to reflect divergent and/or changing meanings, purposes, and values in social action (Lea and Street, 1998, 2006; Leung and Street, 2012; Prior, 2005). So a test based on a prespecified construct that represents a specific kind of language use is at best capable of tapping into only a specific, and in many cases small, part of a much larger and richer language repertoire of the test takers. Thus tests, any test, should be used appropriately so that what they are designed to do is not misused and the outcomes not misinterpreted. The apparent inappropriateness and irrelevance of any test construct become immediately obvious when the values and purposes of key stakeholders involved in a social activity diverge significantly from the assessment construct, as many of the authors in this collection have noted.

Our understanding of the protean nature of language has also been enhanced by research in the fields of English as a Lingua Franca (ELF) and multilingualism. We now understand that in contexts where interlocutors from different language backgrounds choose to use English as the language for communication, they do not necessarily follow the norms of formal correctness and conventions of language use of the native speaker of English. Studies in academic contexts (e.g., Jenkins, 2014; Mauranen, 2012) and in business contexts (e.g., Kankaanranta, 2010; Kubota, 2013) provide illustrative accounts of how participants in ELF-mediated interactions tend to prioritize achieving effective communication over any concern for following or adopting English native-speaker norms and practices.

English language testing is in the main exclusively monolingual in orientation. This observation might sound a little odd at first glance, but given that English is used by a large number of multilingual speakers in ethnically diverse English-speaking communities as well as in lingua franca contexts, we cannot ignore the multilingual dimension in largely English-mediated environments (see Jenkins, 2015). Studies into the diverse and contingent ways in which multilinguals can use their linguistic knowledge and skills in their social interactions in different contexts have added to our understanding of the complex forms of multilingualism that can configure in putatively English-mediated communicative repertoires. The research in code-switching has long alerted us to this dimension of language use (e.g., Auer, 1984, 1998, 2010; Poplack, 1979). Some of the more recent work in translanguage has led to a growing knowledge of how multilingual resources can be drawn on routinely as means for communication in a wide range of multilingual settings (e.g., Anderson and Lightfoot, 2018; Jörgensen et al., 2011; Jörgensen and Møller, 2014; García and Li, 2014; García and Kleyn, 2016; Leung and Valdés, forthcoming). Seen against the backdrop of the complex and dynamic ways in which language is used in social action and interaction, the monolithically imagined and monolingually conceptualized norms and standards, particularly that associated with the putative native speaker, can seem a little out of touch, to say the least.

For the reasons stated above (and many others discussed by the authors in this collection), it is now quite clear that we cannot afford to continue to ignore the built-in narrowness of focus in psychometrically oriented test design and the dynamic dimension of communicative use of multilingualism. The apparent irrelevance of any test construct and standard becomes immediately obvious when the values, purposes, and practices of key stakeholders involved in a social or educational activity diverge significantly from the assessment construct, as many of the authors in this collection have noted.

Another issue that has been raised in the discussions in this volume is the part teachers can play in any potential development and change. Many schooling education systems around the world have tended to put formal standardized summative assessment (such as secondary school graduation examinations) in the hands of professional testing organizations that are not involved in teaching. In such systems, tests and examination papers are designed, produced, and delivered by external agencies. Teachers are at best involved in a peripheral capacity as invigilators and/or markers (with training provided and regulated by the external assessment agencies involved). In other words, teachers' involvement in formal standardized assessment is kept to that of low-level functionary.

A consequence of this long-term outsourcing of assessment is that initial teacher education and in-service professional development have tended to regard assessment and testing as not part of their remit. In additional/second language teacher education, assessment has now appeared as part of the curriculum, as in the case of the DELTA qualification (Cambridge English Language Assessment, 2015) and the pre-K-12 teacher preparation standards (TESOL, 2019). However, it is sometimes presented as an option, and there is a persistent professional sentiment that assessment is the business of the professional testers (Green, 2014). That said, the increasing pressures for public accountability in public education in recent years have led to growing call for teachers to be more knowledgeable and responsible for assessment, as evidenced by the presence of *assessment* in language teacher education curricula (see earlier discussion) and the attention this issue has attracted in this volume.

It should also be noted though that the general tendency to outsource assessment has been disrupted in a small number of educational jurisdictions through the introduction of an element of formative assessment (also known as assessment for learning and learning-oriented assessment) and/or alternative formats of assessment (like the case of using collaborative tasks and portfolios for assessment in Hong Kong, New Zealand, and Scotland). These assessment arrangements tend to require teachers to play an active part in the setting up and conducting the assessment activities, often in their own classrooms (e.g., Assessment Reform Group, 2002, 2006; Black et al., 2003; Carless, 2011; Wiliam, 2011). In the additional/second language education field, there is a growing body of literature that seeks to promote teacher knowledge and skills in assessment (e.g., Leung, 2004, 2007; Leung et al., 2018; Lewkowicz and Leung, forthcoming; Rea-Dickins and Gardner, 2000; Rea-Dickins, 2001). This area of teacher education is now generally referred to as teacher assessment literacy.

The call for teachers to play a more active part in promoting and changing assessment policy and practice is in effect a call for a higher level of teacher assessment literacy. The assessment issues covered in teacher education programs, for instance, the TESOL and the DELTA specifications, suggest that teachers are likely to be provided with an opportunity to understand some of the educational and technical issues such as purposes of assessment, formats of assessment, validity, and reliability. This is no doubt a positive move in teacher professionalization and professional practice. However, asking teachers to be involved in making changes in policy and practice demands something more than higher levels of professional knowledge and practice. It calls for a different kind of professionalism that comprises an element of expertise-informed argument and decision making. I draw a distinction between two kinds of teacher professionalism: sponsored and independent professionalism (Leung, 2009, 2013).

Sponsored professionalism refers to the knowledge and know-how recommended and endorsed by official educational authorities and/or peak professional organizations. In general, this kind of professionalism is represented by qualificatory criteria for certification in teacher education and professional development programs (such as the DELTA qualification); it is also expressed through the criteria for selection for promotion and exemplary service award schemes that carry titles such as "best teacher award." Sponsored professionalism is in effect a form of publicly promulgated benchmark that sets out what a professional can and should be capable of doing. There are such benchmarks of approved and endorsed conduct and practice for a wide range of services and trades, from plumbing to medicine to language testing. The published English language teacher education curriculum statements (see above discussion) on assessment would suggest that teachers who have developed the approved levels of expertise would, in all likelihood, have an understanding of the technical issues related to, *inter alia*, purposes of assessment, validity, reliability, and the functionalities and limitations of different test formats. They would be able to deal with assessment activities and issues in the knowledge that they are in control of the ideas underpinning the work that is expected, indeed required, of them. In other words, sponsored teacher professionalism promotes the ideas, values, and practices embedded within the *status quo* at any one time. The kind of teacher action that can lead to development and change, and to transcend the *status quo*, however, demands something more than sponsored professionalism.

If language teachers are expected to take action to develop and change the existing pedagogic and assessment approaches and practices that they find to be inappropriate or inadequate, then they will need to adopt, as a first step, a more critical and reflexive approach to professionalism, which can be understood as independent professionalism. If language teachers wish to question the educational and social values undergirding the curriculum and language testing regime that they are required to be a part of, they will have to engage in reflexive examination of their own moral and social values and practice. To be reflexive is to be willing to turn our thoughts and action on themselves, making them available for self-scrutiny (Babcock, 1980; Johnson, 2006; Mann, 2016). Teachers working in a program that, say, uses the scores of an essay-based test to assign overall communicative competence levels may question the legitimacy and validity of such use on technical grounds and the consequences for the students on social justice and ethical grounds. If they should come to the view that the vocabulary test is being misused and that the social and educational consequences of misrecognizing students' abilities are unacceptable, then they would now be in a position to make a personal decision: to comply with the status quo or to challenge it.[1] And to challenge the status quo requires a sense of independent professionalism that is premised on informed analysis and supported by social and ethical values. The point here is that teacher support for development and change in language assessment requires independent professionalism, which implicates social and political judgments and agentive actions. The cultivation and nurturing of this kind of professionalism would likely involve adaptations and changes in teacher education curriculum and ethos of professional practice accompanied by supportive policies and societal values.

It is not possible to follow-up on all the important issues covered in this collection of papers in this Afterword. On reflection, I think the title of this volume does an important sign-posting job: It has foregrounded sociopolitical considerations in English language assessment and testing that should receive far greater attention both in the specialist literature and in educational discussions more generally. The contributing authors and the editors in this volume have articulated some of the major challenges facing English language assessment in our time through informed and contextualized observations and analyses. This volume represents a significant addition to the relatively small body of critical discussions in the field to date (e.g., Shohamy and McNamara, 2009; Menken, Hudson, and Leung, 2014; Shohamy, 2001, 2007; Shohamy and Menken, 2015). Given that English is likely to continue to be a major world language and an additional language or a lingua franca for many people, the fundamental conceptual and operationalization issues raised in this volume require careful attention by teachers, policy makers, and language assessment professionals alike. Any future developments will need to take full account of the sociopolitical issues in a context-sensitive manner.

Note

1 Challenging the status quo can be career-threatening. Space and scope preclude a fuller discussion on this point in relation to English language teaching. See Leung (2009, 2013) for an elaboration.

References

Anderson, J. and Lightfoot, A. (2018). Translingual practices in English classroom in India: Current perceptions and future possibilities. *International Journal of Bilingual Education and Bilingualism*. doi: 10.1080/13670050.2018.1548558

Assessment Reform Group. (2002). Assessment for learning: 10 principles. Retrieved from http://assessmentreformgroup.files.wordpress.com/2012/01/10principles_english.pdf

Assessment Reform Group. (2006). The role of teachers in the assessment of learning. July 25, 2011. Retrieved from http://www.assessment-reform-group.org/ASF%20booklet%20English.pdf

Auer, P. (1984). *Bilingual Conversation*. Amsterdam: John Benjamins.

Auer, P. (1998). *Code-Switching in Conversation: Language, Interaction and Identity*. New York: Routledge.

Auer, P. (2010). Code-switching/mixing. In R. Wodak, B. Johnstone, and P. E. Kerswill (Eds.), *The SAGE Handbook of Sociolinguistics* (pp. 460–78). London: Sage.

Babcock, B. (1980). Reflexivity: Definitions and discriminations. *Semiotica, 30*(1/2), 1–14.

Bachman, L. F. and Palmer, A. S. (1990). *Fundamental Considerations in Language Testing*. Oxford: Oxford University Press.

Bachman, L. F. and Palmer, A. S. (1996). *Language Testing in Practice*. Oxford: Oxford University Press.

Bachman, L. F. and Palmer, A. S. (2010). *Language Assessment in Practice: Developing language Assessments and Justifying Their use in the Real World*. Oxford: Oxford University Press.

Bhatia, V. K. (1993). *Analaysing Genre: Language use in Professional Settings*. New York: Longman.

Black, P., Harrison, C., Lee, C., Marshall, B., and Wiliam, D. (2003). *Assessment for Learning: Putting it into Practice*. Maidenhead, Berkshire: Open University Press.

Cambridge English Language Assessment. (2015). *Diploma in Teaching English to Speakers of Other Languages: Syllabus Specifications*. Cambridge: Cambridge University Press.

Carless, D. (2011). *From Testing to Productive Student Learning: Implementing Formative Assessment in Confucian-Heritage Settings*. Abingdon: Routledge.

Davies, A. (2007). Assessing academic English Language proficiency: 40+ years of U.K. language tests. In J. Fox, M. Wesche, D. Bayliss, L. Cheng, C. E. Turner, and C. Doe (Eds.), *Language Testing Reconsidered* (pp. 73–86). Ottawa, ON: University of Ottawa Press.

García, O. and Kleyn, T. (2016). Translanguaging theory in education. In O. García and T. Kleyn (Eds.), *Translanguaging with Multilingual Students: Learning from Classroom Moments* (pp. 9–33). New York: Routledge.

García, O. and Li, W. (2014). *Translanguaging: Language, Bilingualism and Education*. Basingstoke: Palgrave Macmillan.

Green, A. (2014). *Exploring Language Testing and Assessment*. London: Routledge.

Halliday, M. A. K. (1973). *Explorations in the Functions of Language*. London: Edward Arnold.

Hyland, K. (2004). *Disciplinary Discourses: Social Interactions in Academic Writing*. Ann Arbor, MI: Michigan University Press.

Hymes, D. (1964). Introduction: Towards ethnographies of communication. *American Anthropologist*, 6(2), 1–34.

Hymes, D. (1974). *Foundations in Sociolinguistics: An Ethnographic Approach*. Philadelphia: University of Pennsylvania Press.

Jenkins, J. (2014). *English as a Lingua Franca in the International University: The Politics of Academic English Language Policy*. London: Routledge.

Jenkins, J. (2015). Repositioning English and multilingualism in English as a lingua franca. *Englishes in Practice*, 2(3), 49–85.

Jenkins, J. and Leung, C. (2019). From mythical "standard" to standard reality: The need for alternatives to standardized English language tests. *Language Teaching*, 52 (1), 86–110.

Johnson, K. E. (2006). The sociocultural turn and its challenges for second language teacher education. *TESOL Quarterly*, 40(1), 235–57.

Jörgensen, J. N. and Møller, J. S. (2014). Polylingualism and languaging. In C. Leung and B. V. Street (Eds.), *The Routledge Companion to English Studies* (pp. 67–83). London: Routledge.

Jörgensen, J. N., Karrebaek, M. S., Madsen, L. M., and Møller, J. S. (2011). Polylanguaging in superdiversity. *Diversities*, 13(2), 137–54.

Kankaanranta, A. (2010). BELF competence as business knowledge of internationally operating business professionals. *Journal of Business Communication*, 47(4), 380–407.

Kenyon, D. M. and Römhild, A. (2014). Standard setting in language testing. In A. J. Kunnan (Ed.), *The Companion to Language Assessment* (pp. 943–61). Chichester: Wiley.

Kubota, R. (2013). "Language is only a tool": Japanese expatriates working in China and implications for language teaching. *Multilingual Education*, 3(4), 1–20.

Lea, M. R. and Street, B. V. (1998). Student writing in higher education: An academic literacies approach. *Studies in Higher Education*, 23(2), 157–72.

Lea, M. R. and Street, B. V. (2006). The "Academic Literacies" model: Theory and applications. *Theory Into Practice*, 45(4), 368–77.

Leung, C. (2004). Developing formative teacher assessment: Knowledge, practice and change. *Language Assessment Quarterly*, 1(1), 19–41.

Leung, C. (2005). Convivial communication: Recontextualizing communicative competence. *International Journal of Applied Linguistics*, 15(2), 119–44.

Leung, C. (2007). Dynamic assessment—assessment as teaching? *Language Assessment Quarterly*, 4(3), 257–78.

Leung, C. (2009). Second language teacher professionalism. In A. Burns and J. C. Richards (Eds.), *Cambridge Guide to Second Language Teacher Education* (pp. 49–58). Cambridge: Cambridge University Press.

Leung, C. (2011). Language teaching and language assessment. In R. Wodak, B. Johnstone, and P. Kerswill (Eds.), *The SAGE Handbook of Sociolinguistics* (pp. 545–64). London: Sage.

Leung, C. (2013). Second/additional language teacher professionalism - What is it? In M. Olofsson (Ed.), *Symposium 2012: Lärarrollen I svenska som andraspräk* (pp. 11–27). Stockholm: Stockholms Universitets Förlag.

Leung, C. and Lewkowicz, J. (2006). Expanding horizons and unresolved conundrums: language testing and assessment. *TESOL Quarterly, 40*(1), 211–34.

Leung, C. and Street, B. (2012). English in the curriculum—Norms and practices. In C. Leung and B. Street (Eds.), *English—A Changing Medium for Education* (pp. 1–21). Bristol: Multilingual Matters.

Leung, C. and Valdés, G. (Forthcoming). Translanguaging and the transdisciplinary framework for language teaching and learning in a multilingual world. *The Modern Language Journal*.

Lewkowicz, J. and Leung, C. (Forthcoming). Classroom-based assessment—Timeline. *Language Teaching*.

Leung, C., Davison, C., East, M., Evans, M. A., Liu, Y.-C., Hamp-Lyons, L. I. Z., and Purpura, J. (2018). Using assessment to promote learning: Clarifying constructs, theories, and practices. In J. Daviis, J. M. Norris, M. E. Alone, T. H. McKay, and Y.-A. Son (Eds.), *Useful Assessment and Evaluation in Language Education* (pp. 75–92). Washington DC: Georgetown University Press.

Manias, E. and McNamara, T. (2015). Standard setting in specific-purpose language testing: What can a qualitative study add? *Language Testing, 33*(2), 235–49.

Mann, S. (2016). *The Research Interview: Reflective Practice and Reflexivity in Research Processes*. Basingstoke: Palgrave Macmillan.

Mauranen, A. (2012). *Exploring ELF: Academic English Shaped by Non-native Speakers*. Cambridge: Cambridge University Press.

Menken, K., Hudson, T., and Leung, C. (2014). Symposium: Language assessment in standards-based education reform. *TESOL Quarterly, 48*(3), 586–614.

Newton, P. and Shaw, S. (2014). *Validity in Educational and Psychological Assessment*. London: Sage.

Paltridge, B., Starfield, S., and Tardy, C. M. (2016). *Ethnographic Perspectives on Academic Writing*. Oxford: Oxford University Press.

Poplack, S. (1979). "Sometimes I'll start a sentence in Spanish y termino en español": Toward a typology of code-switching. Retrieved from ERIC database. (ED 214394).

Prior, P. (2005). Toward the ethnography of argumentation: A response to Richard Andrews' "Models of argumentation in educational discourse." *Text, 25*(1), 129–44.

Rea-Dickins, P. (2001). Mirror, mirror on the wall: Identifying processes of classroom assessment. *Language Testing, 18*(4), 429–62.

Rea-Dickins, P. and Gardner, S. (2000). Snares and silver bullets: Disentangling the construct of formative assessment. *Language Testing, 17*(2), 215–43.

Shohamy, E. (2001). Democratic assessment as an alternative. *Language Testing, 18*(4), 373–91.

Shohamy, E. (2007). Language tests as language policy tools. *Assessment in Education, 14*, 117–30.

Shohamy, E. and McNamara, T. (Eds.) (2009). Language tests for citizenship, immigration and asylum. Special Issue of *Language Assessment Quarterly*, 6(1).

Shohamy, E. and Menken, K. (2015). Language assessment: Past to present misuses and future possibilities. In W. E. Wright, S. Boun, and O. García (Eds.), *The Handbook of Bilingual and Multilingual Education* (pp. 253–69). Oxford: Wiley.

TESOL. (2019). *Standards for Initial TESOL Pre-K–12 Teacher Preparation Programs*. Alexandria, VA: TESOL International Association.

Weir, C. J. and O'Sullivan, B. (2017). *Assessing English on the Global Stage: The British Council and English Language Testing, 1941–2016*. London: Equinox.

Widdowson, H. (1975). *Language as Communication*. Oxford: Oxford University Press.

Wiliam, D. (2011). *Embedded formative Assessment*. Bloomingdale, IN: Solution Tree Press.

Contributors

Zamzam Abdi did an MA in English studies at Queen Mary University, London, and started working as an ESL teacher. She then completed her PGCE at UCL Institute of Education in 2017. Zamzam is currently teaching high school English, and her interests include issues of representation and diversity in education.

Ali S. M. Al-Issa is an Associate Professor of English Language Education (ELE) at the Department of Curriculum and Instruction, Sultan Qaboos University, Sultanate of Oman. He has presented and published widely about ELE in Oman. He is a recipient of several local and international teaching and research awards and recognitions. Dr. Al-Issa is currently the best cited Omani ELE scholar.

Netta Avineri is TESOL/TFL Associate Professor and Intercultural Competence Committee Chair at Middlebury Institute of International Studies, United States. She also teaches service-learning and teacher education courses at CSU Monterey Bay. Dr. Avineri is an applied linguist and linguistic anthropologist whose research interests include critical service-learning, interculturality, heritage languages, and language and social justice.

Liying Cheng, PhD, is Professor and Director of the Assessment and Evaluation Group in the Faculty of Education, Queen's University, Canada. Her primary research interests are the impact of large-scale testing on instruction, the relationships between assessment and instruction, and the academic and professional acculturation of new immigrant students, workers, and professionals.

Peter I. De Costa is an Associate Professor in the Department of Linguistics and Languages and the Department of Teacher Education at Michigan State University, United States. His research areas include identity, ideology, and ethics in educational linguistics and also social (in)justice issues. He is the coeditor of *TESOL Quarterly*.

Brenton Doecke is Emeritus Professor in the Faculty of Arts and Education at Deakin University, Australia. He has published in the fields of English curriculum and pedagogy, teacher education, and literary studies. He is currently involved in an Australian Research Council research project on literary knowledge.

Leonard A. Freeman is a PhD candidate at the University of Melbourne and an Honorary Fellow at Charles Darwin University, Australia. Leonard has worked in the Northern Territory of Australia for over a decade as a teacher and principal. Leonard is passionate about educational equity and supporting Indigenous students to achieve their potential.

Mari Haneda is currently Associate Professor of World Languages Education and Applied Linguistics at Pennsylvania State University, United States. Her research interests include dialogic learning and teaching, second-language and literacy development, the education of emergent bi/multilingual students, and the professional development of those who teach them.

Gwan-Hyeok Im recently defended his PhD dissertation at Queen's University, Canada. His research interests include validity/validation theories and English as a lingua franca. He investigated validity arguments for score meanings and uses of the Test of English for International Communication used in international business workplaces in his PhD dissertation.

Miso Kim is a PhD candidate in the Department of Applied Linguistics at Pennsylvania State University, United States. She is interested in the influence of neoliberalism on language education, social dimensions of language assessment, translingualism, and Vygotskian sociocultural theory.

Constant Leung is Professor of Educational Linguistics in the School of Education, Communication and Society, King's College London. His research interests include additional/second language curriculum and assessment, language policy, and teacher professional development. He is joint editor of *Language Assessment Quarterly* and editor of Research Issues, *TESOL Quarterly*. He is a fellow of the Academy of Social Sciences (UK).

Seyyed-Abdolhamid Mirhosseini is an Associate Professor at Alzahra University, Iran. His research areas include the sociopolitics of language education and qualitative methodology. He is the editor of *Reflections on Qualitative Research in Language and Literacy Education* (Springer, 2017) and a special issue of *Critical Inquiry in Language Studies* on "Politics of Research in Language Education."

Masaki Oda, PhD, is Professor of Applied Linguistics and Director of Center for English as a Lingua Franca at Tamagawa University in Tokyo, Japan. His interests include sociopolitical aspects of language teaching and communication in multicultural organizations. He is vice president for membership of AsiaTEFL.

James Perren is a TESOL teacher educator, author, editor, community activist, and educational consultant. James earned his Doctorate in Education in Language Arts/TESOL in the Curriculum, Instruction, and Technology in Education (CITE) Department from Temple University, Philadelphia, Pennsylvania. James teaches at Alliant International University in San Diego, California.

Prem Phyak has received his PhD from the University of Hawaii at Manoa, United States. Currently, he is an Associate Professor at the Central Department of Education, Tribhuvan University, Nepal. His research interests include language policy, language and public space, multilingualism and multilingual education, critical pedagogy, sociolinguistics, and TESOL.

Luis E. Poza is Assistant Professor of Multicultural Education in the Teacher Education Program at San José State University, United States. He is a former elementary school teacher whose teaching and research focus on how ideologies of race and language are manifest in educational practice and policy.

Jamie L. Schissel is Associate Professor, TESOL, at the University of North Carolina at Greensboro, United States, in the Department of Teacher Education and Higher Education. She uses participatory action research methods to explore issues of equity related to assessment and educational policies within linguistically and culturally diverse communities.

Sheila M. Shannon is Associate Professor of Culturally and Linguistically Diverse Education in the School of Education and Human Development at the University of Colorado, Denver, United States. She teaches teachers and her research critically examines the education of Latinx students with a focus on ideologies of race and language.

Dongil Shin, PhD, is a Professor of Applied Linguistics in the Department of English Language and Literature at Chung-Ang University, Seoul, Korea. After completing his doctorate degree at University of Illinois at Urbana-Champaign, he has taught and researched language testing (policies), (critical) discourse analysis, language ideologies and subjectivities, mostly in Korean contexts.

Ruanni Tupas is Lecturer of Sociolinguistics in Education at the Institute of Education, University College London. He is the (co)editor of several volumes including *Unequal Englishes: The Politics of Englishes in the World Today* (2015) and *Why English? Confronting the Hydra* (2016). He is currently an associate editor of the *International Journal of the Sociology of Language*.

Gillian Wigglesworth is Distinguished Professor at the University of Melbourne, Australia, and chief investigator in the ARC Centre of Excellence for the Dynamics of Language. She focuses on the language of Indigenous children in remote Australia, the complexity of their language ecology, and how their languages interact with English in the school system.

Paula Winke is Associate Professor in the Second Language Studies Program at Michigan State University. She researches language testing and language teaching methods. She is currently the PI on a language proficiency assessment grant from the National Security Education Program and is the coeditor of the journal *Language Testing*.

John Yandell taught in inner London secondary schools for twenty years before moving to the Institute of Education, University College London, where he has worked since 2003. He is the editor of the journal, *Changing English: Studies in Culture and Education* and the author of *The Social Construction of Meaning: Reading Literature in Urban English Classrooms* (2013).

Index

aboriginal 6, 44
accountability 4, 47, 52, 204
achievement 21–45, 48, 74, 96, 211
African American 94
agency 58, 68–75, 79–82, 115–17, 125, 203, 204, 208
American(s) 19, 47–55, 60–7, 91–108, 118–28, 172, 185, 188, 191, 204, 228
American Educational Research Association (AERA) 91, 106
American Psychological Association 91
Anglo-American 185, 228
applied linguistics 72, 73, 81, 113, 168
Australia 4–9, 15, 20–9, 41–5, 186, 187, 207–30
authenticity 68, 71, 72, 75, 76, 83, 159, 190

benchmark 30, 31, 35, 41, 131, 135, 141, 186–202
bilingual 46, 49, 50–66, 91, 95, 96, 98–100, 122, 168
Bilingual Education Act 56, 93
bilingualism 48, 51, 56, 93, 96, 100
British 8, 9, 17, 173, 185–7, 191
British Council 21–4, 43, 91, 141, 186, 188

CALL (computer-assisted language learning) 119, 126
Cambridge English Exam 134
Cambridge ESOL Examinations 186
CDA (critical discourse analysis) 192, 193, 202, 204
CEFR (Common European Framework of References) 131, 134, 135, 137, 141–4, 188, 189
Chicano 52, 55, 57, 60, 62
China 122, 222
Chinese 133, 173
Christianity 47, 49
classroom-based assessments 70

colonial 3, 52, 95, 114–29, 186, 217
colonialism 49, 92–116, 128
coloniality 52, 113–29
commercial standardized tests 136, 137
commodification of tests 214
Common European Framework of References. *See* CEFR
computer-assisted language learning. *See* CALL
computer-based (test/testing) 74, 160, 171
construct validity 75, 191–9, 204–8
critical
  approach 68
  consciousness 51, 58, 59, 64
  language assessment 69
  language testing 208
  scholarship 113
  thinking 79
critical discourse analysis. *See* CDA
cultural 5, 8, 31, 46, 56, 57, 71–109, 116–26, 138, 159, 185, 186, 190–210
  background 99, 208
  bias 186, 190
  capital 6
  critique 46
  development 11, 12
  factors 101, 190
  hegemony 185
  identity (identities) 4, 6
  validity 69, 92, 101
  values 192
Cyprus 219, 226

decolonization 116
Denmark 222, 226
development aid 114, 123, 124
dialogic 15, 58, 59
digital mentoring 74, 76
discourse analysis. *See* critical discourse analysis, CDA
discourses 12, 14, 114, 119–23, 147, 152

discrimination 14, 47, 96, 97, 191, 202
diversity 28, 52, 77–9, 101, 107
domestic English test 150, 152
dominance 16, 84, 200, 210

economic 47, 56, 77, 116–26, 185, 186, 192, 195, 202, 213
economy 5, 6, 53, 55, 192
educational consultancies 212, 215, 219, 222–8
educational policy (policies) 4, 48, 52, 57, 91, 93, 105
Educational Testing Service. *See* ETS
EFL. *See* English, as a foreign language
ELL(s). *See* English, language learners
ELT. *See* English, language teaching
empowerment 70, 126, 202
England 4, 6–9, 15, 16, 20
English
   competence 166, 171, 172, 180
   as a foreign language (EFL) 32, 39–41, 68, 73, 75
   as an international language 126, 186
   language commodification 226, 227
   language ideology 215
   language learners (ELLs) 61, 74, 76, 92, 100, 106–8, 152
   language schools 167, 172
   language teaching (ELT) 114–17, 124–9, 136, 139, 140, 145, 185–207, 229
   literature 6, 8, 14, 205
   -only 57, 104, 117, 121, 123
   proficiency 47, 49–51, 56–61, 93, 114, 148–55, 166–74, 179, 188, 196, 201
   as a second language (ESL) 32, 39, 40, 54–8, 62–4, 68, 73–8, 86–9, 93
   skills 148, 153, 156, 166, 168
   as a social practice 136
   for Specific Purposes 189
epistemological 98, 192
ESL. *See* English, as a second language
ethnicity 47, 97
ethnocentric 50
ethnographic 59, 167, 214
ETS (Educational Testing Service) 148, 155, 160, 165, 166, 169–74, 179–81
Eurocentric 48, 51, 52

Europe 141–5, 172, 212, 219, 225
European countries 208

feasibility 150, 155
Finland 222
first language (L1) 24, 29, 30, 31, 35, 42, 43, 92, 120, 186
foreign language 25, 29, 30, 39, 42, 73, 77, 133, 135, 142, 144, 155, 188, 205
formative assessment 104
Foucault (Michel) 46, 49, 50, 52, 94, 211
   Foucauldian 57
four skills 135, 138
France 122
Freire (Paulo) 47, 58, 59, 69, 87
French 15, 98, 133, 173

gatekeeping 130, 180, 210, 211, 229
GCSE (General Certificate of Secondary Education) 6, 8, 9, 12, 14, 16, 20
geopolitical dimension of language testing 114
German 133
Germany 222
globalization 123, 185, 204
GMAT (Graduate Management Admission Test) 216, 219, 227
grammar 15, 75, 139, 153, 172, 173, 174
GRE (Graduate Record Examinations) 212, 216, 218, 219, 227

hegemonic English 47–9, 59
hegemony 8, 18, 47, 185, 201, 202
heteroglossic 92, 101, 103–5
high-stakes tests 51, 208, 209
Hong Kong 151, 152

iBT (internet Based TOEFL) 131, 150, 153, 155, 156
identity (identities) 4–18, 41, 47–9, 62–9, 74–85, 122, 125, 208, 213–28
ideological 3–6, 14, 47, 84, 93, 116–25, 136, 186, 205–29
Ideological State Apparatus 4, 6, 14
IELTS (the International English Language Testing System) 131, 134, 143, 152, 185–229
immigrant(s) 46, 49, 54–63, 95, 97, 108
imperialism 113, 114, 185, 186, 204, 206

imperialist   12, 116, 122
India   219
indigenous   23–45, 66
    community   28, 32, 43
    language   23, 29, 30, 36, 38, 39, 42, 43
inequality (inequalities)   5, 113, 124, 191, 193, 202, 208, 229
intercultural   3, 127
    learning   70, 73, 79, 83
    competence   72
interculturality   68–74, 78, 80, 85
internet-based testing   155
Ireland   222, 226

Japan   130–45, 222, 226

(South) Korea (Korean)   122, 133, 148–84, 214, 226

L1, 39, 60. *See* first language
L2, 24, 25. *See* second language
language
    ecology   92
    ideology (ideologies)   47–9, 214, 215
    -minoritized bilingual   91
    policy (policies)   117, 123, 131, 140, 143
    proficiency   50, 73, 83, 92–103, 114, 131–3, 142, 144, 158, 186–210, 217, 227
    teachers   125, 131
    teaching policy   130, 131, 133, 135, 137, 139, 141, 143, 145
Latin America   52
Latino   94, 95
learning experiences   74, 85–90, 171
liberation   58
linguistic
    diversity   28, 50, 76, 101, 102
    ideologies   49, 95
    imperialism   185
    landscape   209, 213, 214, 228
    repertoire   60, 104, 105
listening   120, 134, 139, 140, 181
literacy   3–9, 15, 16, 24–30, 35–42, 55, 58, 75
literacy testing   3–6, 9
literary   9, 14–16
London   7, 9, 20–2, 229

Malaysia   122
marginalization   47, 78, 96, 100, 122, 124, 185, 200
measurement   60, 75, 91, 101–8, 162–7, 180, 189, 200–3
media   75, 131–7, 144–54, 165, 167, 206
Melbourne   6, 7, 26
Mexican   52–5, 60–6, 95, 98
Mexicano   46
Mexico   52, 53, 61, 104
Middle East   190
middle school   76, 158
migrant(s)   29, 54, 58, 59, 63
migration   61, 209–11, 216, 227, 228
monolingual   25, 47–51, 57, 60, 61, 93, 96, 100–3
multicultural   56, 70, 87
multilingual   25, 46, 56, 60, 70, 92, 104–8, 122–9, 209
multilingualism   60, 91, 93, 101–7, 214
multiple-choice   13, 71, 166, 171, 172
Muslim   114, 118
Myanmar   122

national curriculum   14, 17, 20
Native American   94
native speaker   71, 115, 121–7, 216, 217, 228
native-speakerist   114, 122–5, 216
neocolonialism   114
neoliberal   3–8, 14, 18, 114, 121, 185, 195, 204–30
neoliberalism   7, 8, 213
neoliberalist   192
Nepal   208–11, 214, 228
Newbolt Report   15, 20
New Zealand   211, 212, 216, 219, 226
No Child Left Behind Act   57
non-native   124, 125
North America   52, 187
Norway   222
numeracy   6, 23–30, 35, 37, 38, 42

objectivity   12, 93, 94, 98, 103
oral communication   74, 167

PBT (Paper Based TOEFL)   131
pedagogy   3, 7, 9, 28, 58, 68–70, 77, 188, 199, 207

performance assessment   81
(the) Philippines   114, 118–23, 172
placemaking   208–29
placement tests   120, 137, 143, 144, 147, 148, 149, 150
Poland   226
Portugal   226
positionality   68, 69, 79, 81, 82
postcolonial   48, 52, 115–17, 186, 204
power
   dynamics   68, 79, 81, 82, 84
   relations   58, 61, 94, 116, 117, 203
pragmatics   68, 70, 71, 72, 79
praxis   68, 70, 84
private education   150, 153
privilege   5, 78, 79, 94, 208, 212
promotional materials   214
psychometrics   102
public school(s)   56, 154, 156, 175, 177, 179, 183

qualitative   69, 79, 165, 205
quantitative   69, 79, 137, 166

raciolinguistic   47, 48, 60, 95
reading   8–28, 50, 61, 74, 79, 81, 82, 104, 139, 141, 148, 153, 166, 172, 198, 203, 214
reliability   80, 132, 156, 159, 194

scientific racism   94, 97, 103
secondary school(s)   9, 29, 132–40, 149, 153
second language   24, 25, 39, 68, 76, 91–3, 146, 208. *See* L2
second language acquisition. *See* SLA
self-assessments   70, 74, 126
service-learning   68–90
Singapore   152
SLA (second language acquisition)   8, 24, 50, 68, 70, 73, 84, 187
social
   awareness   72
   change   69, 75, 79
   justice   70, 72, 76, 80
   media   75
   networking   74
sociopolitical   49, 79, 91–105, 147–63, 208, 210, 227, 228

South Africa   105
Spain   61, 226
Spanish   46, 52–5, 59–65, 69, 95, 104, 118
speaking   1, 23, 54, 111, 120, 134, 139, 140, 165–81
Standard English   123
standardization   50, 69, 77, 79, 81, 130, 229
standardized
   testing   3–8, 16, 19, 96, 147, 158, 210, 211, 229
   tests   3, 59, 130–44, 208–29
study abroad   209, 219
subjectivity (subjectivities)   3, 7, 11, 13, 195, 201
Sydney   26, 127
symbolic violence   12, 14, 49

task   13, 68, 71–3, 83, 104, 168–79, 203, 205
task-based instruction   68
task-based language teaching (TBLT)   83
technology   74, 121, 123, 131, 153, 156, 187
TESOL (Teaching English to Speakers of Other Languages)   66–9, 73–89, 138, 229
test accommodations   91, 99–108
test development   91, 92, 103
testing regimes   47, 48, 50, 117, 123, 126
test performance   96, 97, 100
test preparation   224
test-taking skills   171
TOEFL (Test of English as a Foreign Language)   131, 134, 143–55, 160, 189, 212, 216–27
TOEFL crisis   41, 147, 150, 153, 162
TOEIC (Test of English for International Communication)   131, 134, 143, 144, 148, 153, 165–74, 179–82
Turkey   122, 126

UK   9, 19, 172, 173, 208, 211, 216, 219–22, 226
United States   7, 46–49, 52, 53, 93, 114, 121
US Agency for International Development (USAID)   118, 119, 128

validity 3, 42, 69, 75, 79–109, 131, 132, 138, 145, 147, 159, 166, 188–206
values 13, 14, 18, 26, 36, 92, 94, 101–6, 114, 155, 186, 193
viability 150, 155
vocabulary 15, 74, 79, 114, 124, 125, 154, 173, 174, 178, 203
Vygotsky (Lev) 3, 20

washback 68, 71, 79, 151–3, 186, 190
Western (society, powers, agencies) 10, 114, 189
whiteness 47–9, 95
white supremacy 92–105
writing 6, 17, 19, 23, 28, 52, 61, 73–7, 81, 104, 115, 134, 139, 148, 152–7, 197, 200–6

www.ingramcontent.com/pod-product-compliance
Lightning Source LLC
Chambersburg PA
CBHW072134290426

44111CB00012B/1871